NGO Involvement in International Governance and Policy

Nijhoff Law Specials

VOLUME 72

The titles published in this series are listed at the end of this volume.

NGO Involvement in International Governance and Policy

Sources of Legitimacy

by

Anton Vedder, Vivien Collingwood, Anke van Gorp,
Menno Kamminga, Louis Logister, Corien Prins,
and Peter Van den Bossche

MARTINUS
NIJHOFF
PUBLISHERS

LEIDEN • BOSTON
2007

This book is printed on acid-free paper.

A c.i.p. record for this book is available from the Library of Congress.

ISBN: 978 90 04 15846 7

Copyright 2007 Anton Vedder, The Netherlands.
Published by Martinus Nijhoff. Koninklijke Brill NV incorporates the imprints Brill, Hotei
Publishers, IDC Publishers, Martinus Nijhoff Publishers and VSP.

http://www.brill.nl

This volume was published within the framework of the Incentive Programme Cooperation
in Legal Research (SaRO) of the Netherlands Organisation for Scientific Research (NWO).

Table of Contents

Introduction

Anton Vedder

This book addresses the theme of the legitimacy of the involvement of non-governmental organizations (NGOs) in global governance and policy. Internationally operating NGOs are increasingly involved in international governance and policy-making. However, notwithstanding the global extent of their impact, a somewhat more than rudimentary system of checks and balances of NGO involvement has hitherto not been developed. The Tilburg-Maastricht research programme on NGO legitimacy that started in 2004 and concluded early 2007 tried to provide materials to fill this gap. This book is one of the end products of this programme. It contains a systematic presentation of its main results.

The programme—just as this book does—focused on the reasons for which NGOs can and cannot be considered to legitimately display power and legitimately affect the lives of many people, and to be legitimate participants in international governance. It tries to deliver defensible principles and a fitting vocabulary for the discussion and the assessment of legitimacy claims for the involvement of NGOs.

This main objective and the corresponding theme of NGO legitimacy should be carefully distinguished from a relevant and familiar yet different theme: the legitimacy of the actual existing global governance order. The debate about the legitimacy of the global governance order considers NGOs primarily from the perspective of their possible contribution to the legitimacy of that global order as a whole. It often focuses, for instance, on the question: to what degree and in what way does the presence of NGOs compensate for or remedy the democracy deficits of international organizations and the power of multinationals? In the research programme, however, the focus was on a more fundamental question. That question was: under what conditions can NGOs themselves be rightfully called legitimate? This question is often dismissed in the larger debates about the legitimacy of the world order.

In order to find defensible principles and a fitting vocabulary for the discussion and the assessment of legitimacy claims for NGO involvement, the programme started with a conceptual analysis—a series of stipulations rather—to clarify and delineate the subject matter and scope of the enquiry. With respect to the notion of legitimacy it was decided to provisionally start out with a three-dimensional notion of legitimacy, which was borrowed from political theories about the state. This notion includes morally normative, regulatory, and social aspects. Legitimacy was regarded as a thoroughly normative notion associated with public moral justification, legality, and representativeness. Such a notion was able to cover all or most of the aspects of legitimacy that tend to recur frequently in the theoretical and practical debate on the legitimacy of organizations.

Secondly, qualitative research was undertaken on the perceptions of the legitimacy of NGOs, NGO professionals, and stakeholders, such as multinationals and governmental organizations. This was done for heuristic purposes in order to flesh out the schematic conception of legitimacy, and to test and improve its practical feasibility.

The interviews made clear what NGOs and stakeholders themselves consider to be the most important sources of legitimacy, and what they view as the most elusive pitfalls regarding the legitimacy of NGOs. The research team wishes to express its gratefulness to the interviewees for their generous cooperation.

In addition to interviews with key persons, two researchers also tried to give a foretaste of phenomena that the near future may hold in store for NGOs. One of them did so by analyzing the websites of a group of traditional, long-established NGOs and of a group of NGOs that mainly exist and operate on the Internet. Thus, she raised all kinds of questions regarding the legitimacy aspects of informational activities of NGOs on the Internet. The other researcher went one step beyond and considered the rise in interactivity that can be expected to occur in the Internet activities of NGOs. She also brought up the question what implications interactive tools might have for the legitimacy requirements to be met by NGOs.

In addition to this qualitative research, enquiries were made into the legal status of NGOs and the extent to which this legal status can or cannot contribute to the legitimacy of NGOs. The focus was on the status of NGOs with international organizations and on the status of NGOs under national law.

Finally, the fruits of the qualitative research and legal analyses were reaped and the broad and schematic three-dimensional concept of legitimacy was reconsidered. The research results were used not only to test the practical feasibility of the concept, but also to explore the mutual relationships between the three dimensions and their criteria, and to enrich them with substantial content derived from the domains in which the NGOs are active. The resulting alternative conceptualizations were further tested, pruned, and enriched by confronting them with relevant theories about, for instance, accountability and legitimacy of state authorities, and general normative principles. The resulting articulation itself will hopefully help to establish a firmer grip on the organizing principles, demarcation lines, and normative priority patterns of the questions and issues that may and should be put forward and—preferably—answered when discussing the relevant features of NGOs.

The authors of this book are greatly indebted to the Netherlands Organisation for Scientific Research, NWO. This organization has funded most of the research carried out within this programme. Thanks are also due to Tilburg University and the University of Maastricht for enabling the researchers to contribute to the programme and to the book. Finally, the authors wish to thank Mr. Dick Broeren of the Schoordijk Institute for editing Chapters 1 to 4 and 7, Ms. Vivian Carter of the Tilburg Institute for Law, Technology and Society for editing Chapters 5 and 6 and Ms. Lin Yuen for her indispensable research assistance and help with the editing of the book.

Chapter 1 Questioning the legitimacy of non-governmental organizations

Anton Vedder *

1. Introduction

Internationally operating NGOs are increasingly involved in international politics and policy-making. They have become powerful players in the international arena. In many respects, their involvement resembles activities and policies that, until recently, were typical of traditional national authorities, and, for that reason, were expected to be performed by those national authorities, or by international governmental authorities rather than by NGOs. Gradually, more and more people are affected by their activities. Notwithstanding the global extent of their impact, a somewhat more than rudimentary system of checks and balances of NGO involvement has hitherto not been developed. This book tries to provide materials to fill this gap. It is about the reasons for which NGOs can and cannot be considered to legitimately display power and affect the lives of many people, and to be legitimate participants in international governance. It tries to deliver rationally defensible principles and a fitting vocabulary for the discussion and the assessment of legitimacy claims for the involvement of NGOs.

This chapter starts out with a conceptual analysis—a series of stipulations rather—in order to clarify and delineate the subject matter and scope of this enquiry. Starting points are given for the specification of the key concepts involved in this enquiry. The aim is not to give an exhaustive description of the most common day-to-day usages of the

* The author is indebted to Anke van Gorp (TNO, Delft), Corien Prins (Tilburg University), and Peter Van den Bossche (Maastricht University) for their valuable comments and suggestions.

Anton Vedder et al., *NGO Involvement in International Governance and Policy*, pp. 1-19.
Printed in the Netherlands. ISBN 978 90 04 15846 7.

terms or a complete lexicographic overview. The demarcation lines between the ways in which the notions are used are not always as clear as could be wished. The aim of this part of the chapter is merely to serve analytical purposes and to draw attention to characteristics and similarities that are significant from the point of view of the main questions of this exploration. Clearly, each of the articulations given leaves room for some discussion and further stipulation. All in all, however, the overview will result in just enough definitional clarity as is relevant to the subject matter of this book.

Then, some questions will be raised with regard to the actual role of NGOs in international governance. How is the involvement of NGOs to be explained at all? And is it more or less natural that NGOs participate in international politics and policy-making in the sense that it is evidently for the best and to be taken for granted, or are critical questions in order? One of the issues arising is the legitimacy of NGOs. Are NGOs the most suitable candidates for involvement in global governance? Why exactly should they be entitled to wield power in the ways they do? (*Mutatis mutandis*, the same issue arises concerning multinational enterprises. For reasons of conciseness and clarity, this book's scope is restricted to NGOs, although some relevant ways in which NGOs resemble multinational enterprises will be pointed out.)

After the legitimacy of NGOs has been called into question, the option of applying traditional concepts of the legitimacy of governmental authorities to NGOs will be critically discussed. This discussion will yield some tentative suggestions for amending and adjusting traditional approaches to assessing legitimacy so as to make them better suited for application to NGOs. A critical investigation of these possible amendments and adjustments will be carried out in the final chapter of this book. Before that investigation can take place, some other steps—intermediate enquiries—must be taken. These are described in Chapters 2 to 6 and will be introduced at the end of this chapter together with some remarks about the methods and methodology chosen in this book.

2.   NGOs

An NGO is generally defined as an essentially non-profit, voluntary citizens' group which is organized at a local, national, or international level, and is locally, nationally, or internationally active. The World Bank (1989), for instance, defines NGOs as 'private organizations that pursue activities to relieve suffering, promote the interests of the poor, protect the environment, provide basic social services, or undertake community development." Most NGOs depend partially or completely on voluntary service and donations from private citizens. The three basic characteristics of NGOs seem to be: (1) being non-profit; (2) consisting at least partially of a voluntary citizens' group (or of a group that consists at least partially of voluntary citizens' groups); (3) and depending at least in part on donations from private citizens or on voluntary activities.

NGOs should be distinguished from governments, political parties, business corporations, activist groups, and social movements, although the demarcation lines between these different types of organizations and groups are not always optimally clear.

Typically, NGOs are not part of a government or a local, national, or international governmental authority. Although NGOs are not governmental bodies, they can sometimes be initiated by governmental organizations or financed by governments. Also, some NGOs perform certain tasks for the government.

NGOs must also be distinguished from political parties, organizations that have or seek to gain seats in parliament. Of course, it is conceivable that NGOs sometimes develop into political parties, or, vice versa, that political parties gradually turn into NGOs.

Although NGOs and business corporations are both non-state actors, business corporations, as opposed to NGOs, are typically profit-driven and not primarily value-based. It is important to notice, however, that many NGOs have lately professionalized to such a degree that in certain respects (business plan, efficiency, certain commercial activities) they resemble business corporations more and more. Simultaneously, there has been a rise in the number of organizations that can be considered NGOs even though corporations lie—at least partially—at their basis: joint ventures of corporations and NGOs, such as the Marine Stewardship Council (see Section 4), and industry associations (voluntary associations of two or more companies that promote common interests or commonly endorsed social purposes). To the extent that these organizations are not profit-driven and at least partially based on voluntary contributions and donations from private persons and organizations, they can be considered NGOs. With regard to industry associations, the input from individual citizens will more often than not be absent, in which case they should not be regarded as NGOs. It is important to notice, however, that the distinction between business corporations and NGOs is, in various ways and in different respects, not as clear-cut as might be expected.

Finally, NGOs must be distinguished from activist groups. NGOs, as opposed to activist groups, are typically organized according to more or less stable structures. These structures can vary from highly hierarchical to flat network-like patterns. The important thing is that the organizations have some stability and can be addressed from outside, even when the individual participants and workers would all be substituted. This is not normally the case with activist groups. Also, NGOs mostly have some sort of legal status under national laws, if only for the sake of tax benefits. Having this status is neither a necessary nor a sufficient condition for being an NGO. Although they can gradually change into NGOs with or without legal status, activist groups usually lack this status.

Sometimes, the use of violence as a way of obtaining results and realizing objectives is explicitly excluded from the definition of NGOs (for instance, Jägers 2002). For reasons of conciseness and clarity, in some chapters in this book the focus is also restricted expressly to NGOs that do not use violence. This does not mean, however, that the avoidance of violence is considered a per se defining characteristic of NGOs. Rather, an NGOs possible readiness to use violence is one of the critical issues to be considered when assessing its legitimacy. Put differently, the use of violence can affect an NGOs legitimacy negatively. The (potential) use of violence relates to the criteria for the legitimacy of NGOs, not to the criteria for being an NGO. Although the issue of the use of violence and its relationship to the legitimacy of NGOs will be touched upon in this book, it will not be dealt with in depth and extensively.

Locally and nationally organized NGOs can have an international scope and action domain. Local or community-based NGOs that have a local scope and action domain are also referred to as grassroots organizations. In this book, the focus will be on NGOs that are internationally active, regardless of how exactly they are organized. These internationally active NGOs often involve grassroots NGOs in their actions and policies. Even so, some international NGOs do refer to themselves as grassroots organizations. Usually, this means is that the local perspective is taken into account and actions are initiated locally and not somewhere far away.

The term NGO is very broad and encompasses a wide variety of organizations. Divergence is typical for the ways in which NGOs are organized and for the scope and objectives of NGOs. NGOs range from large, long-established organizations such as the Red Cross, Oxfam, Amnesty International, and Greenpeace to, for instance, small community-based self-help groups in the South and small networks maintaining websites for the support of other NGOs or individuals. The notion covers religious, academic and professional organizations—often referred to as civil society organizations—and organizations primarily oriented towards aid and advocacy. It may also be beneficial to distinguish between types or categories of NGOs and between different functions and types of activities of NGOs. Bratton introduced the useful distinction between, on the one hand, NGOs that are membership organizations, in which these members help each other, and, on the other hand, NGOs that are service organizations that help others (Bratton 1989, 571). With regard to this latter type, the World Bank (1989) tends to distinguish between two main categories: operational NGOs and advocacy NGOs. Although this distinction clearly bears the marks of the World Bank's typical development perspective, the World Bank is certainly right in assuming that the NGOs currently standing out in the international arena are mostly active in one or both of these fields. Since, in this book, the focus is predominantly on the legitimacy of NGO involvement in international governance and policy-making, the operational and advocacy functions of the NGOs are central. This means that the main focus will be on NGOs that are primarily oriented towards aid and advocacy, while much of what will be said is also applicable to, for instance, civil society organizations to the extent that they also engage in governance and policy-making through aid and advocacy. Having or performing operational or advocacy functions is not considered here as a sufficient or even a necessary condition for being an NGO. Nevertheless, focusing on and distinguishing between these functions seems important from the perspective of legitimacy. (See also Section 4, where an explanation is given of what is meant by involvement in international governance and some of the reasons for this involvement are highlighted).

The operational functions of an NGO relate to designing and implementing concrete action programmes that result directly in changes in the conditions of persons, cultural artefacts, or the natural environment: development, food aid, health care, the protection of historical landmarks, the protection of animal well-being, nature conservation, etc. The advocacy functions of NGOs are aimed at influencing the opinions, policies, and practices of national and international governmental authorities, business enterprises, social groups, and the general public. Although they are indirectly oriented towards changes in the concrete conditions of reality, they do so by influencing intermediaries.

A growing number of NGOs engage in both operational and advocacy activities. Sometimes, it is difficult to determine of which function the activities of NGOs are typical. Advocacy can sometimes take the form of very concrete actions with very specific goals, such as boycotts, picketing, etc. Some groups, primarily involved in advocacy, while not directly involved in designing and implementing action programmes, focus on specific concerns regarding concrete change. From the perspective of legitimacy, it is sometimes necessary to specify further types of actions and policies within the operational and advocacy functions, depending on the possible beneficial or adverse impact on the parties involved.

3.   Legitimacy

Legitimacy is the state or quality of being legitimate. The latter term derives from the medieval Latin *legitimatus*, past participle of *legitimare*: to legitimate. The Merriam-Webster Online Dictionary gives as the first meaning of the entry legitimate: lawfully begotten; born in wedlock; and having full filial rights and obligations by birth. According to this dictionary, secondary meanings are:

–   being exactly as purposed: neither spurious nor false;
–   accordant with law or with established legal forms and requirements or ruling by or based on the strict principle of hereditary right;
–   conforming to recognized principles or accepted rules and standards;
–   relating to plays acted by professional actors but not including revues, burlesque, or some forms of musical comedy.

For the discussion of organizations in contexts such as the one that is central to the purposes of this book—the political context of the international arena—the day-to-day linguistic conventions with regard to legitimacy are not very helpful. Political theory, on the other hand, may offer more or less suitable technical definitions. In this discipline, legitimacy is mostly discussed as a notion relating to state governments. Nonetheless, the definitions put forward can be fruitful for the (heuristic) purposes of this book.

Most theorists concentrate on criteria that need to be fulfilled by a (governmental) authority in order to secure compliance with its rules and establish their supremacy. These criteria are not so much about the technicalities or empirical features that enable an authority to wield power as they are about the right with which it does so. In this context, legitimacy is a thoroughly normative notion mostly associated with (public) moral justification, legality, and representativeness.[1]

Some theorists cherish one-dimensional notions of legitimacy. These authors identify legitimacy mostly with either moral justification, conformity to accordance with rules and procedures, or representativeness. Others put forward mixed and, sometimes, confusing notions, for example those who use criteria of moral justification and conformity to rules and procedures interchangeably and indiscriminately. Finally, there are those who use multidimensional notions of legitimacy, explicitly explaining the relationships between the morally normative, the regulatory, and the social aspects, and carefully explaining why such a multidimensional concept is to be preferred to a one-dimensional one (Beetham 1991).

Since the purposes of this book are heuristic and explorative, a broad approach to legitimacy, encompassing regulatory, social, and moral aspects, seems best fit. Some reflection on the three dimensions of legitimacy may be helpful in coming to terms with the differences between legitimacy when applied to NGOs and legitimacy when applied to state governments. The regulatory, morally normative, and social aspects can be defined in such a way that legitimacy is a matter of conformity to rules (regulatory aspect), justification in relation to moral norms and values (morally normative aspect), and consent or representation of those involved or affected (social aspect).

The search for an applicable concept of legitimacy is urgent, because NGOs are becoming increasingly important at an international level, and are having an impact on the lives of an ever-growing number of people. In certain respects, NGOs tend to wield power in ways similar to governments. These are the main reasons why their legitimacy can be questioned. Direct application of the three dimensions of legitimacy to NGOs, however, would be reckless.

First and foremost, the legitimacy criteria are explicitly tailored to national governments. A national government seeks support for its activities concerning almost all aspects of the lives of its citizens, except certain parts of the personal sphere. An NGO, by contrast, seeks merely permission for certain activities, lobbying, being a discussion partner in trade-offs, and perhaps a restricted willingness to cooperate and support.

---

1   This even holds true for what are known as the empirical notions of legitimacy that are often used in political theory. See Chapter 7, Section 3.

Second, the criteria for legitimacy entail a significant if latent socio-historical component, which may easily go unquestioned as long as legitimacy is reflected on in relation to national governments. The rules to which an organization must conform, the beliefs about the norms and values on which these rules should rest, and the consent that must be given to the organization, will in every state and every society with its own culture and conventions easily take their own forms. These forms will not all be completely different from those in other countries and societies, but major differences will appear nonetheless.

Of course, this is not a problem as long as the scope of the concept is restricted to one country or society. As soon as the scope widens, however, problems may arise because of cultural and conventional differences. And of course, when the concept of legitimacy is applied to NGOs that operate in an international arena against the background of moral and cultural pluralism, similar problems may occur.

Finally, the idea of consent or representation is a difficult one with regard to NGOs. Who are involved or affected? Who can count as stakeholders? How should they express their consent? These questions are not unanswerable; neither do they indicate the hopelessness of the case. For the time being, however, practically satisfying answers to these questions remain to be found.

Two of the three dimensions of legitimacy—the regulatory and social ones—have a primarily procedural character. They do not refer to the degree to which an individual or an organization conforms to certain values and ideals, such as respect for human rights, animal well-being, the protection of the environment, assistance of the needy and the poor, etc. They refer primarily to rules with some kind of formal status or to the formal aspects of the decision procedures of the individuals or the organizations involved. The following questions qualify as procedural criteria. Does a decision that will initialize an activity rest on the consent of all people involved? Are the procedures for decisions and policies transparent and can they be checked? Does an NGO have a legal status under national law? Has an NGO successfully passed the accreditation procedures of an international organization? Does an NGO conform to the legal standards of the country in which it is active? Only the morally normative dimension can include substantive criteria, for instance the requirement that the actions of the organization involved be justified in terms of values and norms with specific content. But this dimension is not restricted to substantive criteria. Accountability and responsibility, for instance, are not exactly substantive, but rather open, procedural moral values. They come, nonetheless, under the heading of the moral dimension. Criteria of the regulatory dimension can sometimes refer to legal standards that articulate other norms than norms about the status or the decision procedures of organizations. Although these criteria as such are primarily procedural, they concern the conformity to norms with a formal status, and these legal norms themselves may therefore justifiably be referred to as substantive legal norms in order to distinguish them from procedural legal norms, which may be understood to relate to the organization and decision procedures of the organizations.

At this point, it is perhaps wise to note that from a moral point of view, the social and regulatory dimensions can be seen as subordinate to the morally normative one. This has to do with the fact that the criteria included in these dimensions can be instrumental in protecting or realizing moral values such as responsibility and accountability. In the final chapter, this issue will be taken up again. There, one of the central questions will be whether it makes much sense to talk about the legitimacy of non-state actors such as NGOs, if the ultimately moral point of legitimacy is not fully recognized.

Before closing the definitions part of this chapter, attention must be paid to three considerations. The first of these has to do with two ways of referring to legitimacy with regard to NGOs. The other two concern the differences between legitimacy and some other familiar notions: legality, accountability, and responsibility.

The notion of legitimacy can be used to refer to the legitimacy of the organization in its entirety, including all of its activities, on the one hand, and to the legitimacy of a particular activity on the other. These two kinds of legitimacy may be labelled as dispositional legitimacy and occurrent legitimacy, respectively. The distinction between the two is of some interest, because failing to take it into account makes it difficult to understand how certain organizations on the whole act legitimately, whereas some of their particular activities may be illegitimate.

Legality is the attachment to or observance of law, or, generally, the quality or state of being legal. Legality can contribute to legitimacy, but it is neither a necessary nor a sufficient condition for legitimacy. In Chapters 5 and 6, the legal status of NGOs and its possible contribution to the legitimacy of NGOs will be dealt with extensively.

Accountability and responsibility have a primarily retrospective meaning. Both terms chiefly refer to the state of being subject to giving an account, an explanation, giving good reasons for behaviour, performances and policies. Although legitimacy may presuppose accountability or responsibility in this sense, it is more. For one thing, legitimacy is not only a retrospective notion. Its main focus seems to be future-oriented, as it explicates the reasons why the organization involved should be considered to be within its rights when performing certain activities. In this very restricted sense, there is also an analogy with the prospective denotation of responsibility which refers to the (in se future-oriented) obligations and duties that come with certain tasks and roles of individual persons. Legitimacy, however, goes beyond accountability and responsibility because it also refers to the question why precisely it is a particular agent (i.e., person or organization) that is allowed to do what it does. In this respect, there is an analogy with many theories of government legitimacy, in which the legitimization explains why the government is justified in having a monopoly on enforcing laws. Legitimacy, therefore, seems to transcend answerability. Of course, this is just an analogy concerning arguments for specific ways of wielding power. It is not meant as a contention that each NGO should have a monopoly on its specific policies.

4.   Reasons for NGO involvement

For some decades now, an exponential growth in trans-boundary traffic and increased globalization of the economy have been manifest. In addition, the production of new international and cross-border technologies has surged. Social and moral problems that appear in the wake of these developments often cannot be solved in traditional ways. Technologies develop at such a speed that traditional governmental bodies cannot keep pace with them. The traditional legislator often lacks the required expertise while legislative processes are so slow that laws run the risk of being outdated as soon as they have entered into effect. The rise of cross-border trade and traffic also confronts the traditional legislator. Although the development of international law and regulation does not stand still, it shows a remarkable pattern. Whereas it is gradually becoming more important than national law, in many relevant areas international law and regulation is as yet lacking while national law and regulation can no longer be applied.

Sometimes, international law and regulation itself creates legal vacuums by prohibiting national policy formation on certain issues, while failing to provide sufficient international legal alternatives. The general outlook of the World Trade Organization (WTO) Agreements, for instance, seems to sit somewhat uncomfortably with regard to national policies in the fields of moral and social concerns, since such policies are often deemed to constitute the first steps in the direction of trade barriers (Vedder 2003, 1-6, 173-182).

The speed of technological developments and the push towards internationalization go hand in hand with a strong diversification of centres of policy-making. Instead of national governments, operating under well-defined constitutional terms, wide varieties of organizations and institutions are involved in the substantive development of international law and policy. Many of these are private parties, such as NGOs and multinational enterprises. In part, these are involved in processes of normal legislation and other formal regulation, for instance as parties with consultative status with international organizations or as discussion partners for national legislators. In addition, many NGOs present themselves as custodians of the observance of elementary principles of international law, such as human rights (Van Genugten et al. 2004). To a large extent, however, NGOs and multinationals are also involved in what could perhaps be called informal regulation. Informal regulation originates not from national, international, or supranational governmental authorities, but from private or semi-private organizations, such as non-governmental and business organizations, and (groups of) citizens, or alliances and associations of these organizations and citizens. Informal regulation takes the form not of legislation but of self-regulation, codes of conduct, agreements, standard setting, etc. The need for informal regulation arises where social and moral problems occur with more or less urgency, some sort of collective action or policy is required because solutions cannot be left to the initiative and the discretion of individuals or even individual organizations, while the bodies which traditionally address issues of this kind, such as governmental authorities, cannot, or just will not, do so.

An impressive set of examples of informal regulation by NGOs and multinationals is delivered by the Marine Stewardship Council, a joint initiative of Unilever and the World Wide Fund for Nature (WWF) (The Marine Stewardship Council 2002). The Marine Stewardship Council was established in order to address the long-term sustainability of global fish stocks and the integrity of the marine eco-system. In 1999, it became an independent non-profit organization encouraging independent certification of fisheries. The Marine Stewardship Council is just one of countless organizations—be it a very sophisticated and effective one—which demonstrate how NGOs and multinationals interfere in international affairs through informal regulation.

5.   NGO legitimacy questioned

The fact that traditional governmental authorities are, more often than not, absent from processes of informal regulation raises profound questions about how norms and policies are established in terms of applicable processes, conditions and standards. As the above-mentioned developments affect private individuals more and more directly, the legitimacy of these types of international governance and regulation processes needs to be specifically addressed. Of course, the legitimacy of traditional and new national, international, and supranational governmental bodies is also a subject that deserves special attention. With regard to governmental authorities, however, some more or less suitable models for assessing legitimacy are already available. With regard to NGOs outside the realm of diagnostic criticism and critique, questions of legitimacy have been raised only to a very modest degree (Edwards 1999, 258-267; for an overview, see Collingwood and Logister 2005).

Of course, there are many publications on the legitimacy of the overall global political order and the overall global governance structure. This literature is indirectly relevant to the purposes of this book. But it is not so much concerned with the legitimacy of NGOs as it is with the ways in which NGOs contribute to the legitimacy of that overall order. Lindblom (2005) even considers the legal status of NGOs in different fields of international law not in relation to the legitimacy of the NGOs themselves but in relation to the legitimacy of international law. It must also be realized that, in political and legal debates, a state's legitimacy is usually conceived of in terms of procedural criteria, such as criteria intended to assure proper representation and the willingness to act according to rules. With regard to NGOs, a clear-cut and partially institutionalized tradition of checks and balances is lacking (see also Chapters 5 and 6).

But are concerns about the legitimacy of NGOs themselves necessary? Are more substantial reasons to question NGO legitimacy conceivable? On first examination, assuming the roles of initiators of political processes and policy-making seems to be not much more than a matter of bare necessity for NGOs. If they would not do it, who would? Some authors even believe that this involvement of NGOs is preferable to a further expansion of international or supranational authorities. This argument will not be examined in this book. The existing situation will be simply taken as a given. The question that remains is whether there are reasons for a critical stand on the idea that NGOs are, by their very nature, appropriate organizations for influencing and forming policies regarding moral and social issues in an international arena? In a sense, the following critical notes merely serve theoretical purposes. They are intended neither to cast serious and principled doubt on the roles of NGOs in the international arena, nor to argue positively in favour of restrictions on their involvement.

Some of the points may sound familiar. This may be especially the case with regard to the arguments that were raised in the past against the idea of attributing social responsibilities to business corporations. That the same arguments—or at least very similar ones—can be brought against NGOs may come as a surprise.

As stated earlier, NGOs are increasingly inclined to fill up the spaces left open by national, international, and supranational governmental authorities. Thus, they gradually fulfil public roles that within in a traditional state are usually performed by governmental authorities. The fact that they take up similar roles does not in itself imply that they must conform to similar requirements regarding their legitimacy. NGOs are simply not governmental authorities. Nevertheless, to the degree that they fill the void left open by governments, their power and the effective use of their power increase. It is precisely this growth of power and its possibly far-reaching consequences that call for consideration in terms of legitimacy. Put simply, with power comes responsibility and a corresponding duty to demonstrate the legitimacy of an assumed role. As the activities of NGOs have ever further-reaching consequences, their ability to demonstrate the legitimacy of their activities becomes more important.

Are NGOs the appropriate organizations for influencing and forming policies regarding moral and social issues? In the debate on globalization, the role of NGOs is often taken for granted. First, there is the empty space which no governmental authority—national, international or supranational—is qualified to fill but which nevertheless needs to be filled. Second, there is a certain tendency to consider multinationals and NGOs as complementary because of their apparently similar natures. NGOs are seen as the only type of players in the field that can act as a counterbalancing power against the supposedly overwhelming power of multinationals that also try to influence policies and policy formation (Oliviero and Simmons 2002, 77-105).

Upon reflection, however, the self-imposed role of NGOs is less natural than it appears to be at first glance. NGOs lack democratic backing. They usually interfere in the lives of people, who are not represented in the decision-making bodies of such organizations. Most internationally operating NGOs have their institutional bases, members, and sponsors in the North, whereas the people affected by their actions live in other parts of the world. Furthermore, the arenas in which NGOs play their roles involve a broad mix of situations characterized by normative conflicts. In the case of a normative conflict, one justified normative claim—such as improving the economic well-being of people—can only be met by going against another justified normative claim—for example, protecting the environment. Because NGOs are usually single-issue organizations—as are many multinationals—in many respects they lack the degree of impartiality ideally needed to deal with situations in which normative conflicts occur. The quality of the outcome of such conflicts is therefore dependent on the accidental presence of countervailing powers advocating on behalf of the conflicting claim.

Finally, it may be assumed that NGOs should be considered as merely private actors whose roles, like any private person's, do not need legitimization. It might be good to keep in mind that although the notion of legitimacy is not normally used with regard to private persons, in a very broad sense, certain requirements associated with legitimacy also apply to private persons. Indeed, in democratic societies private persons are granted all kinds of freedoms, such as the right to speak out, to participate in debates, to undertake action, etc. At the same time, however, these freedoms are not absolute, unconditional, or unrestricted. Private persons can be held accountable for what they say and do. The greater the impact of what they say and do, and the greater the risk their words and deeds might involve other people, the more likely it is that private actors will be held accountable, and the more stringent the requirements regarding their responsibility will be. It seems reasonable to hold that this accountability constitutes a kind of bottom-line legitimacy that applies to the organizations of private persons, such as NGOs and business enterprises, as well.

6.   Towards a concept of NGO legitimacy

To return to the issue presented in Section 3, there is currently no clear and uncontroversial concept of legitimacy that can be applied to NGOs. Nonetheless, the legitimacy of the involvement of NGOs in international governance should be a subject of discussion for various reasons: NGOs have become very important players at an international level, NGO activities affect the lives of an ever-growing number of people, and NGOs are gradually becoming more and more involved in global governance through activities that used to be typical of state governments. Therefore, the main objective of this book is to provide the main elements and principles that can lie at the basis of a rationally satisfying and practically feasible conception of NGO legitimacy. For this purpose, the above-mentioned three-dimensional account of state legitimacy will be taken as a starting point. The criteria included in this account will be adapted to their specific applications and tested against other relevant theoretical and practical insights.

The following chapters aim at providing the background needed to test and, possibly, enrich the elementary three-dimensional concept of legitimacy sketched out in Section 3. Chapter 2 describes the results of qualitative research on the perceptions of legitimacy of NGOs themselves. Interviews with key figures make clear what NGOs themselves consider to be the most important sources of legitimacy, and what they view as the most elusive pitfalls regarding the legitimacy of NGOs. For practical reasons and in order to bring to light possible controversies among NGOs working in different fields, the research presented in Chapter 2 focused mainly on NGOs that are active in the field of human rights on the one hand, and NGOs involved in environmental protection on the other. The results of these interviews may—after critical scrutiny—be used for heuristic purposes, in order to flesh out the schematic conception of legitimacy and to enhance its practical feasibility.

Chapters 3 and 4 give a foretaste of phenomena that the near future holds in store. Chapter 3 concentrates on informational activities of NGOs on the Internet. It describes the results of the analysis of the websites of a group of traditional, long-established NGOs and of a group of NGOs that mainly exist and operate on the Internet. This chapter makes clear that informational Internet activities raise specific legitimacy requirements. Chapter 4 goes one step beyond and considers the rise in interactivity that can be expected to occur in the Internet activities of NGOs. Again the question is brought to the fore what implications interactive tools might have for the legitimacy requirements to be met by NGOs.

Chapter 5 and 6 analyze the legal status of NGOs and the extent to which this legal status can or cannot contribute to the legitimacy of NGOs. Chapter 5 is about the status of NGOs with international organizations. Chapter 6 concentrates on the status of NGOs under national law.

Chapter 7, finally, aims to reap the fruits of the analyses presented in the preceding chapters. It reconsiders the broad and schematic three-dimensional concept of legitimacy, laid out in Section 3 of this chapter. It tries to use the research results discussed in the preceding chapters not only to test the practical feasibility of the concept, but also to explore the mutual relationships between the three dimensions and their criteria, and to enrich them with content taken from the domains in which the NGOs are active.

7.   Advantages and limitations of the approach of this book

The methods used for the enquiries lying at the basis of this book stem from different disciplines. When relevant, they will be explicitly mentioned and discussed in Chapters 2 to 6. The general approach of this book—mainly surfacing in Chapters 1 and 7—can be characterized as a process of constructing a practically feasible and meaningful conception of NGO legitimacy by going back and forth between a first tentative definition of legitimacy, taken from traditional political theory, and relevant reflections and considerations from concrete practice and theoretical debates. This procedure calls for some methodological reflection in order to bring to light the advantages and limitations of the approach.

The chronological order of first claiming that the legitimacy of NGO involvement in global governance can be questioned and then embarking on an enquiry to find an adequate conception of NGO legitimacy may initially seem a little odd. How can the legitimacy of NGOs be reasonably put into perspective without a clear idea of what exactly NGO legitimacy means? The answer to this question is that this is simply how understanding in progress works. The first approach to the legitimacy of NGOs in this chapter was a tentative one. Attention was drawn to certain similarities between the ways in which NGOs and traditional state authorities wield power, and it was observed that if the activities and characteristics involved had been those of state authorities, the questions they raised would have been discussed in terms of legitimacy. At the same time, the upshot of a quick overview of familiar concepts, such as responsibility, liability, legality, etc., was that each of these was either not completely to the point, or somehow too narrow, so that important features of the identities and activities of NGOs might go unquestioned

and unreflected when the focus of discussions or debates would be restricted to concepts such as responsibility, liability, etc. For that reason,
it seems appropriate to use the notion of legitimacy in the context of
NGOs as well. To put it differently, the notion was initially used on the
basis of analogy because of relevant similarities and the absence of other
suitable terms.

Although all the enquiries reported in this book were undertaken
in an attempt to elaborate and expand the tentative three-dimensional
conception of legitimacy in the context of NGOs, the primary or sole
objective of bringing them together is of course not to attain theoretical, semantic clarity. The first analogy-based use was to have a quasi-
shorthand term referring to a tangled net of questions and issues that
can somehow be distinguished from other sets and types of questions
and issues. The original reason for specifically choosing the term legitimacy was that these questions and issues, as well as the activities and
characteristics to which they could be applied, resembled those that are
typical of state authorities. Apart from a few studies by academics and
some people involved in NGOs, discussing these questions and discussing NGOs and governance in terms of legitimacy was and still is fairly
uncommon.[2] Nonetheless, the questions raised are important enough
to merit taking the debate to a wider public. For this to happen, vigorous
progress in the articulation of the legitimacy notion in this context will
be helpful. Such an articulation can help because it sheds light on the
organizing principles and the demarcation lines of the questions and
issues that may and should be put forward and—preferably—answered
when discussing the relevant features of NGOs. Stagnation resulting
from the application of, for instance, rigid state-oriented conceptions of
legitimacy must be avoided. Adaptation to the specifics of NGOs, however, may uncover complicated and sometimes unexpected difficulties
that are better dealt with in advance than left to create confusion and
controversies in discussions with regard to the legitimacy of specific
NGOs or particular NGO activities.

However, it should also be clear that the specific articulation of the
concept strived for is not meant to function as the definitive view of
NGO legitimacy. It is simply impossible to show that a specific articulation of a notion such as legitimacy is the only correct one. The assumption that a correct articulation mirrors the ways in which the notion is
commonly used by the general public, and that empirical evidence can

2   For an overview, see Collingwood and Logister (2005).

be produced to test alternative articulations, would certainly be wrong. Legitimacy is a technical term. It does not belong to the vocabulary of the general public. The use of the term when applied to state authorities and organizations is restricted to certain groups (scholars, for instance). Using the term with regard to NGOs is even less common. For that reason, not even collecting data regarding the use of legitimacy among the very small group of scholars and NGO professionals involved would make much sense. Most importantly, however, the ways in which the notion is actually used is not the main object of concern. The real concern is to find a defensible conception in the sense of a perspective or view that is adequate—not in the sense of being representative of the views commonly held by the general public or the groups most involved, but in the sense of temporarily giving fitting expression to the questions and issues that really matter, to their mutual relationships and connections, and to the normative priority patterns amongst them. The quest, then, is not for lexicographic purity or semantic truth, and not for the ultimate best, but for a good, defensible conception.

The road to such a good and defensible conception is not as straightforward as could be wished. The criteria and conditions that need to be addressed are multifarious and disparate. Some of these are habituallly applied in the assessment of theories and definitions: the general criteria of consistency, coherence, and simplicity or elegance. Most importantly, however, all kinds of substantial conditions and presuppositions are to be taken into consideration. These are in part empirical, having to do with the practical applicability of the notion, and in part normative, prescriptive, setting the standards to which NGOs should ideally conform.

To some extent at least, the empirical requirements can be tested against reality. In Chapter 7, for instance, the data and results of the empirical enquiries described in Chapters 2 and 3 will be used in part to establish marginal conditions of practical feasibility. Something similar will be done with the results of the legal analyses in Chapters 5 and 6: these will be used to assess the extent to which legal status can play a practical role in the legitimazation of NGO involvement in global governance.

Of course, the main difficulties lying ahead are concerned with the normative requirements, which the conception must include. Since completely uncontroversial starting points are lacking in the morally and politically normative domains, an appropriate question would be how it can be determined whether a defensible account of legitimacy with regard to NGOs has indeed been defined? A possible answer might be found in referring to a specific and more or less coherent normative view, such as a utilitarian view of morality or a (neo-) Kantian view of the political order. Explicit normative assumptions for the concrete assessment of a conception would be very illuminating. Unfortunately, explication of the specific normative assumptions underlying stipulations of legitimacy—both with regard to state and non-state actors—is often lacking.[3] Apart from that, if the account were underpinned by a unique normative view, the persuasiveness of the account would in large part depend on the cogency of that view. From the ongoing conceptual and meta-ethical debate between the advocates of the different current and traditional moral and political theories it will be immediately clear that hopes of reaching consensus must be in vain.

Therefore, in Chapter 7, the initial phase of the assessment of the normative aspects of the legitimacy notion will not be restricted to one single view of morality or politics. Instead, suggestions and proposals for a description of the normative dimension of legitimacy will be taken from the empirical studies presented in Chapters 2 and 3 and from a broader range of theoretical perspectives that have been developed in the debate on legitimacy in political theory and, more specifically, the theory of international relations. The suggestions and proposals will be compared with relevant empirical requirements and normative claims that can be associated with various theoretical backgrounds. These theoretical backgrounds will be clarified as much as possible.

It is in this going back and forth—criticizing, pruning and readjusting the suggested content of the legitimacy criteria using the data and insights from various research sources, and vice versa—that the methodical nucleus of this undertaking is to be found. The adequacy or strength of the resulting conception proposal depends on the persuasiveness of the route, the argumentative trajectory, leading up to it. For that reason, its claim to correctness is far from absolute; it does not transcend the cogency of the argument lying at its basis.[4] This approach is nonetheless

---

3   Beetham (1991); with regard to NGOs, see the pioneering work of Atack (1999) and Edwards (1999).

4   The approach resembles the application of what is known as the wide reflective equilibrium method or the reflective disequilibrium method (Carens 2000 and 2004). For examples of the application of this method in conceptual analysis, see Swanton (1992) and (Vedder 1998).

rationally adequate in the light of the absence of uncontroversial, commonly agreed upon starting points and presuppositions.

Chapter 2   Perceptions of the legitimacy of international NGOs

Vivien Collingwood and Louis Logister

1.   Introduction

1.1.   *Main questions and objective*

This chapter examines how NGOs perceive the issue of legitimacy. Its purposes are mainly of a heuristic nature: the perceptions provide a starting point for revising theories of legitimacy, and extend our understanding of how NGOs function and the extent to which they are addressing legitimacy-related issues. This is intended to redress an imbalance in the current literature.[1] As argued elsewhere in this book, traditional theories of legitimacy are largely unsuited to the particular case of NGOs, and there is also a lack of systematic empirical research in this area.[2]

For this research, employees of internationally operating NGOs were interviewed about their perceptions of the legitimacy of their activities. Although the research was focused on NGOs, some stakeholders were also interviewed in order to gather illustrative material that could shed additional light on the perceptions of NGOs. It was thought critical to avoid offering NGO representatives a fixed definition of legitimacy, or a set of concepts that they could adopt or reject as they pleased. The aim was to find out how NGOs approached these issues and identify the terms that they preferred to use. A semi-structured interviewing

---

[1]   For an overview, see Collingwood and Logister (2005).

[2]   An exception is Alan Hudson (2000) who focuses on the move of UK-based NGOs from traditional aid towards greater involvement in advocacy and policy work, and the legitimacy claims that accompany this move.

Anton Vedder et al., *NGO Involvement in International Governance and Policy*, pp. 21-57.
Printed in the Netherlands. ISBN 978 90 04 15846 7.

strategy was thus adopted that was based on a number of core topics arising from the current literature, instead of a rigid set of questions (Patton 2002).

The interviews began with questions about the core topic, legitimacy: to what extent have the interviewees come across the issue of NGO legitimacy in their work? Is it an important issue to the organization? Was the issue originally raised externally (e.g., as a result of criticism from the media or politicians) or internally? How does an NGO view its own legitimacy with regard to its organization as a whole, and how does it justify its different activities? Various aspects of legitimacy were then broken down into sub-topics and probed further, depending upon how the interviewee responded to the initial questions. The topics discussed in the interviews included:

Representativeness and accountability. The literature suggests that some NGOs lack representativeness and accountability, both externally (connection with and representation of supporters' or beneficiaries' interests and values) and internally (structures of representation and accountability within the organization). To what extent do NGOs recognize the dilemmas posed by adequate representation, and how have they responded to them?

The role of *public support* for the organization. Following on from the issue of representativeness, to what extent is support from the general public important in reinforcing the legitimacy of NGOs?

Evaluation and learning. NGOs have been criticized for having insufficient monitoring, evaluation and learning processes in place. To what extent are monitoring, evaluation and learning procedures used, and how useful have NGOs found them?

External relations. NGOs are increasingly working with governments and the corporate sector to achieve change in policy and practice. Some analysts have implied that this results in a loss of independence. How do NGOs reconcile increased cooperation with the public and private sectors with their own aims and principles?

Funding and financial transparency. NGOs are often accused of lacking transparency in their funding. How have NGOs been affected by, and dealt with, this issue?

Future challenges. How do NGOs perceive future challenges to their legitimacy? What are the prospects for increased NGO participation in global governance structures? Should there be limits on NGO participation?

1.2.   Selection of NGOs

The selection of NGOs to be interviewed obviously had critical implications for the project findings. A number of the criteria mentioned in Chapter 1 were used in order to identify suitable NGOs: the organization had to be non-governmental and non-profit; international, in the sense that it had offices or operations in more than one country; and involved in the promotion of human rights or the environment (see also Chapter 1, Section 6).[3] The primary variable criteria used to determine the selection of NGOs were: size, function, and focus. In practice, a number of secondary criteria also came into play. First, proximity: to keep this part of the research manageable, most of the interviews were held in European countries. Second, existing professional networks were used to make contact with potential interviewees. Third, in view of other aspects of the research programme, organizations that made use of information and communications technology (ICT), such as websites or other new media were included.

Taking all of these factors together, the following organizations were selected: Amnesty International (campaigning globally for human rights), Dutch office (AINL) and European policy office (AIEO); Both Ends (BE, promoting environmentally sustainable development); Clean Clothes Campaign (CCC, promoting the labour rights of clothing and sportswear labourers in the South), international secretariat; Defence for Children/ECPAT (promoting children's rights and fighting the sexual exploitation of children), Dutch office;[4] Friends of the Earth (FOEI, environmental watchdog and advocacy organization), international secretariat; Global Witness (GW, watchdog and campaigner

---

3   These criteria were used for guidance rather than in any formal scientific sense; given the limited number of NGOs interviewed, and the subjective nature of the topics covered, it could not have been presumed to select a truly representative cross-section of the international NGO community.

4   ECPAT and Defence for Children (Netherlands) are grouped together in this study because the two organizations share an office and resources in Amsterdam.

against exploitation of natural resources and abuse of human rights); Greenpeace International (GPI, environmental watchdog and advocacy organization), international secretariat; Human Rights Watch (HRW, campaigning globally for human rights), London office and European policy office; the Marine Stewardship Council (MSC, developing global standards for sustainable fishing); Novib, (development and anti-poverty organization), Dutch office, (now renamed Oxfam Novib); WWF (international environmental conservation NGO), European Policy Office; and Pax Christi (PCNL, Roman Catholic peace movement), Dutch office.

The selection of stakeholders to be interviewed was made from a list of actors that interact with NGOs in different ways. For instance, some donate to NGOs, others are partners in policy dialogue. This resulted in the selection of two multinational corporations: Shell and Unilever; two (inter)governmental organizations: the Netherlands Ministry of Housing, Spatial Planning and the Environment and the European Commission; two international organizations: the World Trade Organization (WTO), and the World Bank; and a private funding institute: the Open Society Institute (an organization that can also be classed as an NGO, but is considered here as a stakeholder because of its role in funding NGOs). As with the NGOs, it would be unrealistic to presume to select a truly representative cross-section of stakeholders of internationally operating NGOs.

1.3.   Autumn 2004 – spring 2005: Contacting and interviewing NGOs and stakeholders

When selecting potential interviewees, priority was given to contacting NGO employees who were well acquainted with the everyday activities of the organization, but also involved in policy-making and the ethical dilemmas surrounding decision-making. Executive directors, international policy directors, campaign coordinators, and international media directors were approached. Having set up the interviews, the researchers then conducted additional background research into the policies, structures, and activities of NGOs and stakeholders. Relevant data was collected from the organizations' websites, promotional material, and annual reports, and through desk research. Since the aim of the interviews was to gain a sense of the selected organizations' perceptions of their activities, the questions focused on how organizations presented themselves rather than how others viewed them. The background research conducted formed the basis for the interviewing strategy. Interviewees were not sent questionnaires beforehand, in order to avoiding prejudicing their answers. It was assumed that they would have a sufficient understanding of the interview topics from the research programme summary circulated with the introductory letter.

1.4.   *The implications and limitations of the method*

The methodology outlined above was developed on the grounds that it would offer insights into the perceptions of a range of NGO representatives and stakeholder representatives with respect to issues of legitimacy. It is important, however, to recognize the limitations of the methodology and its implications for the interpretation of the data. Critically, the approach lies in between a large-N study on the one hand—where a large number of organizations is selected according to strict variables and compared—and on the other, a detailed, in-depth study of a few organizations, whereby interviews would be undertaken with a number of individuals and extensive background research carried out. The important implication of this is that generalizations cannot be made about the data. In addition, there are a number of specific issues arising from the methodology used that any analysis needs to take into account:

Lack of balance in accounts of the organization's activities. The methodology used necessitates being careful not to draw too general conclusions from the interviews. This is due to a number of factors. First, the interviewees were asked for their personal perceptions of NGO's legitimacy. Their opinions can therefore not be read as indicative of an NGO's policies or how it functions in practice. Second, it is necessary to acknowledge the fact that an NGO's representatives would naturally wish to portray their organization in the best possible light, and some might be more candid than others in revealing their doubts or concerns. These tendencies would, of course, be countered by doing further research into the organizations and carrying out further interviews with other staff members and people external to the organization. The interviews with stakeholders, for instance, do offer third-party perspectives.

The problem of selection bias. For a number of reasons, the results of these interviews cannot be read as representative of the NGO sector as a whole. For a start, there are thousands of NGOs worldwide, and interviews were only conducted with twelve organizations. This imbalance was countered to some extent by asking interviewees about their experience of working with other NGOs, but the sample is still limited. Second, the organizations chosen were already well known and had established structures and publicity channels. This automatically discounts some more informal or radical groups that might have given a very different perspective on NGO legitimacy. Third, there was some degree of selection bias in the sense that all of the representatives were willing to be interviewed. A more extensive study would also have examined the activities of NGOs and stakeholders that were reluctant to have their activities scrutinized. Fourth, all of the NGOs and stakeholders analyzed come from a narrow geographical and social group: western organizations based with offices in the EU and Switzerland. Although some insights into North-South relations were gained from the interviews, given the vibrancy of the NGO community in many parts of the world, the omission of some of these groups' views from the study is certainly a limitation.

Problems of interpretation. A third set of limitations relates to the fact that, given that this is a qualitative study, the data remains open to subjective interpretation. The language used poses a particular problem: a concept such as legitimacy is hard to define at the best of times, and different interviewees would have understood it in different ways (especially since not all interviewees spoke English as a native language). This makes it difficult, although not impossible, to compare understandings of legitimacy across different NGOs. In order to tackle this problem, the topic of legitimacy was split into different sub-topics, such as representation, accountability, and so forth. The meanings of these concepts could also be unclear, however, and an added disadvantage of this strategy was the fact that interviewees could be prompted by the interviewer's suggestions, rather than bringing up particular topics or concepts themselves.

Issues relating to the comparison of NGOs. Lastly, when interpreting the results, it is necessary to be aware of the extent to which the NGOs interviewed differ in terms of approach, function, working style, and so forth. It is critical to bear in mind how *what* the NGOs do, and *how* they do it, can affect representatives' perceptions of legitimacy. For instance, the degree to which the culture of an organization promotes the challenging and transgressing of international norms, or chooses to work within them. Another issue to bear in mind is the fact that interviewees with different roles were selected; thus, in some cases, a coordinator's perspective will be compared with that of a director. Furthermore, some of the interviews were undertaken with national offices, others with international secretariats, other interviews were carried out with professional lobbying offices.

Given these limitations, how can the interview data best be used? It is suggested that the points discussed above should be seen simply as limitations, and that plenty of conclusions can be drawn from the data as long as these limitations are borne in mind. The data should be seen as a set of *perceptions* from individual representatives of well-established, western NGOs and some stakeholders. These perceptions can be combined with factual evidence and accounts from third parties in order to produce a more comprehensive picture. The opinions expressed in the interviews should not be taken as representative of the NGO sector as a whole, but any agreement or concurrence in the accounts is certainly not insignificant, and may point to views that are held commonly among NGO staff or stakeholder representatives. Most importantly, any assertions need to be taken in the context of the speaker's background and the type of organization on behalf of whom he or she speaks.

In short, the interviews offer a set of perceptions from a range of organizations, which can then be used as the basis for thinking about definitions of legitimacy in the sector as a whole. They should be understood as a source of ideas about legitimacy, rather than a set of factual, generalizable data that allows judgements to be made about whether the activities of these NGOs—and, by extension, those of other NGOs—are legitimate.

2. Issues arising from the interviews with NGOs

2.1. *Is legitimacy a pressing concern?*

A range of opinions are expressed in response to the question, 'Do NGOs consider legitimacy to be a pressing concern?' One group of NGOs acknowledges the existence of the debate, but suggests that it is not a pressing everyday concern. As one interviewee puts it, 'I am not worried about the legitimacy of what we are doing.' Other NGOs suggest that legitimacy is important to the everyday work of the organization. The representative of one human rights organization says that the issue comes up 'pretty quickly', as its partners and stakeholders frequently challenge it to demonstrate its representativeness. An employee of another human rights organization likewise suggests that the question of legitimacy lies close to the core of its activities: 'We are aware of the issue because we know that our power is through reaching out to the outside world via the credibility of our organization.' A conservation NGO based in Brussels suggests that the issue comes up frequently on an internal basis, and that there is much debate regarding the extent to which conservation NGOs are accountable to their beneficiaries in practice. The representative of FOEI agrees with the interviewer that NGO legitimacy is a 'hot issue' and suggests that the debate has taken on momentum of its own.

2.2.   Why is there a debate about the legitimacy of NGOs?

The representatives of the NGOs offer a number of explanations for why concerns have been voiced about the legitimacy of NGOs. Some suggest that these are largely concerns internal to the sector. The representative of the MSC suggests that NGOs themselves raised the issue of transparency some years ago. Another conservation NGO argues that it is important for NGOs themselves to consider legitimacy issues: 'If we're expecting these standards from the private sector, then there's absolutely no reason why they shouldn't apply to the NGO sector as well [...] you've got to be absolutely rigorous in how you charge your way through that territory.' According to AIEO, there is a growing awareness among NGOs of the need for internal transparency and accountability. Other human rights and development NGOs are open to the idea that NGOs need to consider legitimacy and transparency issues as a matter of course.

Many of the representatives of the NGOs express the view that the legitimacy debate is politically or strategically motivated, and used by critics of NGOs (corporations, political parties, other NGOs) to attack the agendas of the NGOs. 'Of course,' one interviewee says, 'if I was going to discredit us, I would say that we're lying or that we're speaking on our own behalf.' A few of the environmental campaigning organizations argue that right wing groups and corporations perceive environmental and human rights NGOs as threatening, while another interviewee sees national criticism coming from the Dutch liberal party (VVD) and key political figures on the right. A representative of HRW agrees that criticism comes from the right, but also from the radical left which sees NGOs as being too close to capitalist interests; from democratic governments, who think that NGOs are insufficiently representative; and from radical NGOs that attack others because they see them as being an obstacle to their own views. Some NGOs think that the debate originates from the fact that NGOs have become more powerful. One representative of a development NGO says, 'I see the attempt to belittle and disqualify us as a compliment to the fact that we're getting quite strong.'

Some interviewees imply that the debate exists because there actually is a real problem with the legitimacy of some NGOs. For example, the representative of an environmental campaigning organization says that:

> there are NGOs who sometimes pretend they speak for the people, and neither do they have a lot of [members] [...] they use the term "the people" very easily, they reflect their own interests (which is fine) but pretending they speak in the people's name. That *this* is questioned sometimes, I find okay.

A human rights NGO likewise argues that there needs to be more transparency in the sector: 'You have many NGOs that are government fronts, the so-called GONGOs, you have lots of organizations that I would take with a lot of caution.' This view is echoed by the interviewee from the MSC. In addition, one human rights organization's representative suggests that in some cases, the existence of a legitimacy debate is less the result of a real problem than of bad communication. For example, this particular NGO has experienced criticism because it is sometimes perceived as aloof, disconnected from events on the ground, and dominated by American personnel.

Lastly, a few NGOs suggest that the NGO legitimacy debate is one aspect of more general interest in standards of governance across all organizations: public, private, and non-profit. This governance agenda finds expression in concerns about corporate social responsibility, accountability, transparency, reporting initiatives, and evaluation. One human rights NGO suggests that this agenda affects NGOs because by working with and receiving funding from governments, NGOs have become part of a 'governance cartel.' This has fundamentally changed their legitimacy, and greater scrutiny on issues of transparency, funding, accountability, and professionalism.

2.3.   Sources of NGO legitimacy

The interviewees cited seven sources of NGO legitimacy in all, directly and indirectly, and it is clear that there are many overlaps between them. In Chapters 3 and 7 of this book, attention is drawn to the sources again in attempts to regroup them systematically from the perspective of the tentative three-dimensional definition of legitimacy.

(1) Procedures. This refers to legitimacy related to transparency, accountability, independence of action, and principled behaviour. The NGOs consider transparency of action to be very important. One environmental NGO states that donor governments are supportive of them because they 'have got mission statements, the fact that we have got performance targets, the fact that we do evaluate [...] We just try [...] to really clearly communicate what we're doing, why, and how [...] every detail every step of the way, why we can do some things, why we can't do others.'

Accountability to funding bodies is another criterion of legitimacy. One NGO says that funding bodies make strict demands of the organization:

> These foundations, they really monitor us, they are very strict [...] we respect the commitments we have signed with them, and of course we would never have this growing support from rich individuals if we didn't explain to them that what we are doing is, generally speaking, of good quality, according to the mandate we have taken.

Another NGO suggests that transparency is perhaps more important to larger organizations, as their funding (and their legitimacy) relies on their visibility.

Another aspect of this is the legitimacy conferred by independence of action and standing up for one's beliefs. An environmental campaigning group argues that consistency of belief and action is a form of legitimacy: 'We are given a certain legitimacy by taking certain personal risks. We stand up for what we believe in.' Certain NGOs draw legitimacy from their refusal to take money from, or bargain with, political or corporate bodies. One international human rights NGO never bargains with governments and is extremely careful not to overstep its institutional mandate, even if this reduces its ability to take positions on certain issues. Some NGOs do not accept money from corporations, so as to retain their independence.

Most of the NGOs interviewed pay considerable attention to the issue of financial transparency, have annual reports and accounts audited by certified accountants, and make records of sizeable donations available to the general public. Some NGOs take money from governments, but refuse to accept sponsorship from corporations. They argue that corporations always want something in return for their money—unlike governments, who are merely distributing taxpayers' money. Some do not have a policy on private sector funding per se, but accept no money from companies that have interests in areas that they campaign on (such as in the diamond or forestry sectors). Other NGOs accept donations from corporations, but reject all forms of direct state funding. A small number of NGOs refuse both state and private sector funding, preferring to rely on donations from private individuals and foundations. Lastly, some organizations are more open to receiving funding from a variety of sources, including the Dutch government, the private sector, and the European Commission.

Predictably, given the variety of approaches, NGOs disagree about the extent to which institutional or corporate funding creates dependency. Some argue that the funding body's aims do not affect its own: funding is granted on the basis of proposals that are independently written by NGOs. One environmental NGO states: 'We write proposals, we say exactly what we're going to say, and it has not once happened that a government—either they say no to a proposal, they can do that, but they have never once said, "yes, but [...]"'. Another suggests that it is easier for a large organization to preserve its autonomy:

> A strong organization is in a better position to negotiate with donors, to prove to them that the priorities that have been decided upon are the good ones. And quite often we believe that the best way to deal with the donors is to build up a good case and to tell them, you should fund that. Not to look for the interest of the donors and to adapt, which is a temptation. [...] I have taken part in many meetings, and I would say that I didn't feel that we were guided by the donors.

One human rights NGO suggests that it is more difficult for NGOs in developing countries and newly emerging democracies to achieve sufficient distance and autonomy from governments.

A couple of NGOs are sceptical about these arguments, suggesting that accepting private sector or state funding always creates some form of obligation. As far as the interview data are concerned, however, there is no correlation between this viewpoint and an organization's general refusal to accept state or private funding. One interviewee makes the point that many NGO staff and funding institution employees have similar backgrounds: 'They live in the same world as the people from human rights organizations or humanitarian organizations, they go to the same meetings [...] they have common spaces. So it's rather obvious that they tend to have rather close priorities.'

(2) Popular support. For some NGOs, the existence of a measurable national and international membership is a critical aspect of legitimacy. The representative of one human rights NGO refers to this, and specifically its democratic credentials, as being a core criterion of legitimacy: 'We have so many members and supporters—people who regularly contribute by giving money or by being active in the organization. So, one of the major sort of legitimacies is the fact that (our organization) has democratic structures [...].'

As with representativeness, the role played by public support in legitimizing an organization's activities varies. Some organizations are member-driven and put great effort into ensuring that members have a say in the direction of the policies adopted. For certain organizations interviewed, members can attend annual general meetings and discuss policies, and there is extensive outreach to member groups. One interviewee commented, 'We (this NGO) are the membership.' By contrast, public support plays only a minor role in other organizations where there is no formal membership as such. Some, for instance, rely heavily upon expertise and effectiveness alone for legitimacy. The extent to which membership plays a significant role also depends upon the office in question; some national offices have very different membership policies due to different historical and cultural circumstances.

Although not all organizations put substantial resources into consulting with members, there is general consensus on the fact that popular mobilization is essential to achieving change, as public support can be used to put pressure on powerful actors such as governments and corporations. These opinions were expressed thus:

> I think [the number of members] will become increasingly important in
> order to have an impact on powerful governments in the South, to have

membership of supporters of some kind in these countries themselves. I think the public face [...] is really important, it's what motivates the companies in the end [...] all the behind-the-scenes work is supported by that inherent threat of mobilizing people to take action. Coalitions are very important [...] in the democratic parliamentary process, because obviously coalitions express the sheer number of citizens that are organized in a coalition and have a lot of influence. If we look at the advocacy strategy [...] the research and the arguments are not enough [...] you've got to mobilize [...] it can be signatures, it can be money given to an organization, it can be via e-mail chains, there's a lot ways to mobilize. But I think that in the end, the power question will make the difference [...] if we have the right arguments but not enough popular mobilization, then the leadership still won't change their behaviour.

NGOs that do involve the public in consultations and decision-making acknowledge that this can sometimes make it difficult for policy-makers to adopt unpopular or challenging policies. This is a dilemma faced by the Dutch section of one human rights NGO, for instance, which found that its decision to cover economic and social rights alongside its prisoner of conscience campaigns was met with some resistance in the Netherlands. Involving the membership in campaigns means having to make an effort to educate them about the thinking behind the organization's policies. This organization thus straddles two roles: an expert role on the one hand (a more top-down approach which relies on supporters rather than members) and a member-driven, democratic approach on the other (see further Text box 1, The dilemmas of being democratic).

Text box 1: The dilemmas of being democratic

The dilemmas of being democratic

One international human rights NGO interviewed distinguishes between two types of organizational structure: one that is democratic, bottom-up, and membership-based, and one that is top-down, expertise-based and focused on attracting more transient, issue-based support. This NGO has traditionally opted for the former model, and has a deep-rooted following in the Netherlands. This structure is not without its drawbacks, however: the need to canvass member opinion can be limiting, and the structure cannot always be replicated elsewhere:

> 'In other parts of the world [...] it's possible to mobilize people on human rights issues, [but] it's much more difficult to actually make them a member. Sometimes they don't have money [...] Sometimes it might be dangerous to be put on lists. Sometimes the commitment to the human rights campaign might be quite ephemeral [...]. And sometimes the tradition [...] of being a member of an organization, mostly by means of paying, doesn't exist.'

As a result, this NGO is turning to a supporter model, whereby it looks for transient, issue-based support and expects less input from its members.

> 'What you see is in a way a loosening of the member concept [...] a shift more to people who adhere to (this organization), who are supporters who maybe don't support us all the time, but on specific issues and campaigns.' This shift is controversial: 'You would have most people in the organization [...] arguing that mobilizing people is [...] so essential to our organization that if you take that away, the organizational concept and the organization itself—if you take that away [...] I think that's what a lot of the discussion in the next ten or fifteen years will be about. You can mobilize people without being democratic. And you can even argue that democracy in some situations, maybe in many situations, puts a brake on the capacity to mobilize.' The tension between the two models is not yet acute, however, 'because in resource terms, we are able to service both systems. We can service the old-style work, which is mostly local groups, and we can service quite high-profile campaigning from the office, which is directed [...] at the Dutch public.'

The potential loss of internal accountability resulting from a shift towards the supporter model could be made up for elsewhere: 'We would have to compensate that by more directly relating to the individuals and groups that we actually want to benefit, the primary stakeholders [...] And we would have to develop clearer protocols and mechanisms for that.' For this reason, 'it's increasingly important to be able to show that what you do is effective or has an impact or is seen by people, on whose behalf we are campaigning, as something that is important or relevant to them.'

Certain organizations draw attention to the legitimacy conferred by another form of public endorsement: financial support. The representative of one environmental NGO states:

> We have a certain democratic legitimacy [...] by having millions of supporters. And while they do not give us a specific mandate, they decide by their membership fee whether they agree with us or not. So, if they disagree with our influence, they have a very simple way of reducing that influence by leaving the organization.

Likewise, a development NGO states:

> We have three hundred thousand (and that's a growing number) paying donors and you could say a paying vote might be better than a once-a-year vote [...] There's forty-five organizations in our General Assembly that together represent about two to three million Dutch people. So, that's our legitimacy in Holland.

WWF's representative also says that WWF derives legitimacy from the fact that half of its income is privately generated.

(3) Effectiveness. A number of NGOs stress the quality of their expertise and the information they provide, and the legitimacy that this gives their organizations. One interviewee, for instance, says that 'we have a science unit, we get the facts right. If you work in an international convention, it's not good enough just to make emotional arguments—you have to support them through science.' He also states that 'we believe in the power of our arguments, which are supported by scientific work.' The representative of HRW emphasizes his organization's expert credentials and the high quality of its information-checking procedures. WWF likewise emphasizes the link between legitimacy, quality of information, and expertise. Another NGO also stresses that its staff are

experts in their respective areas, and that it would never tackle issues in which it did not have expertise.

Text box 2: Managing information

Managing information

Advocacy NGOs are very aware of the need to provide up-to-date, accurate information. This is not only because its reputation (and legitimacy) is grounded in its expertise, but also because information provision can have a real impact on how situations unfold, and can prevent the abuse of human rights. This demands careful information management:

'In Kosovo, for example, we decided to counter one of the major criticisms of a human rights organization, that they produce a report when everyone is dead, and they don't act quickly on denunciation of abuses and atrocities [...]. So we had decided to organize a system of information which was based around Brussels. We had people in Macedonia and Albania, and we had people in New York and Brussels. We were organizing a system by which the researchers were sending information, it was confirmed and checked, and then it was being [...] released from New York and Brussels after a legal counselling. And it was like working on full-time basis, 24 hours, in a rolling news centre. And this was very dangerous, because working in a war zone, the cloud of war is really something that exists. The temptation, of course, for the researchers—because they saw the atrocities—was to become militant and say, "why should I take the risk of obtaining information that I'm not sure by one per cent that hasn't really happened? If I don't say that, there might be more killing". So the temptation was there. We had to really re-conceptualize the management of news and make sure that we didn't have the temptation to send out information without having [...] clearly approved accuracy of information.'

A related aspect of credibility/effectiveness is the fact that the organization is able, as a result of its size and financial power, to maintain a long-term presence in a particular region or devote substantial resources to an issue: 'We're spending a year or two investigating one kind of abuse somewhere in the world where no one else will be.'

Lastly, NGOs see legitimacy being conferred by the ability to actually demonstrate effectiveness, in the form of lasting achievements. For example, the representative of GW argues that its campaigns have been a deciding factor in putting the link between illegal natural resource extraction and abuse of human rights on the international agenda. Likewise, representatives of ANL and GPI emphasize their contributions to international law and changing norms at the international level; and the MSC points to its achievements in developing sustainable fisheries.

All of the NGOs interviewed have monitoring and evaluation procedures, although these rarely extend to impact assessments carried out by third parties or independent bodies. NGOs have an obvious interest in monitoring the effectiveness of their work, not only because donors demand measurable results, but also because in general, it helps them to be more effective. One NGO, for instance, has recently carried out an impact assessment on an area of core importance to the organization: 'We feel strongly that this is one of our most important activities, but we need first of all a better mapping of what we're doing throughout this whole network on the different cases, and then better understand the impact of the different strategies and tools that we use in the context of that case work.' Another describes evaluation as 'one of our current obsessions': 'We want to make sure that we don't just make nice, very ethical statements, but that what we say that we do has impact.' Others also suggest that aside from being able to keep track of achievements, the process of monitoring is also a means of preserving institutional memory—especially when there is a high staff turnover.

A number of NGOs are sceptical about the utility of defining effectiveness too closely, however. A point that is often made by the interviewees is that it can be difficult to explain exactly how a campaign or intervention made a difference. Some examples are relatively clear-cut, such as Amnesty International's success in fighting against the death penalty. In areas such as protection, however, human rights NGOs are less confident: 'It's always hard to say if its your own doing, because sometimes you're working on an issue for a long time and nothing is happening, and suddenly something happens in the outside world.' In some cases, the gradual nature of change can make a long-term success look like a short-term defeat. An NGO cites the case of a campaign against the World Bank, where despite support from the Bank's staff, the Board ultimately rejected its recommendations, 'so you lose at the board level. But these things stay [in the institution and] gradually [make their] way into the policies.'

Despite these difficulties, a couple of NGOs are more upbeat about the possibility of measuring effectiveness, for example, by using measurable indicators. An interviewee from one development NGO argues that 'when people say you can't measure the results of development work, I don't agree at all. We can measure and we should measure [...] I know that [in these assessments] we're adding up apples and pears, but we can still say that there are ten pieces in the bowl!' One NGO, for example, has introduced target-driven programmes: 'They are all completely measurable and we are actually required [by the international secretariat] to measure ourselves against the achievements of those targets and milestones [...] It's a very elaborate system of accountability and reporting.' On the other hand, the usefulness of extensive evaluation processes is questionable. Some NGOs suggest that donors' demands are crippling, that external evaluation models can be badly suited to their goals, and that in the end, it is often hard to learn lessons from complex and unique situations.

Text box 3: The limits of evaluation

The limits of evaluation

As the recipients of substantial funding from governments and international organizations, development NGOs are careful to ensure that they can monitor and evaluate their programmes, and quantify how many beneficiaries they are reaching:

> 'For the last five years, we have asked our partners to indicate the direct reach of their programmes, in numbers of people, and to give an indication of indirect reach. So if you have a micro-credit programme [...] you know you've got seven thousand women you're reaching, and you can do an estimate of [how] with that money, those women are getting their kids to school, now getting food on the table [...] We know that the eight hundred partners that we support are reaching thirty-five million people in direct terms, and about ten-fold indirectly.'

Getting such figures is arduous work, however, and figures alone do not always tell the whole story. In order to do a proper evaluation, one has to look at the details of the programme, not just at the numbers. The interviewee explains this with reference to a report undertaken by the World Health Organization on food security and food intake. Previously,

'food security was always measured at household level. But food security and food intake are two different things. They did in-depth research
and they found out that in Africa, the women usually eat while they're
preparing the food and feed the younger children while they're preparing the food, before it comes on the table to the husband. And in Asia,
they don't: there's no eating in the preparing of the food, that's for religious reasons, and then the food gets put out to the husband and his
friends, and then to the sons, and then to the girls, and the last person
who eats is the mother—which often means she doesn't eat. So in terms
of intervention, if you want to change that, gender policies and assert-
iveness training's the most important thing [...] So that's the interesting
work, I think, that's understanding what the impact actually is.'

(4) *International norms.* This refers to legitimacy derived from the fact
that the organization is pursuing or protecting established international
norms. The majority of interviewees made the point that actions are
rooted in internationally agreed norms, and that this gives legitimacy
to the actions of NGOs. The representative of HRW states that 'we base
our action on the international bill of rights', a point also made by ANL.
A development NGO argues that they 'make demands on the grounds
of internationally agreed morality. We (i.e., the international community) have the Universal Declaration of Human Rights (UDHR), we have
a number of international labour laws, and we have actually agreed on
all these standards.'

Thus, the fact that the organization is acting within firmly established
legal, ethical, or political practices contributes to its legitimacy. The
core of this argument is that the NGO is not transgressing any accepted
code of practice by pursuing its particular agenda. First, a number of
organizations argue that they act within the bounds of international law,
as a result of their consultative or legal status in international conventions. DfC/ECPAT has a formal role in upholding the 1989 UN Convention on the Rights of the Child, for instance, a treaty that was originally
drawn up (in part) by NGOs. The representative of ANL also draws attention to its consultative status with international organizations. Other
organizations also stress the fact that their actions are indirectly (if not
always directly) rooted in established political norms and processes.
The representative of DfC/ECPAT points out that in democratic societies, the changes that NGOs fight for ultimately have to be sanctioned
by parliaments. Many NGOs also emphasize that they gain political le-

gitimacy via partnership with bodies that are formally democratic or representative (a point that is in turn linked to the concept of popular legitimacy): 'Because we work with parliamentarians and trade unions that have huge memberships, and because we work with churches that have huge memberships, we are reinforcing the quality of the representative system.'

Secondly, a number of organizations argue that not only do they work within legitimate political structures, but they also strengthen them. The representative of one environmental campaigning NGO suggests that NGOs reinforce democracy by keeping a check on powerful interests: their presence suggests that society has become more, not less, democratic. As the interviewee puts it, 'We are a very good watchdog, and societies need watchdogs.' A similar point is made by the representative of a human rights NGO: 'I think that it's a cheap shot when they [governments] say that NGOs are not representative. Knowing the crisis of the current modes of representation, I think that NGOs have been providing the best guarantee for democracy to survive.' This point is also made by the representative of Novib, who argues that governments should be supporting the development of civil society because it creates a 'deeper' form of democracy than the ballot box.

(5) Morality. This refers to legitimacy that comes from the organization's involvement in promoting change on moral grounds. Many of the NGOs interviewed make the argument that their contribution to addressing injustice or abuse legitimizes their actions. The core assumption here is that aspects of the contemporary international system are themselves illegitimate, and that NGOs play a legitimate role in changing them for the better.

Central to this line of reasoning is the argument that the issue addressed by the NGO is so important that it is itself a source of legitimacy. One human rights organization makes this point about children's rights when it argues that the extent of public support for their agenda is, in a sense, irrelevant. Even if no public support existed, it would still be important to carry out the work. In a similar way, an environmental/human rights campaigning organization suggests that taking action is imperative, even if it means breaking with the majority view or contradicting diplomatic norms—the ends can justify the means in certain cases. This argument is particularly potent when the NGO is the main, or only, organization addressing a particular issue. An organization might draw legitimacy from being the largest human rights organization in a particular home society, or being the first organization to successfully bring an issue to international attention. Furthermore, environmental groups derive further legitimacy from the fact that they are protecting the common heritage of mankind, thus adding weight to the notion that there are some issues that are inherently worth pursuing.

Some organizations stress that their actions do not transgress widely accepted codes of ethics, such as journalistic ethics, with regard to issues such as the protection of sources or the right treatment of individuals or personnel. One human rights NGO, for instance, is keen to show that its advocacy strategies are in agreement with well-understood principles of ethics, and that it takes ethical issues into account when making decisions ('I'd say that we have very high standards and do not jump to conclusions'), has high standards of accuracy, and makes sure that it can protect its sources. CCC, which campaigns for higher standards in garment factories worldwide, is careful to protect the identity of informants, and takes care to ensure that workers' complaints are genuine. GW, meanwhile, is careful not to use identifiable sources and put people's lives at risk.

(6) Recognition. This refers to legitimacy conferred by partnerships, and the benefits and public recognition that these can bring. A number of organizations suggest that their presence in a network of partnerships, or the fact that they work with governments and powerful actors, gives legitimacy to their actions. One interviewee states that cooperation with other NGOs creates 'complementarity. One cannot do everything by oneself.' It is not just complementarity 'in fields of information and expertise [...] but also efficiency.'

Acceptance by governments is an important factor: 'They take us seriously as a dialogue partner, and that's a source of legitimacy.' Some NGOs also draw legitimacy from their relationship with governments and consultative status at international organizations. One suggests that the fact that they receive funding from the Dutch Government has 'opened many doors', and HRW likewise draws status from the fact that it is respected by governments for the quality of its work. Partnerships with governments also imply that the organization is accountable for public funds, another source of legitimacy. Moreover, the collaborative, trust-based approach to partnerships taken by some NGOs adds to their legitimacy. The assumption is that trust is necessary in order to access particular issues or regions and build consensus for change.

More broadly, organizations draw legitimacy from their links with powerful people or establishment figures, such as senior church figures, scientists, or members of royal families. Legitimacy is likewise drawn from the links and partnerships with international experts; the representative of DfC/ECPAT argues that its work is legitimate because 'we have been asked by colleagues all over the world to do [it].' Another type of partnership legitimacy is identified by the representative of the MSC, who states that the fact that its founding was a result of collaboration between a conservation NGO and a multinational company gives it a special form of legitimacy. Lastly, the different roles and partnerships adopted by NGOs reinforce each other's legitimacy.

Text box 4: Cooperation

Cooperation
Connecting is an important theme for one environmental NGO:

'Together, we are not only more efficient, but also more effective. One might say we are each other's competitors, but we can agree [that] the interests at stake of the people we are working for are considerable, so it is better we are not each other's competitors. That doesn't create any surplus value.'

NGOs engage with the public and private sector at a range of levels, and are aware of the complexities these relationships present. One NGO (see Text box 5, The complex relationship triad) sees itself as having a complex relationship with all three sectors—government, corporations, and civil society. The idea that, in general, it is possible to both cooperate and criticize is a common theme among the NGOs. Another NGO, for instance, works with a range of actors, depending on the issue at stake. Sometimes, principles preclude a working relationship; this NGO would not work with the Catholic Church on sexual health, for instance. Trust-based relationships are seen as critical to achieving progress in particular areas, however: 'When you're based completely on advocacy positions, [the extent of the relationship] doesn't really matter. When you're trying to get permission to do project work in a country, you've got to be pretty careful.'

Text box 5: The complex relationship triad

The complex relationship triad

The Dutch office of one development NGO sees the relationship between civil society, the private sector, and government as a triad that can be conceptualized at the local, national, and international levels. Each has a complex relationship with the others:

'We see ourselves as being part of civil society, and we see ourselves as having what we call a complex relationship with both government and the corporate sector and civil society. What do I mean by a complex relationship? [...] I can illustrate it very clearly with the Dutch Government. We get a lot of money from the Dutch Government, two thirds of our money comes from [them]. We sometimes wholeheartedly agree with the Dutch Government [...] and sometimes, we wholeheartedly disagree [...] And that's the same with the corporate sector: we get some sponsorship from the corporate sector, we criticize the corporate sector. There are businesses that we like and work with [...] there are businesses that we hate [...] and there are a lot of businesses who are somewhere in between, who are trying to work more on socially responsible business. So we argue with them and we push them and pull them and they argue back [...] and we take money from them sometimes, they do sponsorship events with us [...] and we don't feel that means we've got to shut up [...] It's exactly the same with civil society. For example, (approximately) 150 organizations took part in (the Dutch Social Forum [Nederlands Sociaal Forum]), from old people's unions to the churches to *Attac* [...]. But none of that is simple. We were the biggest sponsor of the Dutch Social Forum, so the same power dynamics started playing towards us. Here I am, wanting this, sponsoring it, but wanting it to be an autonomous and free place of discussion.'

(7) Representation. The issue of representation can be divided into two main aspects. First, the question of who or what the organization ultimately claims to represent (external representation); and second, the question of how representation is structured within the organization itself, and the extent to which interests and values are able to filter up and down the organization (internal representation).

External representation. The question 'Who does this NGO ultimately represent?' is acknowledged by a number of NGOs to be a difficult issue and one which challenges them in their day-to-day work. The interviewee from PCNL suggests that it's 'awkward to discuss people's interests in their absence', and that 'you have to break out [of day-to-day work] to make sure that you're connected to the people on behalf of whom you speak.' There is consensus that the problem of representation is solvable, however. One obvious response is to clearly define the target beneficiaries. Some NGOs interviewed claim to represent the end beneficiaries of their actions, and others make demands on behalf of all people who want a just world. By extension, the interviewee from PCNL argues that representation can also be enhanced by maintaining extensive links with representative groups.

Another response is to avoid the term representation altogether, and to use formulas such as 'speaking on behalf of', or 'working with'. One environmental NGO interviewed, for example, does not claim to have a specific mandate for action, since it cannot claim to be acting as a collective view for all its supporters. Instead, it takes a general mandate for action from its supporters. Other NGOs avoid the term represent. According to one, 'represent sounds as if you have a set of structures in place where you can claim a representation function. So I prefer to use a less loaded term, something like "seek to reflect the view of", which is more humble.' One NGO argues that when it comes to members, 'I'm not claiming to seek to reflect their views directly, because I don't know what their views are.' Some interviewees suggest that they do not represent their beneficiaries, but rather work with them and consult them.

Text box 6: The limits of representation

The limits of representation
One representative of an environmental NGO is hesitant to use the word representation because it implies that there is a correlation between what the organization does and what members think—which is not always necessarily true. On some complex issues, representation is virtually impossible. This interviewee gives the example of (not) taking a position on the new EU constitution:

'I think [the European constitution] is a very good case study at the moment ... Referendums in ten countries or so, and questions from our sections—what should be our position? It's similar to the situation in the mid-1990s, when four countries—Finland, Austria, Sweden and Norway—would come to this office and say, should we join or shouldn't we, what would you tell Swedish public opinion or Norwegian public opinion? It's the same with the constitution. I think it's a very good example of where this whole question of ... representation comes in. Who am I speaking on behalf of if I were to say, "Well, I think the constitution's a good thing"? [...] So then you come back to this formulation, "seeking to reflect the view of", and I don't think that's good enough either as a guide for something like this. So I think with the question of the Swedish, Austrians, Norwegians and so on, with the constitution [...] the only safe way to behave [...] is to do a pros and cons analysis. And then you say you're going to gain or going to lose, but also think about the standards that you have for things like accountability in Norway, freedom of information, the environmental standards, and then ask yourself, how useful would those be to export to Estonia, Latvia? [...] So you're not trying to make an opinion yourself, but you're trying to give a sort of analytical tool for people to use.'

Internal representation. Some NGOs define themselves in terms of a grassroots ethos and put great emphasis on the maintenance of participatory and representative structures: 'One of the principles we operate on as a campaign is that [demand for action] has to come from the workers and their representatives.' This is not just a matter of principle, but also a question of effectiveness: consultation is necessary for a network organization: 'We [...] strategize and evaluate together, and I think that's the main way we get to know that we're sort of thinking and going in the same direction.' Participatory structures are important because:

people have the best ideas about how they want to manage their environment, what is important for them, for their livelihoods, and nobody should tell them how to do that best [...] we will work with them to find out what kind of improvements can happen, and we will share information with them on how things have gone wrong in other communities, but it will never be that we step in and say, this is how you do it.

Involving one's partners or members is also necessary for successful implementation of policies. Action ultimately takes place at the local level.

It is clear that often in these organizations, discussion concerning specific issues takes place at the national or local level, and the conclusions then filter up to the international level. Individual country offices and local member groups have a significant amount of policy autonomy in a number of organizations. In those cases, the function of the international office is to coordinate and, if necessary, reconcile the different views. This seems to contradict the idea that NGOs tend to undemocratically impose policies from above, and suggests that debate is more rooted in national structures than would appear to be the case. However, when it comes to actual partner organizations, rather than member groups, there is some scepticism about the extent to which the language of partnership reflects genuine partnership or is merely rhetorical. The third sector is full of NGOs referring to partners, but in the end, 'everybody would like to have partners who are exactly like themselves.' One NGO has witnessed NGOs that do not make enough effort to be representative, either internally or externally. This view is not expressed consistently, however, and one organization overturns many conventional assumptions about NGOs by suggesting that it is the Southern member groups and partners, rather than Northern organizations, which exercise power in the organization, because they are in touch with the key people and issues—ultimately, as the representative puts it, 'they live it.' From this perspective, it is much more difficult for a Northern group to be taken seriously on development issues.

In direct comparison to this grassroots ethos, there are a number of NGOs that take a top-down, globalist approach. Instead of working upwards from local issues, these groups use expertise to identify global issues that are then applicable in local circumstances. For example, a couple of NGOs interviewed focus on a select number of global issues in order to achieve maximum impact, while acknowledging the need to engage with local groups. Moreover, as suggested above, a number of organizations—whether emphasizing global or local concerns—strongly reject the notion that NGOs need to be democratic in order to be legitimate.

Text box 7: Globalism versus localism

Globalism versus localism
NGOs can have very different perspectives on the extent to which grassroots views should feed directly into policy. Two environmental organizations interviewed offer an interesting contrast in this respect.

The first tends to focus on global issues and has a top-down attitude to developing expertise; recruitment is geared to bringing in experts in their respective fields, and campaigns are planned with global strategies in mind.

> 'We've decided to work on a limited number of global issues. We typically don't deal with local issues [...] we see our special responsibility (as working) on global environmental problems: for example, oceans, overfishing, dumping at sea, climate change, genetic engineering, deforestation of ancient forests. That does not necessarily (mean) in all cases that the sum of local concerns ends up to be a global concern. So, while we work with local organizations and try to be respectful of them, we try to have a global view, express that very clearly, and follow it through.'

The culture of a second NGO interviewed is notably different. This second organization is the archetypal bottom-up, participatory organization:

> 'Nothing happens here, or should happen, top-down.' A key concept behind its activities is the principle of self-determination: the notion that local people should have the right to determine their own development, and that local people tend to know what is best for themselves: 'People have the best ideas about how they want to manage their environment, what's important for them, for their livelihoods, and nobody should tell them how to do that best.' As a result, the international secretariat focuses on coordinating knowledge and resolving contradictions between the different groups, rather than directing global policy from the centre: 'We spend a lot of time developing communications systems and democratizing parts of the decision-making, so that people [...] get information on time in the right language [and] can provide input.'

Both NGOs acknowledge that neither approach to running an environmental organization is necessarily the best—and that the differences between them can be complementary. As the second says of the first, the organization 'starts from a knowledge base [...] and then that translates into what needs to happen in practice. And that's fine, it's just different. We start from the knowledge that is in the grassroots, and it's the variety and diversity of that knowledge that makes it interesting and good—and nobody can replace that. It's just a different perspective.'

A number of organizations engaged in internal consultation emphasize the fact that achieving successful representation is a challenging and time-consuming process, especially when extensive cultural differences must be bridged. For some NGOs, internal consultation is time-consuming and it is difficult to create a representative structure that functions well: 'It's a difficult question and we're struggling with it internally [...] how we should relate to these groups.' Similar views are expressed by others who identify a number of tensions between supporters of representative working methods, and supporters of more direct democratic working methods within the organization. There is also a cultural split in the organization between those national groups that are organized on a hierarchical basis, and those which are more participatory; and different attitudes to campaigning (whether based on lobbying or direct action) can also contribute to tensions within the network: 'Commitment does not have to be a majority standpoint to be legitimate.' A certain viewpoint does not have to be the opinion of the majority to be legitimate.

NGOs employ a number of strategies to overcome these problems. One NGO states that if affiliated sections cannot come to some form of consensus on an issue, then the issue is dropped. Others also have formal and informal procedures for disaffiliating or disciplining groups that fail to follow the organization's line. An alternative strategy is to avoid organizational structures that lead to conflict rather than consensus. One NGO, for instance, having witnessed the conflicts within other organizations, deliberately avoided becoming a membership-voting organization, and instead adopted a consensus-based model of decision-making.

Text box 8: Representation and cultural differences

Representation and cultural differences

Large international NGOs can encounter tensions when different cultural models conflict. This problem is clearly set out by an employee of an environmental NGO:

> 'One of the conflict areas is democracy through representation versus direct democracy, and that is something that we really struggle with in the network. Because in many European countries, [democracy is] through representation, no question. And for Latin American countries, this is sometimes very hard, because they really want direct democracy, and in every decision, everybody has to be involved. And there's no right and wrong here [...] For example, [with] the board, the Asians and Europeans will say, "we have been elected to be here, we are accountable, so we can make decisions". But the Latin Americans will say, "no, we have to go back, check it all out, because otherwise we can't say anything" [...] Because for the Latin Americans, any kind of representation is seen as a hierarchy, and they're very, very anti-hierarchical groups. And then in Africa you have a whole different concept of representation [...] there's much less consultation, it's much more directive. And there, within the culture, you can't have a directive organization sit around the table with everyone around the same level, because it just doesn't work. He's the boss, and he will still listen, but he will not say, "you have the same force as I do". So that's also [something] that we have to accept.'

2.4.   Challenges for the future

At the end of the interviews, representatives from the selected NGOs were asked to identify issues that they thought would present challenges in the future, both in terms of legitimacy and more generally. The most frequently expressed concerns are listed below.

First is the question of how NGOs can move their agendas forward and, in particular, influence the actions of states and corporations. A couple of organizations argue that there has been much progress in standard setting, but there are still limited means of enforcing standards. This is a particular problem in the area of international standards, where many gaps in policy remain:

> The basic premise is that we document human rights violations and we say to national governments, the governments responsible, that they should deal with this, that they should change policies or practices. The hole, or the gap, is what the responsibility of the international community is [...] that's the area where we don't have a doctrine.

Moving agendas forward is also related to the issue of relevance; some NGOs are consciously looking for the areas in which they can have the most impact, or added value. One human rights NGO suggests, for instance, that in an era of 24-hour media coverage, NGOs need to pay more attention to in-depth analysis. Another perceives similar dilemmas:

> The human rights organization certainly has to think more broadly about its responsibilities and how it connects with other issues, in order to make itself more relevant. This means a different way of recruiting people, of contextualizing the reports, it needs more maturity. We are still at the first steps of the intellectual concept.

Second, international NGOs need to develop structures that are relevant to local groups and interests as well as global in scope. There are a number of challenges associated with this. For example, how to reconcile the balance between local and global issues in an NGO's portfolio: One human rights NGO describes the delicate balancing act between preserving the organization's Western identity and the risk of its message being diluted:

> You have a choice between staying more or less a Western organization, as we were, and run the risk of losing legitimacy in the sense that you remain to be seen as Western and not being global and universal—and adopting a much broader mission and running the risk of diluting yourself too much.

A related question is how outreach policies can be developed that will attract members and/or supporters, and how can these policies be reconciled with different sorts of internal representation? For instance, to what extent should an organization have democratic membership structures? As one interviewee states,

The word 'democratic' is an essential word, I think that's what a lot of the discussion in the next ten or fifteen years will be about. You can mobilize people without being democratic. And you can even argue that democracy, in some situations, maybe many situations, puts a break on the capacity to mobilize.

Yet another issue is how organizational structures can be developed which will overcome cultural differences. NGOs highlight the differences in approaches to campaign strategy and decision-making in Northern and Southern countries.

Third, there is the question of how far NGOs should play by the rules of the countries in which they deploy their activities when intervening or carrying out research. If an NGO encounters a situation in which bending the rules might ultimately result in an important change in policy, should it do so? One of the NGOs interviewed occasionally benefits from clandestine research (i.e., sending in researchers without the permission of the national authorities)—a fact that has caused some debate within the organization. This dilemma is particularly acute for NGOs working in closed countries or under repressive regimes, in which cases it might be very difficult to obtain information.

Fourth, NGOs face the challenge of developing effective working relations and networks, while at the same time preserving their own identities and particular concerns. One interviewee is critical of the proliferation of NGOs, suggesting that greater cooperation is necessary. In some areas, however, working together is particularly difficult—as in the case of drawing up international standards and conventions. GPI points out that in the 1980s, it was one of the few NGOs contributing to discussions on international environmental conventions, whereas now hundreds of NGOs have an interest in such discussions.

Fifth, there is the question of the extent to which NGOs should be subject to quality standards or specific criteria at the international level. Some are open to the idea of standards for NGOs, particularly those relating to financial transparency. The key is developing appropriate standards. As one interviewee puts it,

You don't say that it's difficult and therefore it can't be done [...] for certain types of, let's call them membership- or supporter-based organizations, you can apply one set of standards. If you're network-based and so forth, then you possibly apply a different set. But you don't walk away from the need.

The MSC has important experience in this area, as standardization and accreditation is a process that it has been through as a member of the International Social and Environmental Accreditation and Labelling Alliance. Others argue that fixed standards for, say, giving access to participation in international organizations would always be open to abuse by powerful actors, and would set dangerous limits on democracy. One NGO, for instance, thinks that a transparency criterion would be acceptable, but that other actors should not be able to determine how an NGO should be structured or defined: 'I would tend to think that democracy by itself tries to avoid too many criteria for participation in debates and internationally that should be the case.'

Lastly, NGOs see the changing political climate as a challenge—and in particular the increasing limits on freedom of expression and organization that have accompanied governments' responses to international terrorism. Many NGOs see the perceived war on terror as a threat to their political space, making them increasingly vulnerable to charges of collusion or political smears. One development NGO suggests that 'the tension's going to get worse [...] with the "war on terror", there's a very, very conscious attempt to decrease our civil space.' NGOs are aware that they will need to be especially transparent and accountable in their actions in order to counter such accusations.

3.   Illustration: Stakeholders' views

Interviews with some stakeholders reveal a wide range of forms of cooperation between NGOs and stakeholders. The variety in these relationships results in an equally diverse range of perceptions of the legitimacy of NGOs. A representative of a multinational corporation puts it thus: 'In all topics we work with NGOs. They can act as the voice of citizens and in that sense they are very useful for us. NGOs are organizations through which we receive information about the public opinion about our work and our projects.' Politicians and trade professionals argue that 'there has been a broad realization of the importance of the inclusion of NGOs and the public opinion into what were before considered behind closed doors negotiations. So, you have the institutional dialogue and you have a constant informal dialogue with them.'

In addition to governments and intergovernmental organizations, institutes and foundations also cooperate with NGOs to achieve their aims. One interviewee, an employee of an international foundation, states that 'although we focus our attention on local government reform, we work through NGOs in a wide variety of everything from policy centred to formal associations to technical assistance groups.' Because the NGOs involved act in the stakeholders' interests, these institutes try to improve the effectiveness and efficiency of NGOs. One interviewee states that 'we try to come up with some policy recommendations how to sustain the NGO sector in certain parts of our interest region. We support NGOs who work for [us] as a network and we help them to become independent institutional partners.'

Text box 9: A threefold relationship between stakeholder and NGO

A threefold relationship between stakeholder and NGO
A representative of a large donor organization described the relationship with NGOs as threefold:

'First, it is as a relationship with a partner in policy dialogue. This is something that has developed over the last ten, fifteen years. Second, it is through supporting programmes and projects implemented by NGOs. Third, it is a relationship that builds capacity in NGOs. This is done, not only through transfer of funds or support, but also by training, internships, etc. People work [here], give presentations on different issues, and that is the way we build capacity.'

It is interesting to note that stakeholders conceive of NGOs as a means to strengthen their own legitimacy. Most of the stakeholders interviewed are aware of a debate about the legitimacy of NGOs, and have a different perspective on this from those outlined earlier in this chapter. Opinions on the value of questioning NGO legitimacy vary from statements such as 'I think NGOs need to be more legitimate', and 'NGOs are artificially constructed by subsidies that are not part of the market. Let them also be part of the market [because the market excludes illegitimate NGOs]' to statements such as, 'How do you really define their legitimacy [...] or why would you?', and more suspicious views such as 'A discussion about legitimacy in a way is a discussion that governments would like to have to keep NGOs quiet.' Some interviewees also suggest that it does not make sense to talk about the legitimacy of NGOs in general terms: 'You know, it seems strange to me to talk about a legitimacy question of a general nature, since the work of NGOs is so different depending on the kind of issues they're addressing and the approaches they're taking. [...] So to talk about one model of legitimacy is kind of a mistake.'

Implicitly or explicitly, the stakeholders interviewed express their opinion about the seven sources of legitimacy distinguished in Section 2.

(1) Procedures. On procedures, there is a division of opinion among stakeholders. Generally, the stakeholders interviewed agree on the importance of criteria of transparency, accountability, credibility, having a good administration, and so on. Some stakeholders view this type of legitimacy with suspicion. Others doubt the decisiveness of these criteria: 'I think that an organization that is not transparent, but meets other requirements, can be legitimate.'

(2) Popular support. Some stakeholders conceive of an NGO's public authority or public support as the main source of its legitimacy. Others point to the fact that popular support might disregard the views of minority groups: 'NGOs sometimes reflect a minority view. [...] this is not to say that the NGOs should just reflect what is the popular view in a country. Then you'll never get change, you'll just get the status quo.'

(3) Effectiveness. Most stakeholders agree on the importance of expertise and resulting criteria such as efficiency, effectiveness, and even speed. One stakeholder states that '[we work with] NGOs because of the expertise that the NGOs have, because of the legitimacy it also brings [...] and also because [we] realize that NGOs can reach certain places that [we] cannot reach.' Another stakeholder points to the importance of constructive cooperation for the legitimacy of NGO actions: 'Honesty, credibility, and being part of the solution. We are not looking for NGOs that just want to criticize us. We want NGOs that are part of the solution of the problems.'

(4) International norms. Many stakeholders point to the importance of complying with the law of the country where an NGO is operating. Others stress the importance of the presence of NGOs in international organizations for a system of international democratic governance. Some also suggest that being part of such a system can contribute to the legitimacy of the participating NGOs.

(5) Morality. The stakeholder interviewees argue that conformity with moral values is in itself insufficient for being legitimate. One interviewee says:

I think it is always good to have moral values, but that is not enough. [...]. If you mention human rights, for instance, you are not only talking about morality but also about law because human rights have now become law. So it's not because it's religion or because it's good, but because it's the law.

(6) Recognition. Stakeholders stress the importance of cooperation between NGOs and their stakeholders through policy dialogue, by sharing expertise, and by cooperating to solve jointly perceived problems.

Text box 10: Recognition

Recognition
With regard to the recognition aspect of network legitimacy, a representative of a large international organization states:

'This is something we've been talking about for a long time. Why shouldn't you cooperate with NGOs if they are proven specialists in a certain field? Why shouldn't you do research together? [...] This is a very sensitive topic here: politically impossible, not acceptable. [...] You shouldn't force NGOs to cooperate, because 99% would say: goodbye, we're not going do this. Maybe you should distinguish between soft and hard legitimacy. Cooperation is legitimacy of a soft kind.'

(7) Representation. With respect to internal representation, there is no unanimity. One interviewee says:

It is important to apply principles of democracy. Fine, but I think you should tell us how you can apply them to a professional organization and then you can talk about it, because obviously you cannot have every new decision in an organization voted on by everybody, because that is simply not reasonable [*sic*]. I think NGOs should work for democratization and democratic values, but they do not necessarily need to be democratic themselves.

Regarding external representation, some interviewees point to the importance of representing the views of beneficiaries, while others stress that the people on the ground might have other interests than the NGOs—for example, with regard to environmental issues.

Just as the interviewed representatives of NGOs do, the interviewed stakeholders stress the importance of knowledge and expertise. One stakeholder points to the legitimacy enhancing effect of representation/ participation generated by close partnerships with beneficiaries:

> [NGOs] need to have a relationship with the people whose problems they address. [...] they need to have a relationship when they are listening to these people. So if an NGO is addressing environmental problems in a particular country, it should be listening to the people of that country and represent these people's problems in the debate.

4.   Conclusion

The aim of this research was to gather and examine a set of perceptions from a range of organizations that could be used as the basis for analyzing understandings of the legitimacy of NGOs. As emphasized at the outset, these findings should be understood as a source of ideas about legitimacy, rather than data that allows us to make judgements about the legitimacy of particular activities of the NGOs.

It was found that many of the NGO representatives interviewed considered the legitimacy of NGOs to be an issue of concern, although not always a valid one. Some of the interviewees suggested that the legitimacy debate is politically driven, and that arguments about the representativeness, accountability, and transparency of the NGOs mask attacks on their reform agendas. Other interviewees were more willing to concede that some aspects of the activities of the NGOs lack aspects of legitimacy, and this is linked to a more general concern about standards of governance across many different kinds of organizations.

All of the interviewees referred to a range of overlapping sources of legitimacy: procedural criteria, popular support, effectiveness, international norms, morality, recognition, and representation. In Chapters 3 and 7 of this book, the concepts mentioned will be regrouped systematically from the perspective of the tentative three-dimensional definition of legitimacy. Interestingly, the representatives of the stakeholder organizations referred to similar sources of legitimacy when asked about their views on NGOs. Some suggested that the legitimacy of an NGO must come from a range of sources, rather than rest on one aspect of legitimacy alone. In this, they seem to echo the concerns expressed by some of the NGO interviewees. The latter referred to situations in which conformity to certain criteria—which under normal circumstances would increase legitimacy—could undermine the legitimacy of the NGO involved, such as conformity with the national laws of an oppressive regime.

What the interviews also suggest is that NGOs have put great consideration and effort into issues such as representation, relations with other civil society actors, and policies on funding and corporate sponsorship. In the course of the interviews, extremely sophisticated views and evidence of comprehensive policies were encountered in many areas. It is therefore critical that any discussion of the legitimacy of NGOs comes back to these existing policies and engages with the fact that NGOs and their core stakeholders are already tackling the issue.

Chapter 3   Internet activities of NGOs and legitimacy

Anke van Gorp

1.   Introduction[*]

The number of international NGOs and their involvement in international regulation on issues related to the environment, development and human rights has grown enormously over the past decade. A fairly recent phenomenon that adds a new dimension to the legitimacy discussion is the growing importance of the Internet in today's society and the use of this technology by NGOs. Extensive Internet and e-mail campaigns have shown the usefulness of the Internet for NGO activities. The existence of Internet-only NGOs—NGOs that operate solely on and through the Internet—would raise interesting issues, with regard to the regulatory aspect of legitimacy in particular. For instance, such NGOs cannot be registered in a domestic country (see Chapter 6). The research identified no such Internet-only NGOs. However, some NGOs, although having registered offices in the offline world, heavily depend on the Internet for the way they operate. Network NGOs that aim to provide information about human rights and environmental issues from all over the world are particularly dependent on the Internet. For these NGOs, the Internet is an inexpensive way to inform people, and e-mail a low-cost and fast way to communicate with partner groups from other continents. Even though Internet-only NGOs were not found, there are NGOs that make extensive use of the Internet and this raises interesting issues concerning the legitimacy of these NGOs. An example of such an issue is whether NGOs use their websites to publish

---

[*]   The author would like to thank Anton Vedder and Corien Prins for their comments on earlier versions of this chapter.

Anton Vedder et al., *NGO Involvement in International Governance and Policy*, pp. 59-110. Printed in the Netherlands. ISBN 978 90 04 15846 7.

information about their financial and organizational structure. If they do, this may contribute to the regulatory aspect of legitimacy.

Vedder (2006) proposes a distinction between dispositional legitimacy, the legitimacy of the NGO as a whole, and occurrent legitimacy, the legitimacy of certain activities of an NGO (see also Chapter 1). Although most of this chapter deals with occurrent legitimacy, the legitimacy of specific website activities, some data—information on the website about the NGO—is also relevant to dispositional legitimacy.

The two questions that will be addressed in this chapter are the following. How do NGOs use the Internet or, more specifically, their website? How do NGOs perceive the legitimacy of their website activities? These two questions will be answered empirically by analyzing NGO websites. The empirical data will be used to formulate normative ideas about the legitimacy of Internet activities of NGOs. (The final section of this chapter will focus on the reliability of the information on NGO websites. Chapter 7 will provide a more thorough analysis of the concept of legitimacy based on all contributions to this book).

In Chapter 2, traditional NGOs were examined as to their ideas about the legitimacy of NGOs. The method used was interviewing; in this chapter, websites will be analyzed. The research questions in this chapter are directed at the use of the Internet for external communication, discussions with donors, the mobilization of people, etc. With the research method used, the ways in which the Internet is used as an internal organizational tool cannot be determined. Of course, clues such as intranet links may be looked for on the website indicating that the website is not only used for external communication but also for internal communication. But the absence of an intranet link or a separate member login does not justify the conclusion that the Internet is not used for internal or organizational purposes. If online meetings are scheduled or a link to the intranet is visible, it is fair to say that the Internet is used to a certain extent, but the importance of the intranet for the organization cannot be reliably gauged. In this chapter, therefore, only external communication is addressed.

2.   Selection of Internet NGOs

The past decade witnessed optimistic accounts that the Internet would be instrumental in realizing a more democratic system of global governance by facilitating communication between people. An international discourse with participants using the Internet was expected to help achieve a more direct and inclusive form of democracy. The success of what is often referred to as the Battle of Seattle in 1999 raised these expectations even more. During the Third Ministerial Meeting of the World Trade Organization (WTO) in Seattle, large-scale protests and demonstrations were held leading to massive fights between the police and activists. The protests were organized mainly with the use of the Internet and mobile telephones. In recent years, the potential of the Internet to create more direct democratic involvement of citizens and global solidarity between very different groups has been put into perspective. The effectiveness of discourse and communicative action is doubted because it is difficult to assess the validity and reliability of claims people make on the Internet. According to Salter (2003),

> In order for a speech act to be accepted, the hearer must be able to accept its truth, the corresponding normative basis, and the sincerity of the speaker. Of course, such criteria might be unattainable on the Internet.

On the other hand, the exchange of rational arguments that can be assessed impartially and without knowing who has made the claim may be conducive to a proper discourse about the merits of a claim. This could help attain a deliberative democracy as described by Habermas (1988 and 1996). As yet, the Internet potential has not been fully explored, so it is unclear whether the Internet will in time contribute to making the world order more directly democratic. In anticipation of this development, Chapter 4 offers supportive suggestions.

For small, low-budget activist groups the Internet provides new opportunities: cost effective and fast communication and networking facilities, sharing ideas on the Internet with other groups from all over the world, and hacktivism—hacking out of ideological motives, for example disabling a company website for a good cause. Probably because of these new opportunities for such groups, literature about cyberactivism focuses relatively often on activist networks, within the anti-globalization movement especially (see Van Aelst and Walgrave 2004, Rosenkrands 2004, Clark and Themudo 2006), and some contributions in (Ayers 2003). These dispersed and large networks of individual activists, collectives of activists, and NGOs rely on the Internet and e-mail. It may even be wondered whether these anti-globalization networks could exist without modern information and communication technologies (ICT).

2.1.   Website selection

In this chapter, the focus is on NGOs. These NGOs can be linked to NGO networks or not. The following three distinctions are important: the distinction between activist groups or collectives and NGOs; the distinction between NGOs and Internet NGOs; and the distinction between campaigns and Internet NGOs. These distinctions are not clear cut and there may well be activist groups resembling NGOs, and NGOs that are very loosely organized and resemble activist groups.

The first distinction is that between activist groups and NGOs. An NGO is an organization and has some form of formal organization and legal statutes. Activist groups may very well organize themselves but the resulting organization is an informal one which may change in response to people joining or leaving the activist group. In NGOs, the organization is more stable and less dependent on the actual persons who constitute the membership (see Chapter 1). The focus on the legitimacy of NGOs implies that the websites studied are NGO websites and that websites of individual activists or very loosely organized collectives are outside the scope of this chapter. So, although the Internet is used by a host of different protest and activist groups, the focus is only on NGOs. For more information about activism on the Internet, please McCaughey and Ayers (2003) and Van de Donk et al. (2004).

The second distinction is between NGOs and Internet NGOs. Scanning the Internet with a number of search engines (Yahoo, MSN, Google) and various search terms did not identify NGOs existing exclusively on the Internet. Internet-only NGOs probably do not exist at the moment. NGOs need the online as well as the offline world to do projects, secure funding, etc. Most NGOs, even those that make extensive use of the Internet, have offices and projects in the real world. Some NGOs focus on ICTs and the Internet because they think that communication and access to information can help countries develop sustainably. For these NGOs, the Internet is not only a communication and organization tool, but also the object of their efforts. NGOs that are networks with a large, global membership in particular, would probably not have existed without modern ICT. In other words, a very strict definition of Internet NGOs as Internet-only NGOs would inevitably rule out the existence of Internet NGOs. This would, however, disregard interesting features of NGOs that rely heavily on the Internet for their operations but have a tangible foothold in the real world. For that reason, Internet NGOs will be defined as NGOs that make extensive use of the Internet and are not well-known NGOs of long standing. They were either established after the emergence of the Internet and other ICTs or changed or restructured following Internet and ICT developments. For ease of reference, these young NGOs will be termed Internet NGOs, although strictly speaking their existence is not exclusively digital and most traditional NGOs also have websites and use the Internet.

The third distinction, that between NGOs and campaigns, is relevant because campaigns that are run predominantly on the Internet—such as NikeWatch and CokeWatch—are not themselves NGOs; these campaigns are in fact run by NGOs (NikeWatch by Oxfam, CokeWatch by the International Labor Rights Fund).

In summary, websites of Internet NGOs were searched for. For the purposes of this chapter, Internet NGOs are defined as relatively young NGOs for which the Internet is important. Campaigns and activist collectives are not included in this analysis.

In addition to these demarcations, the criteria for the selection of Internet NGOs are that: 1) the NGOs should be international; and 2) they should focus on human rights, the environment or economic development. These two criteria are the same as the ones used in Chapter 2. Also, websites were selected on subject: some NGOs address environmental issues, some human rights issues, and others a combination of human rights and environmental problems. Moreover, some NGOs were selected that focus on ICT in relation to human rights, the environment or economic development. From a practical point of view, the websites had to be available in a language understood by the researcher, in this case Dutch, English, French, German or Spanish.[2]

As can be seen from the selection criteria, this chapter does not give a complete overview of Internet NGOs. This limited study can, however, provide some general ideas of the purposes most NGOs use their websites for and whether differences may be expected in the use of the Internet between more traditional NGOs and the younger Internet NGOs that make extensive use of the Internet.

---

2   As the NGOs that have been selected are international organizations, most websites will probably be available in one of the languages mentioned, notably English.

2.2.   Selected websites

EDRI (European Digital Rights) (www.edri.org) EDRI's objective is to defend civil rights on the Internet. Membership is restricted to non-profit NGOs that aim to defend and promote civil rights in the information society. EDRI was founded in 2002.

RSF (*Reporters Sans Frontières*) (www.rsf.org): RSF aims to defend press freedom in all media, radio television, newspapers, the Internet. Its public is the general public and reporters. RSF was founded in 1985.

Virtual Globe (www.virtualglobe.org): Virtual Globe was created by the Institute for Global Environmental Strategies in 2000 and aims to: (1) 'provide a data center for environmental [...] NGOs in developing countries'; (2) 'support the fundraising activities and worldwide partnerships for [...] NGOs in the developing world'; and (3) 'disseminate the reality of global environmental issues each local [...] NGO faces, so as to have them reflected in the process of policy-making by governments and international organizations.'

HRI (Human Rights Internet) (www.hri.ca): 'HRI is dedicated to the empowerment of human rights activists and organizations, and to the education of governmental and intergovernmental agencies and officials [...] on human rights issues and the role of civil society.' The Human Rights Internet was founded in 1976 as the Human Rights Documentation Network but changed its name when it incorporated the Internet into its mandate in the 1990s.

EarthAction (www.earthaction.org): EarthAction wants to mobilize people from around the world to press their governments (or sometimes corporations) for stronger action to solve global problems. EarthAction started in 1992.

McSpotlight (www.mcspotlight.org): According to the website, McSpotlight is the 'biggest, loudest, most red, most read Anti-McDonald's extravaganza.' The McSpotlight website was launched early 1996 and is run by volunteers from the McInformation Network. It aims at collecting as much information as possible about McDonald's and the 1990 McLibel case.

BehindTheLabel (www.behindthelabel.org): This is a website and campaign run by UNITE HERE (a US union of textile workers and hotel and hospitality workers). The campaign started in 2000. Please note that campaign websites as such fall outside the scope of this research. This website has been included for comparative purposes.

Banana Link (www.bananalink.org.uk): Banana Link aims to alleviate poverty and prevent further environmental degradation in banana exporting communities and to work towards a sustainable banana economy. Banana Link was established in 1996. The Banana Link website was completely restyled and a renewed website was launched in April 2006. This analysis only covers the older website.

AlterNet (www.alternet.org): AlterNet regards itself as an infomediary and wants to provide views and news that cannot be found in mainstream media in the US. AlterNet was created in 1998.

Idealist (www.idealist.org): This website is a portal for everyone interested in non-profit organizations and issues, non-profit careers, volunteering, events, and resources. The website was started by Action Without Borders in 1995.

APC (Association for Progressive Communication) (www.apc.org): 'APC is a global network of civil society organisations whose mission is to empower and support organisations, social movements and individuals in and through the use of information and communication technologies to build strategic communities and initiatives for the purpose of making meaningful contributions to equitable human development, social justice, participatory political processes and environmental sustainability.' APC was founded by several NGOs (the oldest dating from 1985) in1990.

CryptoRights (www.cryptorights.org): CryptoRights aims to promote global justice through the protection of human rights and humanitarian workers, journalists and the information they collect. CryptoRigths was founded in 1998.

IICD (The International Institute for Communication and Development) (www.iicd.org): IICD assists developing countries to realize locally owned sustainable development by harnessing the potential of ICTs.

The IICD was established by the Netherlands Minister for Development Cooperation in 1997.

Panos (www.panos.org.uk): Panos wants to stimulate informed and inclusive public debate around key development issues in order to foster sustainable development. Panos helps in creating local debate by assisting local journalists and using InterWorld Radio. Panos UK was started in 1986; the Panos network was started in 1996.

OneWorld (www.oneworld.net): OneWorld is a network of organizations with over 1,600 NGO members. OneWorld aims to bring news and views of these member NGOs. Member NGOs work to promote human rights and to fight poverty. OneWorld aims to help people communicate with each other using different kinds of ICTs (OneWorld TV, OneWorld Radio, and the website). OneWorld was launched in 1995.

Virtual Activism (www.virtualactivism.org): Virtual Activism was developed to contribute towards closing the ever-increasing digital divide, by helping NGOs to make websites and to train people from NGOs. It cannot be concluded from the website when Virtualactivism was created but the earliest entries are from 2003.

For comparative purposes, five websites of traditional NGOs that were discussed in Chapter 2 are included in the analysis in this chapter: Novib, Greenpeace, Amnesty International, Friends of the Earth International (FOEI), and Global Witness. Some NGOs have both an international and a national website. For that reason, the international as well as the national (Dutch) websites of two NGOs (Amnesty and FOEI) have been analyzed.

3.   Method of website analysis

In order to establish the purposes NGOs use their websites for, the websites were analysed with regard to what is available on them. The method for this analysis is similar to content analysis: the content of websites was categorized and listed, see Bryman (2004) and for an example of content analysis application, Van Gorp (2003). An inventory was made of the way NGOs use their websites. Most of the categories are loosely based on Vegh's (2003) ideas about different types of Internet actions and on an article by Naude et al. (2004) about interactive possibilities on NGO websites. Vegh (2003) grouped Internet actions by activists and NGOs into three general categories: awareness/advocacy; organization/mobilization; and action/reaction. Another important distinction to be made is whether the interactive possibilities of the Internet are used by the NGO (Naude, Froneman et al. 2004). Raising awareness might be interpreted as giving information to the general public. This can be unidirectional, the NGO posts information on its website. An NGO can also decide to not only give information to the general public or other NGOs, but to also invite comments or let people post their information on the website, this is more interactive. This means that informing can be unidirectional or interactive; the former will be referred to as informing, the latter as interaction. For the purposes of this research, an adapted version of Vegh's distinction combined with the ideas about interactivity expressed by Naude et al. was used, resulting in four main categories of what NGOs do on the Internet: informing, interacting, mobilizing, and performing ICT activities.

To be able to say more about the websites than just which purpose(s) they are used for, the four categories of activity mentioned were operationalized in a way similar to Norris (2001) and Van Aelst and Walgrave (2004). In her research, Norris used lists with criteria to characterize websites of political parties. Van Aelst and Walgrave used a similar method to characterize anti-globalization websites. As in their analyses, websites could score 0, 1 or 2 points on a criterion. The operationalization of the four purposes consisted of defining criteria indicating that a website is used for one of the four purposes. An example will illustrate this. Whether a website is used to mobilize people could be and was determined by registering the opportunities offered to become a member, join (Internet) actions, donate money, and visit events. This approach showed in greater detail to what extent which purpose(s) the websites are used for. The specific operationalizations and criteria can be found in Section 2.2.1.

The analyses of the websites were based on the information on the websites, including annual reports. The NGOs were not asked for permission to use the information on their websites because the websites are publicly accessible. Moreover, in the case of Internet NGOs, the information on the websites is the main source of information about the NGOs.

Other methods of Internet research may be interesting but have their limitations or are very expensive. Some studies use a social network analysis to depict the connections or links between organizations and individuals. For example, Garrido and Havalais (2003) depicted the network on the Internet concerning the Zapatista movement. The links between organizations in social movements might be relevant to the social dimension of legitimacy. It is, however, not clear what a link on a website means; the link may be there, but there may not be direct contact between the NGOs that have links to each other's websites on their websites. Cooperation between NGOs is relevant to the social aspect of legitimacy, but it is not obvious whether a link on a websites indicates actual cooperation. Another method might be to look at the hits of NGO websites and relate this to popular support and the social aspect of legitimacy. However, this relationship is also problematic because viewing a website does not indicate whether someone agrees with the NGO: someone may be directed to an NGO website by a search engine while he or she is not even interested. A third method might be to ask people what they think of an NGO website and whether on the basis of the website they think the NGO is reliable. This research method would be very interesting and yield valuable results with regard to the social aspect of legitimacy but it is too expensive and time-consuming for this study. Moreover, this method requires a prior and thorough content analysis.

A problem with website analysis is that websites can be very dynamic; they can be changed constantly. The analysis presented in this chapter should be seen as the analysis of a snapshot (in time) of the website taken at the time the research took place: January to March 2006. This means that some information reported here may since have been altered or even removed, or that websites may have been changed drastically.

Another problem is that websites can be dormant and it is difficult to interpret this. Websites can remain unchanged and contain old information for quite some time. This might mean that the NGO is no longer active and has ceased to exist. Alternatively, it might signify that the NGO is currently not active but may resume its activities at a later time. The lack of updates may also be due to the lack of people who are willing and able to update the website; volunteers or employees might be busy with other tasks (although NGOs focused on ICT neglecting their websites could arguably raise some eyebrows). For the purposes of this research, websites that have not been updated for at least a year will be referred to as dormant.

A specific problem with regard to the analysis of websites of Internet NGOs is that it is difficult and sometimes even impossible, to check whether a particular Internet NGO does in fact exist or is merely a money making scheme. Despite the information on the website, in some cases there may even be a telephone number or an address, it remains hard to verify whether the Internet NGO is a bona fide organization or a front operation remains hard.

To conclude, the method used in this research has its limitations. The sample is selective and too small to draw statistically significant conclusions. The analysis presented is an analysis of the websites at a specific moment in time. This means that results of this study cannot be generalized on statistical grounds and that they depend on the moment on which the research was done. So, general conclusions that are valid for all NGOs cannot be drawn. The research method is, however, suited for the heuristic purposes of this chapter. The websites analysis provides ideas of what kind(s) of information NGOs give on their websites and how NGOs use their websites.

3.1.   NGO website activities

As explained in the previous section, four categories of website activities of NGOs were formulated: informing, interaction, mobilization, and ICT-related activities. In this section, the operationalizations will be specified. A score of 0 means that the feature or information is not available on the website.

3.1.1.   Information

Websites can be used to give public information about the NGOs and their aims to interested members of the general public. First of all, this can be information about the NGOs themselves. From the perspective of legitimacy, it is important to know what the aims and values of the NGOs are and whether they address these on their websites. It is also relevant to know whether the websites include information about the organization and decision-making procedures. Some NGOs have elaborate biographies of the people who work for them or who are on the board; this was also noted. NGOs might also define themselves by referring to earlier campaigns and successes. Information about earlier campaigns gives additional information about the aims and values because it makes clear what the NGOs actually do. Hence, the following points were scored with regard to general information about the NGOs.

Organization
>Score 1:   some information about who is responsible for what issues in the NGO;
>Score 2:   elaborate information about the organization of the NGO and decision-making procedures in the NGO.

People
>Score 1:   only names and/or photos or only of director;
>Score 2:   names and/or photos including biographies.

Aims, mission, and values
>Score 1:   short and very general;
>Score 2:   elaborate and more specific.

Earlier campaigns and successes
>Score 1:   only some earlier campaigns;
>Score 2:   all earlier campaigns and results of these campaigns.

Of course, the information may also be about other topics. For example, some NGOs use news about a situation somewhere in the world for their campaigns and for mobilization purposes. Other NGOs aim at providing information about, for example, human rights and maintain a database with all kinds of information about human rights, the environment, economic development, etc. In this part of the analysis, the websites were scored on providing information about topics other than their organization. Five criteria concerned general information, three criteria campaign information.

News
>Score 1:   only information about campaigns or directly related to campaigns;
>Score 2:   information broader than only about campaigns and directly relevant to campaigns. (Information on themes that are also campaign themes were allowed for, the difference with score 1 being that the news comes from very different sources and some of it is not directly related to campaigns.)

Newsletters
 Score 1: infrequent newsletter (less than four issues a year) or per-
          sonalized information about the subjects that someone has
          expressed an interest in;
 Score 2: frequent newsletter.

Links
 Score 1: only internal links to other parts of the NGO (network),
          campaign websites, etc.;
 Score 2: internal and external links.

Database
 Score 1: limited scope, such as only news items relevant to cam-
          paigns or only training materials;
 Score 2: large database with good search functions.

Events
 Score 1: a list of events that website visitors might be interested in
          and which are not organized by the NGO, for example ex-
          hibitions in museums or lectures.

NGOs may be expected to refer to their campaigns on their websites. In
this part of the website analysis, the campaign information provided was
scored. An item related to events was included. NGOs organize events,
such as protests, petitions, or letter campaigns. In this category, events
were restricted to events NGOs organized themselves or cooperated in.

Aims
 Score 1: short and very general;
 Score 2: elaborate and more specific;

Successes
 Score 1: mention of results only;
 Score 2: description of results and related to actions undertaken.

Events
 Score 1: limited overview of events (for example, only e-mail peti-
          tions) or outdated information;
 Score 2: regularly updated lists of all campaign and other events.

3.1.2.   Interaction

Naude et al. (2004) analysed the websites of ten South African NGOs from a communication perspective, and one of their conclusions was that these NGOs tend to use the Internet unidirectionally: information is given. The two-way communication that the Internet might be used for was not visible. The authors ascribed this to the limited technical and communication skills available at these NGOs. Claims about the Internet being a new commons for discourse presuppose that the Internet is used to exchange arguments. It is therefore interesting to see whether the results of Naude et al. (2004) can be confirmed. Do NGOs use their websites only to give information or do they also allow or stimulate people to give information or their opinions? The websites were analysed for opportunities for interaction with NGOs, with other people on NGO websites, and for sharing knowledge in a community of people interested in a particular subject.

E-mail address for comments
>   Score 1:   e-mail or physical address available, but only—and explicitly—for questions regarding the website or inquiries, not for comments on the NGO or its aims;
>   Score 2:   comments and questions about the website and projects as well as the NGO and its aims are welcomed.

Discussion forum
>   Score 1:   available but not really in use (for example, because it has been hacked, or no new entries are being posted);
>   Score 2:   discussion forum or bulletin board available, in use, and easily accessible (registration may be required, but paid membership must not be a condition): discussions   may be initiated by website visitors on subjects relevant to the NGO or its projects and campaigns.

Response options
>   Score 1:   Only specific information given on the website may be reacted to, for example a comment box at the end of an article.
>   Score 2:   All information on the website may be reacted to. (This is different from the discussion options because the response item is limited to reacting to information. Website visitors may start discussions on the discussion forum).

Posting information
>   Score 1:   Specific information may be posted at designated places on the website, for example the events calendar or job announcements.
>   Score 2:   All kinds of information may be posted anywhere on the website. (This is different from the discussion item because the discussion forum usually is a separate part of the website.)

Sharing knowledge
>   Score 1:   on a closed forum or at the NGO's request (for example, job postings);
>   Score 2:   posting features for stories and news from local communities in written, audio, and video format.

3.1.3.   Mobilization

Websites may be used to invite people to become active or to donate money. In this part of the website analysis, the options offered to people to become active were scored. Most NGOs invite people to donate money through their websites. Some NGOs offer membership, others—while not offering membership—invite people to join a campaign. People may become active by, for example, sending e-mails to their government, or by helping in a spam attack. Websites may also be used to ask people to participate in demonstrations, boycotts of products, etc. There is, of course, some overlap between mobilization and campaign information, because people can only be mobilized if information about the events is available. This is, however, not a problem, as the same information on the website can be arranged in different categories. These categories are not mutually exclusive; some information is meant to inform as well as mobilize people, other information is not meant to mobilize people.

Membership/joining a campaign
>   Score 1:   Only NGOs may apply for membership or join campaigns.
>   Score 2:   Individuals may also apply for membership or join campaigns.

Donations
>   Score 1:   Donations may be made through the website.

Events calendar
    Score 1: few or outdated events (for example, conferences);
    Score 2: several types of up-to-date actions and events.

E-mail, letter campaigns, or consumer actions
    Score 1: no more than two actions, and sometimes not directly accessible on the website but linked;
    Score 2: several actions in several forms (for example, letters, e-mail flyers, information for consumers).

Hacktivism
    Score 1: cryptographic keys or tips for Internet use, for people in countries where the Internet is censored especially;
    Score 2: calls and tips for spam actions, spoof sites.

3.1.4.   ICT-related activities

In the previous section, it was observed that there are NGOs that not only use ICTs, but focus on helping people to develop economically by giving them access to ICTs and information. In this part of the analysis, the activities of NGOs on their websites with regard to access to information and the use of ICTs were scored. These activities can be divided into training and support, facilitating knowledge sharing, and research and development. Research and development may be aimed at the development of open source software to be used by NGOs or communities, but it can also focus on ways of secure communication on the Internet (e.g., cryptographic keys). Facilitating knowledge sharing on the Internet may be achieved by supporting online communities, but also by using radio broadcasts in remote parts of the world. These radio broadcasts can be made available on websites. Through the combination of the Internet and radio, information from the Internet may be received in parts of the world with only very little infrastructure. (Radios do not require a highly developed or complex infrastructure at the receiving end; a crank radio or a crystal radio suffices).

Online support
    Score 1: guidelines on how to use an application (for example, RSS);
    Score 2: help with creating websites.

Online training
> Score 1:   combination of online and offline training;
> Score 2:   full online training programmes.

Facilities for knowledge sharing
> Score 1:   online knowledge sharing;
> Score 2:   online and offline knowledge sharing (for example, radio).

Open source software development
> Score 1:   development of open content and a limited range of open
>   software available;
> Score 2:   development of open software.

Cryptographic keys
> Score 1:   cryptographic keys via link, or tips for secure Internet use;
> Score 2:   open source cryptographic keys on website.

3.2.   *Legitimacy and NGO websites*

In Chapter 1, Beetham's dimensions of legitimacy as applicable to states were used as a starting point for a discussion of the legitimacy of NGOs. In this chapter, this discussion will be used to analyse NGO websites with regard to dimensions of legitimacy. Beetham introduced three dimensions: regulatory, social, and moral. The regulatory dimension is not only about compliance with laws, but also concerns rules and procedures with some formal status. The social dimension can take different forms, explicit as well as implicit. The moral dimension refers to moral norms and values.

It is probably not feasible to define three clear-cut categories and group information found on NGO websites neatly into these three categories. The difficulty is that some information about legitimacy is directly related to one dimension but indirectly to another. Nevertheless, an attempt was made to categorize website information in accordance with Beetham's three dimensions.

3.2.1.   Regulatory dimension

NGOs sometimes refer to international law, such as human rights law, but also to national law, for example with regard to registration and financial accountability. In the website analysis, it was noted whether or not and in how much detail reference is made to national and international law. It should be noted that some international law, for example human rights law, has a moral foundation, so this could also be part of the moral dimension of legitimacy. It may be assumed that NGO websites give information about their procedures and finances. The availability and detail of annual reports, financial statistics, audit reports, and clear eligibility requirements for support are related to the regulatory dimension of legitimacy. If NGOs meet certain standards, for example with regard to transparency and accountability, they may be accredited by such organizations as the World Bank (see Chapters 5 and 6). Mentioning accreditation on websites was included in the analysis.

Reference to international law
    Score 1: limited reference to one international treaty or declaration;
    Score 2: extensive reference to several international treaties and declarations.

Annual reports
    Score 1: short summary of activities and results of the preceding year;
    Score 2: extensive annual reports.

Financial statistics
    Score 1: short table with general financial information only;
    Score 2: extensive table including detailed financial information.

Audit report
    Score 1: An audit report for a particular fiscal year is provided.
    Score 2: Every annual report includes an audit report.

Clear eligibility requirements for support
    Not applicable: the NGO does not give support;
    Score 1: criteria for members NGOs;
    Score 2: criteria for people seeking support.

Accreditation
    Score 1: accreditation received from a local organization;
    Score 2: accreditation received from one or more international organizations.

3.2.2.   Social dimension

The social dimension refers to support and consent from different groups: people affected by the NGO project; NGO members; or organizations donating money to or cooperating with the NGO. These groups may be referred to with the terms representation of affected people, public support, and recognition by other organizations, respectively.

Representation of affected people. Some NGOs are known as grassroots NGOs. This means that they partner with (organizations or groups of) affected people. The websites were analysed with regard to references to grassroots. As connections with affected people may also create knowledge, they could be regarded as pertaining to performance. For the purposes of this research, these connections are considered part of the social dimension of legitimacy, because grassroots NGOs themselves perceive their relationship with (groups of) affected people as going beyond the mere instrumental quality of obtaining knowledge; grassroots NGOs view groups of affected actors as their partners and not only as sources of information.

Public support. Membership of an NGO or making donations to an NGO could be argued to imply endorsement of the goals and projects of the NGO. Thus, the number of members or donations could be an indication of the social dimension of legitimacy. It is important to note that membership or donations do not necessarily express consent; people may have other reasons for donating money or joining an NGO, (such as the prospect of gifts).

Recognition. Donations by and cooperation with governments, companies or other international organizations may be regarded as a form of recognition for some NGOs. Other NGOs have a policy of not accepting any funding from companies or governments because they wish to remain independent. The websites were analysed for cooperation with and donations from governments and companies, but whether cooperation and donations are indeed a source of legitimacy depends on the kind of NGO and its aims. Cooperation with and recognition by international organizations such as the UN, but also by very large well-known NGOs, is usually seen as a source of legitimacy. Some NGOs have steering committees or boards whose members include well-known, popular, knowledgeable or powerful people. Although the existence of boards and steering committees is linked to procedures and rules, this study will consider these bodies as belonging to the social dimension of legitimacy. The fact that people are willing to sit on boards or steering committees may be seen as support or consent and this might induce other people to support an NGO.

Reference to grassroots
Score 1:   reference to and cooperation with groups of affected people, but without decisive influence of these groups on NGO policy;
Score 2:   groups of affected people are an essential part of the NGO, not only cooperation but partnership.

Number of members
Score 1:   indirect, only number of member NGOs given;
Score 2:   number of members or supporters given on website.

Donations by governments
Score 1:   only one government mentioned and in little detail somewhere in a list;
Score 2:   one or more detailed references, and mentioning government donations used explicitly as a source of legitimacy.

Donations by companies
Score 1:   only one company mentioned and in little detail somewhere in a list;
Score 2:   one or more detailed references, and mentioning corporate donations used explicitly as a source of legitimacy.

Donations by NGOs
Score 1:   only one NGO mentioned and in little detail somewhere in a list;
Score 2:   one or more detailed references, and mentioning NGO donations used explicitly as a source of legitimacy.

Reference to other powerful organizations
Score 1:   only one powerful organization mentioned and in little detail;
Score 2:   more, and more detailed, information about cooperation with and recognition by powerful organizations.

Supervision by steering committee
   Score 1:   a board;
   Score 2:   a separate steering committee.

3.2.3.   Moral dimension

NGO websites will very likely include information related to the moral dimension of legitimacy. It may, however, be expected that moral norms and values are only explicitly mentioned in sections describing the aims of NGOs. In the analysis, website sections that deal with the aims or mission or values of the NGO were scored on how elaborate (level of detail) they are.

Aims, mission, and values
   Score 1:   short and very general;
   Score 2:   elaborate and more specific.

There is a group of factors, referred to as sources of legitimacy in scholarly literature, but also in the interviews in Chapter 2 and in the analysis of websites, that cannot be grouped neatly under the headings of the three dimensions of Beetham's legitimacy concept. For this group of factors, this study uses the term performance. NGOs focused on bringing about changes in the world directly, often regard their effectiveness as an important source of legitimacy (see Chapter 2). As measures of effectiveness, earlier successes, expertise and experience are mentioned. Some NGOs have expertise as a result of their grassroots connections, but expertise can also be based on research conducted by an NGO. With regard to NGOs focusing on advocacy, reference is often made to the credibility or reliability of the information they provide instead of effectiveness (see Chapter 2). In this study, the reliability of information on NGO websites is regarded as relating to performance, but it could also be claimed that NGOs, and advocacy NGOs especially, have a moral duty to provide reliable information, thereby pertaining indirectly to the moral dimension.
   It is difficult, and in some case even impossible, to check claims on a website, but it can be established whether websites address the reliability of the information. Different criteria to judge whether information on the Internet is reliable are proposed in books and courses about searching information on the Internet. Some of these criteria were incorporated in a reliability score. A high reliability score means that there

are many clues that can be used to assess whether the information on the website is reliable. Consequently, a high score on reliability does not necessarily mean that the information on the website is true. A website might aim to entertain people, if it includes disclaimers, suspicious sources, or authors with names such as Donald Duck. The information on such a website may be assumed not to provide serious or correct information. Such a website could, however, score high on reliability, because people can see that the purpose of the website is not to give reliable information, but to entertain. Some NGOs include a disclaimer on their website that they cannot be held liable for damage resulting from the use of information provided by the website or a disclaimer that certain opinions and views on the website need not be the views and opinions of the NGO. If a disclaimer is used with regard to some information, that information might be perceived to be less reliable. A disclaimer does not mean that the information is not true, but it is more difficult to judge whether information is reliable, if the NGO providing the information does not want to vouch for the reliability of the information. If credibility is interpreted as the tendency of people and organizations to trust NGOs to provide good and reliable information, then a website analysis cannot be used to draw conclusions about the credibility of the NGOs, as this depends on the people viewing the websites.

Reference to effectiveness or earlier successes
  Score 1: only limited information about effects and successes;
  Score 2: an extensive list of successes.

Author of information mentioned
  Score 1: a few references to the author;
  Score 2: several references to the author.

Moderation system (for open access websites especially)
  Score 1: There is moderation of a limited part of the website and moderation is only used to prevent abusive language.
  Score 2: Moderation is not only used to prevent abusive language but also to maintain focus.

Disclaimer regarding information on the website
  Score 1: disclaimer with regard to a limited part of the website;
  Score 2: disclaimer covering all the information on the website.

Sources
  Score 1: sources or references only included in certain documents
          or information;
  Score 2: sources or references included in most of the information.

Regular updates
  Score 1: at least every 3 months (note that websites were analysed
          between 17 January and 10 March 2006);
  Score 2: at least weekly.

It may be imagined that the regulatory dimension of legitimacy is the
most important one, as it is mentioned first and was analysed in detail.
This, however, is not the case. It is simply easier to analyse NGO websites on issues related to the regulatory dimension of legitimacy, because NGO websites generally provide annual reports, financial statistics, etc. It is much harder to analyse the moral dimension because the
moral norms and values underlying the aims and goals of NGOs are not
always addressed explicitly and usually only in one part of the website
called Aims or Mission.

4.   Results

On the basis of the list of selected Internet NGOs and traditional NGOs,
some preliminary and general conclusions can be drawn. One, Internet
NGOs range from single company oriented activist groups/NGOs, such
as McSpotlight, to NGOs such as OneWorld and EarthAction that focus on all kinds of global problems not just the environment or human
rights. McSpotlight does not have an office or a formal organization,
and it therefore shares a number of characteristics with activist groups.
The distinction between environmental, human rights and development NGOs is easier to make with regard to traditional NGOs than
with regard to Internet NGOs. Two, NGOs or trade unions sometimes
create websites that are not meant to inform people about the organizations themselves, but about campaigns, for example www.behindthela-
bel.org. (This website was included for comparative purposes only, as
BehindTheLabel is not an NGO, but a campaign.). Three, most Internet
NGOs were started in the (second half of the) 1990s. Some were created
earlier (Panos and HRI), but they were transformed into their current
shape in the 1990s (Panos became an NGO network, HRI an Internet
database).

In the following two subsections, the results of the website analysis will be presented. Where scores on subcategories or numeric differences in scores are relevant, the scores in question will be presented in tabular form.

4.1.   NGO website activities

4.1.1.   Information

The following tables present the scores on the information subcategories.

Tables 1-3: Scores on the three subcategories of information (the number in round brackets is the maximum score).

Table 1

	EDRI	RSF	Virtual Globe	HRI	Earth Action	McSpot-light	Behind TheLabel	Banana Link
Organization (8)	5	4	5	7	6	1	3	2
General information (9)	6	3	6	9	3	5	5	6
Campaign information (6)	4	1	Na	4	4	5	3	4

Table 2

	AlterNet	Idealist	APC	Crypto-Rights	IICD	Panos	OneWorld	Virtual Activism
Organization (8)	6	8	5	7	6	7	4	6
General information (9)	7	5	6	0	3	8	6	3
Campaign information (6)	na	3	4	2	5	2	2	3

Table 3

	FOEI	Oxfam Novib	Global Witness	Amnesty NL	Amnesty Int.	Green-peace NL	Green-peace Int.
Organization (8)	8	7	6	7	7	8	8
General information (9)	5	4	5	9	7	6	6
Campaign information (6)	5	6	4	4	4	4	4

The scores give an indication of how much information can be found on the website; a high score means that a great deal of information is given. A high score on general information means that the websites provide much information from different sources on different subjects or themes. As is clear from the tables, some of the Internet NGO websites are not really used for giving general information; the information provided may be limited to one subject or one company (for example, Banana Link and McSpotlight). For others, such as AlterNet and Virtual Globe, giving general information is their goal, and while they do so abundantly, they do not run campaigns. The traditional NGOs score relatively high on giving general information as well as campaign-related information. Text boxes 1 and 2 contain the mission statements of HRI and Greenpeace International.

Text box 1: HRI Mission Statement
         (source: www.hri.ca)

Founded in 1976, HRI is a leader in the exchange of information within the worldwide human rights community. Launched in the United States, HRI has its headquarters in Ottawa, Canada. From Ottawa, HRI communicates by phone, fax, mail and the Internet with more than 5,000 organizations and individuals around the world working for the advancement of human rights.

Our Mission Statement reads as follows:

HRI is dedicated to the empowerment of human rights activists and organizations, and to the education of governmental and intergovernmental agencies and officials and other actors in the public and private sphere, on human rights issues and the role of civil society.

HRI seeks to accomplish the above by:
–   Facilitating the application of new technologies toward the furtherance of human rights through transferring knowledge and expertise particularly to Southern nongovernmental organizations (NGOs) and other civil society organizations;
–   Producing and providing access to human rights databases and a unique and comprehensive documentation centre;
–   Carrying out human rights research and disseminating the results to concerned institutions and activists;
–   Producing human rights resources including the Human Rights Tribune, annual publications and directories in digital, hard copy and microfiche formats and making them available to NGOs and international institutions;– Fostering networking and cooperation among NGOs, as well as other civil society organizations, to integrate human rights with social and sustainable development issues; Strengthening civil society and NGO access to and participation in international fora; and
–   Supporting the role of NGOs in the promotion of civil society and assisting governmental and intergovernmental organizations in the application of good governance practices and the protection of human rights through technical assistance, training and educational programs.

Text box 2: Greenpeace International mission statement
           (source: www.greenpeace.org)

Our Mission
Greenpeace is an independent, campaigning organisation that uses non-violent, creative confrontation to expose global environmental problems, and force solutions for a green and peaceful future. Greenpeace's goal is to ensure the ability of the Earth to nurture life in all its diversity.

Greenpeace organises public campaigns for:
–   The protection of oceans and ancient forests.
–   The phase out of fossil fuels and the promotion of renewable energy to stop climate change.
–   The elimination of toxic chemicals .
–   The prevention of genetically modified organisms being released into nature.
–   An end to the nuclear threat and nuclear contamination.
–   Safe and sustainable trade.

Greenpeace does not solicit or accept funding from governments, corporations or political parties. Greenpeace neither seeks nor accepts donations that could compromise its independence, aims, objectives or integrity. Greenpeace relies on the voluntary donations of individual supporters, and on grant support from foundations.

Greenpeace is committed to the principles of non-violence, political independence and internationalism. In exposing threats to the environment and in working to find solutions, Greenpeace has no permanent allies or enemies.

Greenpeace has been campaigning against environmental degradation since 1971 when a small boat of volunteers and journalists sailed into Amchitka, an area north of Alaska where the US Government was conducting underground nuclear tests. This tradition of 'bearing witness' in a non-violent manner continues today.

Greenpeace has played a pivotal role in, among other things, the adoption of:
  –   A ban on toxic waste exports to less developed countries.
  –   A moratorium on commercial whaling.
  –   A United Nations convention providing for better management of world fisheries.
  –   A Southern Ocean Whale Sanctuary;
  –   A 50-year moratorium on mineral exploitation in Antarctica.
  –   Bans on the dumping at sea of radioactive and industrial waste and disused oil installations.
  –   An end to high-sea, large-scale driftnet fishing.
  –   A ban on all nuclear weapons testing – our first ever campaign.

The traditional NGOs (except Global Witness) and approximately half of the Internet NGOs provide information about their organizations and decision-making procedures. The other Internet NGOs provide little or no information about their organizations. For example, it cannot be established who the people behind McSpotlight and Banana Link are and how they are organized. Banana Link has an office, so staff could be identified through a visit to the Banana Link office. McSpotlight has no official office, only an e-mail address. Global Witness only gives some information about the relation between the Global Witness Trust, Global Witness Limited and the Global Witness Foundation. The names of three directors are included in the annual report. No other information about the organization is revealed on the website or in the annual report. Global Witness provides more information about its campaigns in what it terms its vision. Greenpeace only sums up its main campaigns, but, unlike Global Witness, does provide information about its organization and decision-making procedures.

Text box 3: Greenpeace International organizational structure
                (source: www.greenpeace.org)

How is Greenpeace structured?

Greenpeace is a global environmental organisation, consisting of Greenpeace International (Stichting Greenpeace Council) in Amsterdam, and 27 national and regional offices around the world, providing a presence in 41 countries. Each office is governed by a board, usually elected by a voting membership of volunteers and activists. Each board appoints a representative, called a Trustee, who meets once a year with all other national or regional offices' trustees to agree on the long-term strategy of the organisation, make changes to governance structure where necessary, consider any applications for new national or regional offices, set a ceiling on spending for Greenpeace International's budget and elect the Board of Stichting Greenpeace Council.

Trustees from National and Regional offices elect 7 members of SGC Board of Directors, which appoints the Executive Director of Greenpeace International. At this moment the Board is chaired by Anne Sumemr and the Executive Director is Gerd Leipold. He leads and coordinates international campaigns, monitors National and Regional office performance, and provides global services to national and regional offices.

Some NGO websites, of both traditional and Internet NGOs, have events calendars with lectures, discussions, expositions, etc., that website visitors might find interesting. These events are not organized by the NGOs, either independently or with partners. There are also events specifically related to campaigns. Both Oxfam Novib and Amnesty International the Netherlands only have events calendars in Dutch; the English sites of these NGOs do not include events calendars.

Most events calendars for the campaigns of both traditional and Internet NGOs are either empty or not up-to-date. Some websites appear to be dormant, when the events calendar only includes 2002 and 2003 events especially. The McSpotlight site had been dormant since late 2003, but in January and February 2006 new entries were posted. The CryptoRights website has been dormant since 2004, most information dating to 2003 and earlier. Text box 4 shows the most recent CryptoRight press releases (as accessible in March 2006).

Text box 4: Top news on the CryptoRights website
(source: www.cryptorights.org, accessed March 2006)

Top News & Media Releases

Jan. 16, 2004:
CRF Thanks international team for translating HighFire into 7 languages:
CRF sends thanks to Hernán Collazo, Roland Fritz, Nicoletta Godbout, Tomas Kuliavas, Alex Lemaresquier, Marcio Merlone, Mij, Philippe Mingo, Michael Prinsen and Marcos Tadeu for helping make HighFire:Mobile available in German, Spanish, French, Italian, Lithuanian, Dutch and Brazilian Portuguese.

Oct. 3, 2003:
CRF Teams Up with Squirrelmail:
CRF welcomes support from Squirrelmail team for HighFire; CRF's work to benefit all Squirrelmail users, Too.

Aug. 18, 2003:
CRF Presents HighFire Alpha at Crypto 2003:
Seeks the Contribution of the Security Community BoF & Rump session presentations to include first hardware demo of CRF's human rights communications security system.

Apr. 2, 2003:
CRF Launches HighFire Project at CFP2003:
Human Rights Communications Security System will help NGOs Protect Privacy, Data Integrity First phase of project is introduction of Communications Assessment Tool (CAT); NGO participation sought.

Mar. 31, 2003:
CRF quoted on "PATRIOT Act II"
New anti-encryption provisions troubling. In a major AP Newswire article carried by hundreds of papers around the country, CRF and other organizations came out against new privacy-threatening legislation.

4.1.2.   Interaction

From the interaction scores of both the traditional and the Internet NGOs, the conclusion may be drawn that most websites do not use many opportunities for interaction and discussion with the general public (see Tables 4-6).

Tables 4-6: Total scores on interaction
            (the number in round brackets is the maximum score).

Table 4

	EDRI	RSF	Virtual Globe	HRI	Earth Action	McSpotlight	Behind TheLabel	BananaLink
Interaction (10)	5	1	2	4	3	6	2	1

Table 5

	AlterNet	Idealist	APC	Crypto-Rights	IICD	Panos	OneWorld	Virtual Activism
Interaction (10)	5	5	6	3	4	6	7	3

Table 6

	FOEI	Oxfam Novib	Global Witness	Amnesty NL	Amnesty Int.	Greenpeace NL	Greenpeace Int.
Interaction (10)	2	3	2	4	1	3	3

All NGO websites specify e-mail or physical addresses through which information about the organization or the website may be obtained. Most addresses are given with clear instructions on the kinds of questions that may be asked (e.g., a separate e-mail address for questions regarding the website). On the FOEI website, an e-mail address is given, but visitors are discouraged from using it, because FOEI receives so many e-mails. For this reason, other NGOs include a FAQ list.

It is remarkable that only Amnesty International the Netherlands, EDRI, McSpotlight and Idealist have functioning discussion sites. The EDRI discussion site is limited to one subject, the data retention campaign. On the discussion site of Amnesty International the Netherlands, visitors may comment on propositions (every month, a new proposition is posted). During the research period, some propositions triggered meaningful visitor responses, others did not (e.g., 'hi!'). The McSpotlight discussion site is currently not active, and only a few of the discussion threads created earlier may be accessed. The Idealist bulletin board requires registration and is a site with many lively threads, where people seek and give advice, about careers in the non-profit sector especially. Greenpeace has devoted a separate section of its website to cyberactivism, and it would appear that its discussion forum must have been very lively and active, as it has been closed due to the large number of visitors. The Virtual Activism discussion forum was hacked during the research period.[3] The UK OneWorld website has a discussion forum, while other OneWorld sites do not.

On most sites, posting information is restricted. Some selected persons or member NGOs maintain weblogs or write columns. The Alter-Net website, for example, hosts many columns and weblogs. Website visitors may respond to some of these, but cannot post their own weblogs. Most websites created by NGOs that can be regarded as networks of partners from different countries allow partners to post information, for example Panos and OneWorld.

In the interaction category knowledge sharing refers to whether individuals or communities exchange information on websites. The ICT-related category includes a score on whether or not NGOs develop knowledge sharing facilities. All Internet NGOs that focus on ICT for developing countries, except Virtual Activism, offer knowledge sharing facilities on their websites. APC's ActionApps and CryptoRights volunteers are examples of knowledge sharing, albeit restricted to a very specific group of users, software developers. IICD, Panos and OneWorld allow for knowledge sharing, in or between communities in developing countries especially. Knowledge sharing occurs in closed or open Dgroups on the Internet, but Panos and OneWorld also use other media such as radio and television for knowledge sharing purposes. Radio broadcasts can be put on the Internet where people may listen to them or broadcast them somewhere else (see Text box 5). Panos also publishes books, for example, on mountain people. McSpotlight allows for knowledge sharing between activists against McDonald's.

---

3   After the data collecting period, the discussion site—although no longer hacked—remained unavailable. A new chat site requiring registration was opened in April 2006.

Text box 5: Downloadable InterWorld Radio files

Feature: Ghana: Hard Currency
Tourism in the West African country of Ghana is on the up, and the foreigners are bringing in much-needed hard currency. Plans to triple tourism have been agreed between the government and its donors – the World Bank and the International Monetary Fund.

Feature: AIDS memoirs
Just a few years ago, Nchelenge district in the north of Zambia was being devastated by HIV/Aids. Reporters David Bweupe and Chilufya Mumba take a journey to meet the men and women who have rediscovered hope.

The traditional NGOs do not use knowledge sharing facilities on the Internet except for knowledge sharing between partner or member NGOs.

4.1.3.   Mobilization

Virtual Globe, IICD and Panos have very low scores in this category and probably do not aim to mobilize the general public. This would appear to hold true for Virtual Globe that aims to be an environmental data resource for NGOs. IICD implements projects in Southern countries in partnership with local NGOs; its objective is not to mobilize the general public. Panos is a network NGO that wants to stimulate communication in and between communities in Southern countries as well as a public debate about developmental issues in Northern countries. In this regard, it is a little surprising that, even though Panos seeks to initiate a public debate on key developmental issues, it does not use its website to mobilize the general public to start this discussion. The website provides local stories of people from developmental countries—input for a societal debate—but the website does not offer an incentive to website visitors to start a debate.

Most NGOs have included a feature for donating money securely, the exceptions being BehindTheLabel (a campaign website from Unite Here), Banana Link, APC, and IICD, who do not solicit donations on their websites. NGOs usually offer of a number of payment options (see Text box 6).

Text box 6: Donation methods
(source: the Alternet and Novib websites)

Alternet allows for credit card, mail, fax and PayPal donations.

On the Novib website one can become a regular donor or allow Novib to transfer an amount of money once.

Approximately one third (six out of sixteen) of the Internet NGOs in this research are network NGOs that accept other NGOs as members or partners, but not individuals. The other Internet NGOs welcome individuals as members, except BehindTheLabel. Within the selected group of traditional NGOs, FOEI is a network NGO. Only NGOs may apply for membership, individuals may join campaigns and actions. Amnesty International and Greenpeace consist of national sections or units which individuals may join. Membership of Global Witness is not open to either NGOs or individuals. Global Witness may be considered an expertise NGO: experts work on (i.e., research and monitor) some selected subjects, such as blood diamonds and illegal logging.

E-mail, letter campaigns and consumer actions are popular mobilization methods and it is remarkable that, although the traditional NGOs all use one or more of these methods, not all of the Internet NGOs do. On the NGO websites, hacktivism is restricted to the availability of (links to) cryptographic keys and a handbook for safe cyberblogging. There are no calls for spam attacks, spoofsites, etc. There are hacktivist collectives, for example Electronic Disturbance Theater, Electrohippies Collective, and °Tmark (Vegh 2003), but these seem to operate separately from the Internet NGOs.

4.1.4.   ICT-related activities

As may have been expected, the initiatives of the Internet NGOs that focus on human rights, environment and development through ICT with regard to ICT-related projects, demonstrate greater variety than those of the traditional NGOs. Whereas Virtual Activism, RSF, HRI, EarthAction, and AlterNet only include training or support features, APC, CryptoRights, IICD, Panos, and OneWorld have several ICT-related activities other than training and support.

APC, IICD, Panos, and OneWorld develop facilities for knowledge sharing. APC and IICD develop facilities on the Internet for sharing knowledge, which means that communities need to have Internet access before they can participate. IICD also supports projects in which hardware and software are implemented in developing countries. Panos and OneWorld also use radio and television for knowledge sharing, allowing communities that do not have Internet access to join. Radio in particular needs little infrastructure and is thus a suitable knowledge sharing facility in remote areas.

APC, CryptoRights, IICD, and OneWorld develop open source software. Ideally, open source software enables people in developing countries to use computers without having to pay for expensive software licences. Somewhat surprisingly, two traditional NGOs that focus on environmental problems—FOEI and Greenpeace—also develop open source software, independently or in cooperation with others.

The websites of APC, IICD, OneWorld, and RSF refer to cryptographic keys, but do not provide them on their websites. Only Crypto-Rights—perhaps not surprisingly—provides pgp keys on its website.

4.1.5.   Conclusions about NGO website activities

None of the NGOs studied is an 'Internet-only' Internet NGO. One website—BehindTheLabel—was created for a campaign that relies heavily on the website itself. McSpotlight might be considered an Internet NGO, but it is questionable whether it is an organization at all. It seems to be a kind of anti-McDonald's database including interaction options. There is very limited information about the organization—it is mentioned that McSpotlight is run by a group of volunteers from different countries, some of whom may be involved directly or indirectly in the McLibel case—but there is no indication of who these volunteers are and what they do for McSpotlight. The website had been unchanged for months before the research started.

The traditional NGOs use their website mainly to give information and to mobilize, with the exception of Global Witness, which does not use its website for mobilization. Generally, the interaction opportunities are rudimentary, being mostly e-mail or physical addresses and sometimes discussion forums. The discussion forums of the traditional NGOs showed fairly low activity rates (Oxfam Novib and Amnesty International) or were closed down because of too much activity (Greenpeace).

The Internet NGOs also use their websites to give information. A number of NGOs use their websites predominantly to that end: BehindTheLabel, Virtual Globe, HRI, and Virtual Activism. The volumes of general information and campaign information vary greatly. Virtual Globe gives general information and does not really run campaigns. HRI gives a great deal of general as well as more specific campaign information. About half of the Internet NGOs provide only limited or no information about their organizations and decision-making procedures, for example, the McSpotlight and Banana Link websites.

Besides giving information, some Internet NGOs use their websites to mobilize people, interact with people and implement ICT-related projects. Only Oneworld seems to combine all categories of activities on their website. EDRI, Idealist, AlterNet and Panos use their websites mainly to give information and interact with people. Mobilization activities on these websites are restricted to applying for membership and donating money.[4] ICT-related activities are less prominent or unavailable on these websites. Banana Link, EarthAction and RSF use their websites mainly to give information and mobilize people. People are mobilized to send letters, e-mails and postcards to politicians and companies. The Banana Link website also provides addresses of shops that sell fair-trade products. Whereas RSF and EarthAction seem to focus only on adults or adolescents, Banana Link has developed educational material and also focuses on children. CryptoRights aims to mobilize ICT professionals as volunteers, and addresses human rights workers and journalists who might need these volunteers' help. CryptoRights also offers online training and support, and provides open source software encryption keys. The McSpotlight website gives information about McDonald's, allows for interaction and tries to mobilize people to act against McDonald's. Information on the website covers different subjects related to McDonald's, ranging from nutritional facts to labour rights. The APC and IICD websites give information, allow for interaction and support ICT-related projects. These websites pay little attention to mobilizing people, neither solicits donations, but both have events calendars.

4.2.   Legitimacy and NGO websites

4.2.1.   Regulatory aspect

The traditional NGOs refer to international treaties, such as the Universal Declaration of Human Rights. Amnesty International even includes the complete texts of the international treaties and declarations

---

4   On the AlterNet website, anti-war bumper stickers are offered for sale.

referred to on its website. The Internet NGOs refer to international law much more sparingly. RSF includes a reference to freedom of expression and the International Criminal Court, and in the BehindTheLabel campaign there is some reference to the rights of workers, but the international legal basis of these rights is not specified. The Virtual Globe website refers to the Johannesburg Summit, because Virtual Globe was launched as a result of that summit. The CryptoRights website refers to the First Amendment to the United States Constitution. Panos includes more references to international law. All international treaties and declarations concerning human rights and labour rights are based on international regulation but could also be part of the moral aspect of legitimacy. These declarations and treaties are based on moral ideas, human rights law in particular.

Only five out of sixteen Internet NGOs present annual reports and financial statistics on their website (Idealist, APC, IICD, Panos and RSF). This does not necessarily mean that the other Internet NGOs have no financial statistics at all; they simply do not provide them on their websites. Some Internet NGOs, for example Virtual Globe, have one or only a few donors; it is conceivable that these Internet NGOs provide their donors with some financial statistics. Slightly more Internet NGOs (seven out of sixteen) provide information about individuals and organizations that may apply for support. The group of Internet NGOs providing financial information and the group providing eligibility criteria do not completely overlap. For example, OneWorld and Virtual Activism give clear eligibility criteria for support, but do not have information about finances and annual reports on their websites. CryptoRights provides pgp keys for general use, but support and training only for human rights workers and journalists.

Financial statistics, annual reports and audit report are taken very seriously by all traditional NGOs, although the Amnesty International website and the website of its Dutch section differ in this respect. On the national website much more attention is paid to financial transparency than on the international website. The Dutch website provides elaborate justification of the money spent—as do the websites of Greenpeace, Oxfam Novib and FOEI. In the Netherlands, NGOs and whether they spend donations well have been extensively debated. This may have induced NGOs to provide detailed information about their finances on their websites and in their annual reports.

Accreditation does not seem to play an important role for the Internet NGOs. APC is the only one to mention its accreditation explicitly (by the Economic and Social Council (ECOSOC) and the UN). The other Internet NGOs have not been accredited or consider their accreditation of too little significance to warrant reference on their websites. The Dutch websites of the traditional NGOs all mention that they have received a national certificate for charities. A charity may only qualify for this certificate, if it meets certain requirements, pertaining especially to transparency and the use of funds.

4.2.2.   Social aspects

Some of the traditional NGOs (FOEI, Oxfam Novib, and Amnesty International) and half of the Internet NGOs (EarthAction, Banana Link, APC, IICD, Panos, OneWorld, Virtual Activism, and—to a lesser extent—Virtual Globe and HRI) point to their grassroots orientation. Most of these NGOs may be regarded as networks, the exceptions being Virtual Activism and Banana Link. Banana Link participates in a network that addresses human rights and ecological problems in the banana trade. An NGO is free to decide to be a grassroots NGO. Some NGOs do not intend to be grassroots organizations, such as Greenpeace, RSF or Global Witness. If, however, an NGO manifests itself as a grassroots organization, it does so explicitly and repeatedly on its website. HRI and Virtual Globe occupy the middle ground. They work with partners, but seem to be organized centrally. NGOs subscribing to certain values or meeting certain requirements may become partners. However, this means that they may, for example, post information. It does not in fact mean that they have consultation rights with regard to the policies of HRI or Virtual Globe.

   With regard to public support, Idealist is the only Internet NGO to refer to its members and even to the number of website visits in the previous months. The network Internet NGOs, such as APC, Panos, OneWorld, and EarthAction, refer to the number of NGO members. Most other Internet NGOs do not refer to the number of supporters or the level of public support they receive. EDRI lists all its members to substantiate its claim that it is a European organization drawing its membership from the entire European Union. The traditional NGOs refer either to the number of members (Amnesty International, Oxfam Novib, Greenpeace) or to their member and affiliated NGOs (FOEI); only Global Witness does not refer to either its members or public support.

   Regarding the recognition by knowledgeable and powerful organizations or individuals, it is noticeable that EarthAction mentions Leonardo di Caprio as one of its supporters. Leornardo di Caprio may not be considered a particularly knowledgeable or powerful person with regard to environmental and social problems, he is, however, popular. EarthAction would appear to think that Leonardo di Caprio's support may help the organization reach its goals and mobilize people. In fact, a number of celebrities support NGO or UN campaigns, for example, Bono or Angelina Jolie. Some other NGO websites include references to people or organizations supporting their campaigns, or to the UN as a knowledgeable and powerful organization.

Approximately a third of the NGOs have steering committees. NGO steering committees usually include experienced and powerful people among its members from various strata of society.

Some NGOs consider government funding a seal of approval, others refuse donations from governments or companies in order to remain independent. Global Witness, FOEI, Oxfam Novib, IICD, Panos and Virtual Globe mention that they obtain government funds for their projects. The other NGOs, traditional and Internet NGOs alike, do not, some even decline government funds. For example, Greenpeace adheres to a principle of independence from both corporations and governments. RSF, IICD, and Panos accept donations from companies and cooperate with companies, the other NGOs do not do this. Of the traditional NGOs, only Amnesty International and Oxfam Novib cooperate with companies, but they do so only with a select group of companies that focus on fair trade, or banks that support sustainable development. Global Witness rules out cooperation with companies that are involved in the trades or countries that it investigates.

4.2.3. Moral aspects

Most NGOs very clearly express their aims, missions, and values on their websites. Text Boxes 1 and 2 contain samples of NGO missions and values. Some NGO websites include explicit references to ethics. EarthAction, for example, states that its campaigns are based on ethics, experience, and wisdom. Some traditional NGOs have separate sections on values, principles, or basic rights (Text boxes 7 and 8).

It should be noted that the results with regard to references to human rights or labour rights could also be included here. Traditional NGOs tend to refer to universal rights of this kind on moral grounds. Also, performance criteria such as the reliability of information on NGO websites could be included here. The moral basis of the regulatory aspect, the social aspect and the performance of legitimacy will be discussed more extensively in Chapter 7.

Text box 7: Rights identified by Oxfam Novib
              (source: www.novib.nl)

Rights based approach

Oxfam Novib regards poverty as being equal to a lack of rights. Due to a lack of basic rights, people that live in poverty do not have (sufficient) access to power, material resources and basic services. This leads to hunger, exclusion, exploitation, a lack of opportunities and inequality.

That is why we have divided our work up into five rights which reflect the various poverty dimensions. These are rights which are acknowledged throughout the world and which are based on a wide range of agreements, conventions and declarations:

Right to a sustainable existence

Everyone has the right to sufficient and healthy food, to safe and paid work and to a clean, safe and supportive environment. Honest world trade and ethically responsible investments are badly needed.

Right to basic social services

In order to improve your living conditions you need a proper education and good healthcare. Oxfam Novib focuses particularly on education for women and girls.

Right to life and safety

In the event of natural disasters and armed conflicts, Oxfam Novib provides emergency aid, together with Oxfam International. At the same time we lay the basis for sustainable development, for example by training counterparts to act effectively in the event of life-threatening situations.

Right to social and political participation

Civic organisations and political parties must be free and able to act democratically. Each citizen must be able to have a say in decisions that affect his life.

Right to identity

People are discriminated against because they are women, homosexuals, disabled or Indians. Such exclusion occurs the world over. That is why Oxfam Novib is working on integration and equality. Violence against women is an area of particular attention.

Text box 8: Amnesty International core values (statutes)
          (source: www.amnesty.org)

Core values
Amnesty International forms a global community of human rights defenders
with the principles of international solidarity, effective action for the individual victim, global coverage, the universality and indivisibility of human
rights, impartiality and independence, and democracy and mutual respect.

4.2.4.   Performance

The traditional NGOs and the Internet NGOs differ with regard to the
information they provide about their successes on their websites. All
traditional NGOs include a list of successes, whereas only half of the
Internet NGOs refer to successful campaigns or actions, and most of
them do so briefly. For example, RSF mentions the release of impris-
oned journalists, but there is no separate section listing all releases of
journalists RSF has campaigned for. EarthAction, on the other hand,
provides a long list of its successes and results similar to the lists of traditional NGOs (see Text boxes 9 and 10).

Text box 9: A sample of the successes listed on the EarthAction website
          (the full list numbers 21 successes between 1992 and 2004)

Over the last 12 years, EarthAction has planned and carried out 83 global
campaigns addressing the world's most serious environment, development,
peace and human rights issues. Here is a selection from the many successes
that our Network has played a key role in bringing about:
–   The International Criminal Court that will try individuals for crimes
     against humanity is now being established.
–   Over 80% of the ozone-depleting substances listed in the Montreal Pro-
     tocol have been phased out. Elimination of the last 20% is underway.
–   Clayoquot Sound in British Columbia, one of Canada's last remaining
     temperate rainforests, was rescued from imminent destruction from
     logging and in 1999 was established as a UN Biosphere Reserve.
–   The Venezuelan government set aside plans to allow mining and log-
     ging in the Imataca Forest Reserve, one of the most biologically diverse
     regions on Earth, and consulted with indigenous peoples, environment
     and human rights organizations and local officials to make a new plan to
     protect the Forest Reserve and the indigenous communities within it.

Text box 10: Sample of successful campaigns
              *(source: the Good News section of the Amnesty International website, which
              includes photographs)*

Maldives: Release of artist and internet dissident
Prisoners of conscience Ahmad Ibrahim Didi, internet reporter, and Naushad Waheed, an artist and cartoonist, were released in February 2006 after four years imprisonment in the Maldives.

"Ahmad Ibrahim Didi and Naushad Waheed were tried in grossly unfair trials simply for expressing their peaceful opinions," said Abbas Faiz, South Asia researcher at Amnesty International. "Their release today is welcome but long overdue."

Guantánamo: Action works!
Since AI started highlighting specific cases of Guantánamo detainees, 15 of them have been released from US detention. Of those detainees transferred to their home countries, 7 remain in detention and 8 have been released.

Traditional NGOs appear to use their successes as a way to muster support. Amnesty International shows that its letter writing actions produce results and that people do not write letters in vain. Its website not only contains information about released prisoners of conscience, but also accounts of released prisoners of the impact the letters had on the treatment they received during their imprisonment.

With regard to the reliability of the information published on the Internet, about half of the traditional and Internet NGOs include the names of authors in some articles on their websites. Weblogs and columns express personal views and inevitably include the name of the author. Most traditional and Internet NGOs refer to sources to some extent. Only RSF, Virtual Globe, EarthAction, CryptoRights and Oxfam Novib do not do so. Some information, such as campaign information, may be considered original information provided by the NGO, and no author or source is therefore referred to, as is exemplified by the websites of Greenpeace and Amnesty International. Information resulting from the NGO's own research usually does not identify one or more individual authors or sources, as the NGO is both the author and the main source.

If a bulletin board or discussion site is available, then there is usually a moderator as well. There are rules about what information can and cannot be posted; insulting language, for example, is not allowed on the Idealist bulletin board.

Virtual Globe has included a disclaimer in its conditions to the effect that it cannot be held liable for the information on the website. Other Internet NGOs have posted disclaimers in, for example, the book list or the links, stating that the views in the books or in the links are not necessarily shared by the NGOs, as, for example, the Virtual Activism book list, and HRI links. McSpotlight has added disclaimers to information on its website that has been provided by McDonald's (for example, the nutritional value of McDonald's food as stated by McDonald's).

At least three websites of Internet NGOs were dormant during the research period: Virtual Globe; CryptoRights; and Virtual Activism. McSpotlight was been dormant from approximately late 2003 to 2005, but since January 2006 signs of website activity have been reported. Three other websites include a great deal of outdated information: HRI; EarthAction; and BehindTheLabel. In other words, only nine out of sixteen Internet NGO website were updated regularly. The traditional NGO websites were all updated regularly.

4.2.5.   Conclusions about NGO websites and legitimacy

All NGOs studied for the purposes of this research give information related to the moral aspect of legitimacy. They all provide information about their missions, aims, and values on their websites.

In general, the traditional NGOs have higher scores (more than half of the maximum score) on more aspects of legitimacy, the regulatory aspect especially. It is worth noting that none of the traditional NGOs realized high scores on the reliability criteria. Their scores on these criteria are mostly due to their regular updates and some inclusion of authors and sources. The fact that certain information is published on the websites of well-established NGOs, such as Amnesty International and Greenpeace, may be argued to constitute sufficient proof of the reliability of the information to some website visitors.

The Internet NGOs generally have slightly lower scores on the different legitimacy aspects than the traditional NGOs, except for the information reliability score. Contrary to the traditional NGOs, approximately half of the Internet NGOs have high scores on reliability of information. CryptoRights, BehindTheLabel, McSpotlight and Virtual Activism have low scores on most legitimacy aspects. McSpotlight only provides information related to the moral aspect of legitimacy and the reliability of information. CryptoRights provides some information related to the moral and regulatory aspects. The total scores of APC, IICD, and Panos are at least as high as those of the traditional NGOs.

The traditional NGOs have high scores on the regulatory aspect of legitimacy (except for the Amnesty International website), and on financial statistics, audit reports, and annual reports in particular. Of the Internet NGOs, only Idealist, APC, IICD, and Panos have high scores on these criteria.

OneWorld, Panos, EarthAction and APC describe themselves as NGO networks and provide a great deal of information with regard to the representation of the different partners. Banana Link and IICD do not describe themselves as NGO networks, yet also provide much information related to the representation of people in communities within their networks. Banana Link is not an NGO network, but a member of an NGO network that addresses social and human rights, and environmental issues in the banana trade. EDRI describes itself as an NGO network, but does not provide any information regarding the representation of the network members on its website. In conclusion, reference to representation is not limited to network NGOs and not all NGOs that describe themselves as NGO networks refer to representation on their websites.

5.   Conclusions

In this section, the five main conclusions of this research are presented. A first conclusion of this study is that most NGOs, Internet NGOs as well as traditional NGOs, use the Internet to provide information. This means that questions concerning the legitimacy of Internet activities of NGOs should also address the information function of their websites. This point will be discussed in the next section. As concluded in the previous section, approximately half of the Internet NGOs provide a great deal of information that website visitors may use to assess the reliability of the information published on the Internet. The traditional NGOs provide far less information that may be used for that purpose. Virtual Globe and Idealist include disclaimers to the effect that they cannot be held liable for the information published on their websites. Idealist refers specifically to the information posted on its website by others, such as job ads. Such a disclaimer can be argued to reduce the perceived reliability of the information on the website, for if an NGO does not trust the information published on its website, why should anyone else?

Some Internet NGOs have disclaimer stating that the views expressed in the books on their booklists or accessed through the links on their website are not necessarily shared by the NGOs. It would seem unlikely that disclaimers of this kind aversely affect the perceived reliability of the information on the websites. Disclaimers are not found on the traditional NGO websites.

A second conclusion is that there are no Internet-only NGOs. There are NGOs that are focused and more active on the Internet but these NGOs too need the real world for offices, lobbying, etc. There is, however, a difference between the younger Internet NGOs and the traditional ones. The traditional NGOs use the Internet for information, mobilization, and—to a limited degree—interaction purposes. The Internet is used supplementary to other media, such as newspapers and television. The Internet NGOs use their websites for the purposes of giving information, mobilizing people, interacting to some extent, and for ICT-related projects. Some of these NGOs do not use other media than their websites and e-mail to provide information. The younger Internet NGOs—with the exception of APC, IICD, and OneWorld—refer to fewer legitimacy aspects on their websites than the traditional NGOs do.

A third conclusion is that none of the NGOs provides information about all elements of the three legitimacy aspects and performance. Some elements of the legitimacy aspects seem to be excluded by the missions and values of some NGOs. For example, Greenpeace and Global Witness do not provide any information related to the representation of affected people and members, since they do not wish to represent anyone.[5] It is probably best to allow for different operationalizations and interpretations of the four legitimacy aspects depending on the aim of the NGO. An example of this is that if the main aim of an NGO is to present information to the general public about unjust situations somewhere in the world, the reliability of that information is very important. Hopefully, the information is also effective and successful in raising awareness of the issue but accreditation and financial transparency are probably less important.

A fourth conclusion is that, although some of the NGOs try to use the interaction opportunities of the Internet, these opportunities are not used to their full extent. Most NGO websites include e-mail addresses that people may use to make inquiries. Interaction opportuni-

---

5   Greenpeace aims to represent nature.

ties offered on NGO websites usually are bulletin boards, discussion forums or sections where website visitors may respond to propositions. If websites offered full access to all of its visitors, the risk of nonsensical and insulting entries being posted might be very real. It is therefore understandable that NGOs monitor and supervise their websites, and allow people to post information only on designated webpages, even if this does hamper interaction. Complete freedom to post and react to information on the one hand, and the reliability of information on the website on the other hand, may possibly be in contradiction with each other, even if illegal information is deleted by a moderator.

A fifth conclusion is that there is no direct relation between the availability of financial statistics or audit reports and donation options on the websites. Most NGOs offer a number of donation methods on their websites, the exceptions being BehindTheLabel, Banana Link, APC and IICD. All traditional NGO websites (except for the Amnesty International website) provide a great deal of information related to the regulatory aspect of legitimacy, financial transparency in particular. Only half of the Internet NGOs provide some information related to financial transparency. It is remarkable that both APC and IICD, which do not solicit donations, include a considerable amount of information with regard to the regulatory aspect of legitimacy on their websites.

6.   Some specific normative legitimacy issues

In this section, the results of the empirical analysis of the NGO websites will be used as input for a normative reflection on the legitimacy of Internet activities of NGOs. First, the necessary reliability of the information on the NGO websites will be elaborated on. Second, a few remarks will be made about the way Internet could increase the legitimacy of NGOs by helping to build or strengthen communities.

6.1.   Reliability of information on NGO websites

Legitimacy questions regarding the provision of information might seem a bit strange. In principle, everyone is legally allowed to publish all kinds of information on the Internet, unless the information is illegal, such as child pornography. However, it is too simplistic to conclude that if NGOs refrain from putting illegal information on their websites, their Internet activities will be legitimate. A problem is that in different countries different information is illegal. For example, China has imposed a censoring regime on the Internet. Some information provided by NGOs will be illegal in certain countries; the information about Chinese cyberdissidents on the RSF website is probably not legal in China. Does this mean that providing that information is not legitimate? This is a difficult question. Information can be illegal according to some repressive regime, but then, providing this information need not be immoral, and the regime itself might be illegitimate. With regard to providing information on their websites, NGOs should prima facie refrain from publishing information that causes harm or information that has been obtained by causing harm. In other words, an NGO should not have a rare bird killed in order to take photographs of it for publication on its website, because the photographs would have been obtained by causing harm. This is a prima facie duty that can be outweighed by other duties. There may be situations where information might cause some harm, but where the benefits of providing this information outweigh the harm. One could say that cyberdissidents that criticize a government harm the government, but this harm can be outweighed if certain human rights or environmental issues are exposed and made public, so people may pressure the government to change its policy. From a moral point of view then, there may be reasons for including information on NGO websites that might damage a company or government. Is it sufficient for NGOs to prima facie do no harm with information on their websites in order to be legitimate? In the following, it will be argued that the information needs to be reliable and complete.

In cases where the information is meant to persuade people to act in a certain way or to change their beliefs, the legitimacy question is very relevant.[6] If people are persuaded to donate money, or change their beliefs or behaviour, the information needs to be reliable and people need to be able to ascertain the reliability of the information provided in order to ensure that people may make informed decisions.

With regard to judging whether information on a website is reliable, Vedder and Watchbroit (2004) introduced the distinction between content and pedigree criteria. On the basis of this distinction, reliable information will be interpreted as information that is properly justified (Vedder and Wachbroit 2004). Reliable information may not necessarily be true, but there are reasons justifying the belief that it is. Judging

---

6   Note that this point is relevant to beneficiaries as well as donors. Beneficiaries also need to be able to make informed decisions about accepting support or changing their behaviour.

whether information is reliable, then, is judging whether the justification meets certain standards.

According to Vedder and Wachbroit (2004), content criteria are 'a function of the content of the information itself'. One could think about the evidence that is provided for a claim, its consistency, etc. Information may be inconsistent within itself, for example when someone claims that a person is alive and not alive. Information might also be inconsistent with some piece of general, elementary knowledge.[7] If an NGO claimed on its website that the people in Ghana need help because the ice caps on which they hunt for polar bears are melting, people with some knowledge of geography would know that Ghana is an African country, and that there are no ice caps in Africa (although some African mountain tops may be covered with snow or ice) and certainly no polar bears. This information is inconsistent with some rather basic geographical knowledge. It is difficult to judge the reliability of information given by NGOs on their websites by using content criteria. The NGOs that have been studied in this research deal with all sorts of problems all over the world and most people do not know how poor people in, for example, Jamaica are, or what the human rights situation in former Soviet states is. This means that most people are only able to use limited content criteria to judge the reliability of information.

Vedder and Wachbroit (2004) introduced a second criterion, the pedigree criterion. Pedigree criteria are 'the conditions or criteria of reliability that are a function of the source of the information.' These criteria specifically refer to established credibility-conferring institutions, such as academic institutions or professional societies. Information from a source or author that has provided reliable information before is deemed more reliable than information from a source that has proved to be unreliable. Information from a knowledgeable or professional source is usually considered reliable. The place where information is located is an important pedigree criterion. Information provided on a website of a well-known NGO that has provided reliable information in the past, such as Amnesty, will probably be considered more reliable than information on the website of an NGO that is an unknown quantity. Therefore, the pedigree criteria pertaining to NGO websites mainly

---

7   Different people will probably hold very different views on what constitutes basic knowledge, depending on their experiences, education and social context. Interesting though this issue may be, it falls outside the scope of this chapter.

consist of the reputation of the NGO itself if it is well-known and has a good reputation, its sources, authors of information, and supporters, and perhaps its connections with other well-known NGOs, or its status as an accredited organization.

Based on the idea of autonomy, it could be claimed that people need to be enabled to make an informed decision about changing their beliefs or supporting an NGO. As said before, most people may be assumed to have only a limited amount of knowledge available to them to judge the reliability of information on the Internet using only content criteria. For that reason, the pedigree criteria are, for most people, very important to determine the reliability of information on websites. The importance of pedigree criteria means that NGOs need to provide information related to pedigree criteria. In other words, providing information related to pedigree criteria is a necessary condition for the legitimacy of information provision by NGOs on their websites. This means that the information on NGO websites not only needs to be reliable, but should also include information about pedigree criteria allowing people to judge for themselves that the information is reliable.

Some traditional NGOs are regarded as reliable sources of information and the very fact that some information is available on their websites is a pedigree criterion in itself. People will rely on information on the websites of these well-known NGOs with a good reputation. The fear of losing their good name will encourage well-known NGOs to check the information before they put it on their websites.

Reliability of information on the website is probably even more important for the Internet NGOs. Unlike such NGOs as Amnesty International and Global Witness, the Internet NGOs are not recognized experts in their respective fields. The Internet NGOs cannot regard the familiarity of their names and their reputations as constituting pedigree criteria by themselves. This means that the Internet NGOs have to provide a great deal of additional information allowing people to judge the reliability of information. Articles should, for example, refer to evidence, but also include authors and sources. EarthAction uses another strategy by presenting Leonardo DiCaprio as a supporter on its website. This could be seen as a way of providing information about pedigree criteria, although it is questionable whether the support of a famous actor is indicative of the reliability of the information on the website. Another point to be made with regard to Internet NGOs is that their offices or projects often cannot be visited. The McSpotlight website, for example, does not include an office address. Its office might be someone's living room. If someone doubts the sincerity or reliability of traditional NGOs, he or she may decide to visit the NGO; with Internet NGOs, this may not always be an option.

Therefore, it is more difficult or even impossible for people to judge whether Internet NGOs are sincere or not, and Internet NGOs should provide much information about pedigree criteria.

Another point related to the reliability of the information is the availability of all the information relevant to people. This point is not only important with regard to the Internet, but with regard to the provision of all information. If an NGO website or television commercial is created in order to persuade people to change their beliefs, donate money, or send letters, then the aims, values, and mission of the NGO and the campaign need to be clear. People need to know what they subscribe to. They need this information to decide whether they share these beliefs. If the NGO provides reliable information, but not all information relevant to people to make a well-considered and informed decision, then consent may not be assumed. This could mean that, although an NGO attracts many members or donations, it cannot boast wide support, because its supporters do not know what values they subscribe to. An NGO, for example, provides reliable information about one of its goals, building schools in less developed countries in order to further the education of children in these countries. Suppose that the NGO has a religious background and aims at converting children to Christianity using these schools. Atheists who are convinced that religion and education should not be mixed, may support the goal of educating children in less developed countries, but they will almost certainly not share the aim of converting children to Christianity. The same may hold for people in the communities where the schools are planned; they may very well wish their children to be educated in order to increase their chances in life, but they might not want their children to be converted to Christianity. Therefore, if the NGO only provided information about the school building projects, this information would be insufficient, even if the information about the school building project were reliable.

This example demonstrates the tension between effectiveness and reliability or completeness. The NGO might solicit more donations and build more schools, if it provided unreliable or incomplete information. Although effectiveness is important, the ends do not justify the means in this case. Respect for autonomy and giving people the opportunity to make well-informed decisions about supporting an NGO or accepting help from an NGO requires information to be reliable, and include all information relevant to the persons making the decision to change their beliefs and/or support an NGO. To conclude, information provided on NGO websites must be reliable, include sufficient details on pedigree criteria to allow people to conclude that the information is reliable, and should be complete, with regard to the values and aims of the NGO especially.

6.2.   *Interaction using the Internet*

Although most NGOs studied do not use all interaction opportunities the Internet provides, most of them allow for some interaction. If the interaction were used for community building in grassroots NGOs or in knowledge sharing groups, the interaction could support the development of shared norms and values. This is especially important when different norms and values may be expected between the different groups involved in projects (see also the last chapter of this book that addresses moral plurality in more detail). An example would be a grassroots NGO that has projects all over the world. Groups from different parts of the world are likely to have different norms and values, and real-world meetings are probably rare—depending in large measure on the resources of the NGO. In cases such as this, the Internet could be used to help build the community and to arrive at shared problem definitions, norms and values. These shared norms may be considered a basis for the moral aspect of legitimacy. Studies of virtual communities reveal that it is currently problematic to build a community using only the Internet (Ayers 2003; Nip 2004). There is only limited trust online and it is difficult to define shared problem frames. The Internet can probably be used in addition to other forms of communication; face-to-face meetings in particular are very important. Therefore, interaction through the Internet as well as through other means of communication could be argued to enhance the legitimacy of NGO projects.

A problem with Internet interaction is that it is very difficult to verify whether someone is who he or she claims to be. A way to solve this problem is to ask people to register. Access to certain information may be restricted to members, who may, for example, be required to log in using their membership identification code. This might, however, prevent some people who would have liked to participate to actually do so, for example because they do not feel comfortable with being registered. Technologically, registration data can be protected, but in some parts of the world registered membership of an NGO could be dangerous and the question is whether people may rely on technological methods used to protect registration data.

In summary, even though the use of the Internet to develop shared norms and values is not without problems, the Internet could probably support and strengthen existing communities. In Chapter 4, near-future scenarios will be described for ICT-supported opportunities to develop shared norms and build communities.

Chapter 4   A step beyond: Technologically enhanced interactivity and legitimacy

Corien Prins

1.   Introduction

Picture a future world where many of the online tools that children now have at their fingertips are used powerfully by NGOs to advocate and campaign in challenging new ways. In such a world, NGOs are actively engaged in educating the general public via virtual games. Based on their earlier successes with e-commerce applications, NGOs apply recommender systems to signal correlations in societal perceptions by making links between two or more political views based on user feedback through their websites.[1] Instant messaging and weblogs will by then have become routine instruments in creating awareness, trying out certain ideas, coalition building and bringing relevant information to the attention of international organizations. This is a world in which the strategies employed by NGOs are to a large extent determined by the opportunities new digital tools offer.

---

[1]   Recommender systems are gaining popularity in the e-commerce domain. One example is an application available for users on the Internet called MovieLens, where visitors can obtain movie recommendations based on ratings by website visitors, but also rate or review any movie themselves and recommend these to others, or share movie recommendations in discussion groups. Mobile location based services through cell-phones are currently also available. For instance, people with similar preferences within the same geographical perimeter of approximately 30 metres. For more details on these applications, see Mobasher, Bamshad, Robert Cooley, and Jaideep Srivastava (2000) Automatic Personalization Based on Web Usage Mining. Web usage mining can help improve the scalability, accuracy, and flexibility of recommender systems. *Communications of the ACM. Association for Computer Machinery* 43, no.8: 142-151.

Anton Vedder et al., *NGO Involvement in International Governance and Policy*, pp. 111-134. Printed in the Netherlands. ISBN 978 90 04 15846 7.

At first glance, this scenario may seem a little far-fetched. Today, true technology-amplified action by NGOs is a far from common scenario. The majority of these organizations have not yet moved beyond the use of websites and e-mail, and have not yet learned or noticed the capabilities, value, and strategic potential of the new interactive digital tools described above. But the tools are in fact at their disposal. All applications and techniques mentioned are already being used or applied by other actors in the online world, both for commercial and public purposes. What is more, some of the tools mentioned are indeed part of the present-day strategy of some NGOs. So why would NGOs and other social movements in, say, ten years, not broadly benefit from these new opportunities? One way or another, once NGOs start to experiment with ways to use these tools, and the knowledge of their strategic potential has had sufficient time to mature, they will no doubt serve as increasingly important instruments in the work, role and influence of NGOs. This raises questions about the accountability for the use of these tools and the available formal and informal checks on such use. And, when focusing on this book's central theme—the legitimacy of NGOs—it may be presumed that a more intensive reliance on digital strategies could have an effect on several of the dimensions that constitute legitimacy. But what exactly will this effect be? Below, a glimpse of the potential impact of interactive digital tools on NGOs and their legitimacy will be presented.

In discussing the questions raised above, this chapter starts from the presumption that the discourse environment in which NGOs operate has an effect on the legitimacy issue and the three legitimacy dimensions (to be discussed below). In applying this perspective, this chapter aims to explore what the new interactive digital tools might mean for legitimacy and on what basis such tools could develop contributions to the (understanding of the) concept of legitimacy and its dimensions. The exploration partly builds on the research results presented in Chapter 3 of this book. However, whereas that chapter focused on websites and on the information and services provided through websites, this chapter's perspective is interactive digital tools. By way of example, two applications mentioned above will be elaborated on: simulation games and personalized information distribution. Section 2 will consider the opportunities these new tools may offer NGOs to pursue their objectives and exercise their influence. In Section 3, the discussion will then turn to the possible implications of the employment of new interactive tools. More specifically, the legitimacy issue will be focused on. Digital simulation, for example, has the potential to help consolidate the legitimacy of an NGO and its activities by explaining and justifying its course of action to its constituency and the world at large. However, it may also entail risks and ambiguities for NGO legitimacy. Finally, in Section 4, an attempt will be made to develop a framework for understanding the impact on and conceivable contribution to legitimacy of interactive digital tools. In the conclusion it will be argued that the criteria for legitimacy cannot be analyzed irrespective of the particular forms, practices and strategies that NGOs use in their dealings. It must thus be acknowledged that new digital tools will transform practices of legitimatization.

2.   Interactive digital tools

2.1.   Introduction

From the available literature on Internet use by NGOs, a picture emerges of a growing interest in the use of this medium to manage and disseminate information, collaborate on knowledge sharing, and mobilize capacity. As early as the late 1990s, representatives of social movements were arguing that new technological opportunities, such as the Internet, offered much more than mere efficient instruments for their traditional activities and strategies. Information and communication technology (ICT) would require them to rethink their role (ECDPM 2000). Recent studies and surveys indeed show that the Internet and other ICT tools are employed in a wide range of new strategies that may change the way social movements work, NGOs included. Such strategies range from simple one-way information distribution to politically motivated cyberactivism (Vegh 2003; McGirk 1999).

Most commentators argue that the emergence of digital tools does have implications for the activities of NGOs (Surman and Reilly 2003; Clark and Themudo 2006). However, they differ in their opinions on how and to what extent exactly the use of ICT influences the work and position of NGOs. Although most appear subtle about the contribution of new ICTs to shaping and enforcing the position of NGOs, political activists, and social movements, some are more explicit: 'There is little doubt that the Internet has dramatically increased the effectiveness of advocacy NGOs and especially their capacity to influence public opinion' (Kurtz 2002, 245). Others, in contrast, do not believe that the new digital means will ever radically change democracy and the role

NGOs play in that process, in either a positive or negative way (Van Aelst and Walgrave 2004). To quote Siurala, 'it seems that Internet as an instrument does not as such create new political activism nor does it fundamentally alter the political landscape' (Siurala 2000, 9). Chapter 3 showed that most NGOs use their websites mainly to provide information.

Various reasons are offered to explain the scepticism about the changes ICT might bring for NGOs and the legitimacy of their activities. Two reasons in particular stand out. First, academics, commentators and social movement watchers doubt whether virtual tools and contacts can ever replace the indispensable interpersonal networks of the physical world. The Internet, it is argued, does not offer the emotions and thrills of real and direct interpersonal interaction (Etzioni and Etzioni 1999). 'It is difficult to run a meeting that lacks the visual cues and the immediate feedback that you have in "flesh meet"' (Lebkowsky 1999). And Diani (2001) argues that when interaction is solely based on Internet communication, it lacks the required basis of trust for building long-term relationships. A second reason for the scepticism is that ICT does not allow for identity building. In studying the well-known example of cyberactivism set by the Zapatista solidarity network, Olesen concluded that despite the existence of networked patterns and ties, this network cannot be regarded as a social movement. What is lacking is the element of collective identity seen as central to social movements. The network 'is primarily a network of information exchange and less one of identity exchange and construction' (Olesen 2004, 100). Chapter 3 of this book showed that if the Internet were to be used to help build and maintain a community, such use could contribute to the legitimization of NGO activities, because it might facilitate the discourse on relevant norms and values. However, the conclusion of Chapter 3 was that it is difficult—if not impossible—to build such communities only with the use of the Internet. The Internet could play a role here in addition to other ways of communication.

It could, however, be claimed that it is too early to draw any final conclusions on the real potential of ICTs. A first argument would be that experiments and models to promote interactive social activism by means of digital tools are rather new and experiences seem to come up constantly. And it is the very effect of these new interactive tools that has thus far been poorly theorized. The majority of the surveys and studies on the use of ICTs by NGOs, cyberactivists, and other social movements deal with information distribution and communication facilities. But what will be the implications of digital tools that allow for bonding and sharing emotions in a virtual setting? They might perhaps introduce a mechanism for online identity construction. The popularity of gaming, virtual worlds, and other interactive digital tools is a good illustration of the possible effect of the new interactive opportunities. But there is more. Gaming can offer small laboratories of democracy and political simulation and thereby create virtual learning and testing environments that do not require real-life situations. It is characteristic of gaming that it is an active, not a passive, form of interaction. Therefore, games have a very real potential for education, because those who play them must make all choices themselves. Players learn from earlier experiences and from examining their decisions, and they are offered tools to explore how alternative options might have developed. Online games and virtual worlds might be instrumental in creating environments that allow for values similar to those in the physical world, such as face-to-face communication, political debate, trying to figure out a balance of arguments, and making decisions. Gaming might even entice political activists and human rights watchers on the one hand and their opponents on the other hand, to sit down and try to understand the complexity of certain problems and the arguments behind their disagreements.

Another effect of the use of interactive multimedia tools is that due to the very characteristics of this type of instrument, it may affect the decision-making of individuals and therefore have an impact on mass opinion formation. Studies of the influence and effectiveness of digital media for persuasive purposes have shown that various characteristics of digital documents appear instrumental in changing the attitude and mood of people towards a certain topic (Krahmer, Van Dorst, and Ummelen 2004). Also, research into the psychological theory of the affect heuristic has shown that a first impression (a strong and emotional one in particular) may determine a decision, even if the decision is cognitively counterbalanced by subsequent facts. A good or bad feeling towards a certain situation (i.e., positive or negative affect) influences the perception of this situation, even when the situation itself does not logically warrant the perception (Finucane et al. 2000). In other words, depending on the specific stimuli used in simulation games (a certain visual presentation of a certain human rights violation), a person's emotional response—and therefore his or her judgement of the violation—might vary, and thus be influenced. Moreover, studies on public estimations and mass opinion formation have shown that interpersonal associations prominently shape the processes by which individuals choose what policies, candidates, or issues to support. Based on the earlier work of Aaron Wildavsky, Gastil et al. (2005) recently asserted that cultural cognition plays a dominant role in the tendency of individuals to form perceptions of societal and political issues that reflect and reinforce their world views. Through an extensive survey the authors showed that cultural orientations operate as a fundamental orienting force in the generation of mass public opinion.

Secondly, the forms of moral and political engagement among young people are changing and it will only be a matter of time before NGOs will (must) adapt their communication strategies to the new interactive and reciprocal communication patterns. As Lasse Siurala, Director of Youth and Sport of the Council of Europe, observed a couple of years ago, 'At the same time the forms of youth involvement are changing from fixed long-term commitments to an ever wider variety of looser, ambivalent and even contradictory commitments, and from "rational discourses to emotional, expressive and aesthetic forms of engagements" '(Siurala 2000). In suggesting that his organization should act on this development, Siurala stated: '[I]t is not only a question of developing the technology, but more so a question of adapting the strategies of governments, municipalities, political parties, NGOs and civic action movements to reciprocal communication with audiences than cascading down decisions— "communicative strategies" and competencies of "mass listening"' (Siurala 2000).

Of course, activism, identity building, and bonding by means of interactive tools have their limitations. Moreover, real-life use of and experimentation with new technologies progresses slowly, which makes it difficult to paint a balanced picture of the possible advantages and challenges of the use of new technologies. Thus, it is far from easy to fully grasp the implications of ICTs for the legitimacy of NGOs. Nevertheless, an exploration of the potential role and influence of these tools as well as of the impact of certain features of these tools on the legitimacy of NGOs might further the understanding of future developments. What is more, it is interesting to observe that some social movements, NGOs, and international organizations have already started to make use of new interactive digital tools.

2.2.   Games and digital simulation

Virtual games appear an excellent tool to make a political argument through simulation. Numerous political activists use this new instrument to make their argument. And the Internet appears an excellent vehicle in making their political tool available to a worldwide audience. For example, in 2005, an Israeli peace group launched a game called *Wild West Bank* (http://www.brand.co.il/unik/westbank) to show how difficult it would be to evacuate Jewish settlers from settlements surrounded by Palestinians.[2] Other examples of the role virtual worlds and gaming might play in creating political awareness and an understanding of the complexity of certain political problems, are games titled *A Force More Powerful, Industrial Waste* and *Food Force*.[3] The first of these is sponsored by the International Center on Nonviolent Conflict (ICNC), which describes itself as 'an independent, non-profit, educational foundation that develops and encourages the study and use of civilian-based, nonmilitary strategies to establish and defend human rights, democracy and justice worldwide' (http://www.nonviolent-conflict.org). Commentators describe the game as a unique collaboration of experts on non-violent conflict and game designers to build a simulation game that teaches the strategy of non-violent conflict (Boyer 2005). The game is designed for use by activists, but also aims to educate the media and general public. It also serves as a simulation tool for academic studies of non-violent resistance. 'A dozen scenarios, inspired by recent history, include conflicts against dictators, occupiers, colonizers and corrupt regimes, as well as struggles to secure the political and human rights of ethnic and racial minorities and women' (http://www.afmpgame.com).

Another example is the computer simulation-documentary called *Pax Warrior*. Having the 1994 Rwandan genocide as its theme, this virtual world based on counter-factual scenarios was created by activists on human rights and genocide in close cooperation with Canadian academics. The central goal of this digital tool is not to stop the genocide, but to educate its players about the complexity of dealing with situa-

---

2   More details on this initiative presented by Linda Gradstein are available at http://www.npr.org/templates/story/story.php?storyId=4717381 (accessed 26 November 2006).

3   See *A Force More Powerful* (http://www.afmpgame.com), *Industrial Waste* (http://www. spiritgames.co.uk/gamesin.php?UniqueNo=762) and *Food Force* (http://www.foodforce .com).

tions where human rights are violated. In reviewing the simulation tool, Cascio (2005) describes its potential and its limitations as follows:

> If counter-factual scenarios are well-constructed, they can show us how we can make better choices in the future, and allow us to look anew at whether and how we could work to change the results of decisions already taken. At the same time, we should recognize the limitations of counter-factual scenarios. Our real-world choices are not limited to an established set of A through E options; sometimes solutions emerge when we approach the situation in innovative ways, whether we're talking about humanitarian emergencies, political struggles, or responses to climate disruption. Pax Warrior, like all counter-factuals, is best thought of as a trigger for discussion, as a way of prompting the 'what haven't we thought of here?' questions. It's a catalyst for thoughtful conversation about humanitarian problems, and we can certainly use more of those.

Some simulation tools allow players to become involved in learning about and responding to disasters and to play the role of international NGOs. Basile Pissalidis, a senior programme associate with InterAction, a US-based development and humanitarian NGO, vividly describes his experiences with a tool and concludes: 'An entire cohort of important people has learned a great deal about NGOs, and how they can work effectively with NGOs during the disasters that nature will surely send their way' (Pissalidis 2002).

Finally, NGOs, activists and other social movements are not the only organizations that use games and digital simulation to communicate their message to the general public. Interestingly, *Food Force* was created for the United Nations World Food Programme. This game is designed for children between the ages of 8 and 13, and puts them in the role of food aid team members. The game simulates activities such as finding, buying, shipping and delivering food aid around the world (Cascio 2005).

2.3.   *Recommender systems*

The second example of the potential of new interactive digital tools relates to what are known as recommender systems. Simply put, recommender systems signal correlations in user preferences by establishing links between perceptions, notions, or other views based on user feedback (Prins 2006; Lips et al. 2005). Contrary to the aforementioned simulation tools, the use of these systems has not yet surfaced in the domain of human rights organizations and other social movements. Notable examples are, however, broadly available both in the public and private sectors. One of the best-known applications is the personalized recommendation of books on the website of Amazon.com. Through the use of cookies, every customer of Amazon.com is recognized by the website the moment he or she enters the site. Based on a user's preferences, click streams, recommendation algorithms, personal data, cookies and item-to-item collaborative filtering, Amazon.com recommends products that are on sale or have just been released, for example, in real-time (Linden, Smith, and York 2003). Although today recommender systems are mainly to be found on the Internet, other technologies and services, such as location-based services (LBS), radio frequency identification (RFID), smartcards, and biometrics, are expected to follow closely and offer even better opportunities for tailor-made or individualized services. In essence, recommender systems allow organizations to provide information and services to a large audience on an individualized and yet worldwide basis. And, what is more, these systems allow companies and organizations to learn about their customers' habits, preferences, lifestyles and opinions. Clearly, this offers interesting opportunities for social movements and NGOs as well.

What makes this new phenomenon attractive to NGOs is that it may, for instance, facilitate the provision of access to certain information to a specific group of people. Information distribution to selected (groups of) individuals might be predetermined by their attachment to a group, their cultural or societal position or predisposition, etc. Also, personalization services seem well suited to determine who will view or read a particular document on certain human rights issues and who will not. Techniques that facilitate this new type of inclusion and exclusion may be especially useful to accommodate the varying political interests of people. For NGOs, the new opportunities might be useful in that they will be able to do a better job of providing the right information to the right persons. Without personalization and profiling techniques, they must make wasteful investments in distributing information of which it is unclear whether their members or the general public will appreciate it.

In thinking about other possible opportunities, it is interesting to refer to the work of Masum (2002) who developed a system called TOOL that—in his words—'could demonstrate *the power of sharing and analyzing our opinions and implicit valuations* of the universe around us.'

It would allow that 'a population's opinions on a variety of personal and social issues could be aggregated into a social analogue of GNP (maybe "GHP", for gross human product) that would more directly measure the wealth levels experienced by the population.' The author argues that TOOL

> could be used to reduce opinion-search costs, to observe and analyze opinion streams, and to reward opinion generators objectively. The end result of these steps will be an *adaptive decision substrate*, complementing and enhancing the collective observation and decision processes of markets and human consciousness. This substrate will become just as ubiquitous as our current-day monetary system, and just as essential for carrying out trade, directing human attention, and incentivizing society.

Other researchers in the domain of social recommendation mechanisms take it one step further when elaborating on the opportunities that lie ahead:[4]

> While most recommender systems continue to gather detailed models of their 'users' within their particular application domain, they are, for the most part, oblivious to the larger context of the lives of their users outside of the application. What are they passionate about as individuals, and how do they identify themselves culturally? As recommender systems become more central to people's lives, we must start modelling the person, rather than the user.

As said before, recommender systems have not yet surfaced in the domain of human rights organizations and other social movements. But the phenomenon is quickly gaining popularity and it seems only a matter of time before NGOs and other social movements will recognize that the use of these systems is an important, if not inevitable, strategy to deploy in all their activities, which will enable them to profit from advantages such as improved relationships with members and potential members, channelling information to members and other interested people around the world, a higher performance on achieving organizational goals (e.g., policy effectiveness), and improved use of organizational means.

---

4   See http://www.media.mit.edu/research/ResearchPubWeb.pl?ID=955 and http://web.media.mit.edu/~hugo/research/#corelate.

Now that some of the key opportunities that interactive digital tools might offer to NGOs have been set out, the effect of the use of these tools on the legitimacy issue will be examined in more detail.

3.   Implications for NGO legitimacy

3.1.   Introduction

In principle, an inquiry into the link between new digital tools and NGO legitimacy should start with a clear a priori perspective on the concept of legitimacy and how it is to be applied to these internationally operating organizations. Such a definition would offer the starting point for an elaboration on what type of digital dealings of NGOs might be perceived as legitimate and which criteria would need to be fulfilled. Unfortunately, and as was shown in earlier chapters in this book, defining legitimacy is not an easy task. Scholars have struggled to grasp the concept and numerous definitions have been advocated. One key perspective found in literature is that there is no such thing as one strict definition of the concept. On the contrary, various theorists accept a mix of legitimating motives rather than one ideal type. In this sense, NGOs have various sources of legitimacy at their disposal and thus create a specific legitimation mix of elements (Steffek 2003). This perspective is very much in line with the central point taken in this book. Earlier chapters in this book showed that legitimacy has a multifaceted nature. The empirical work presented in Chapter 2 showed that NGOs draw on seven sources of legitimacy in order to establish or enhance their legitimacy. And in trying to set some tentative steps towards the criteria that make up the concept, the first chapter of this book sketched a stipulative definition of legitimacy, thereby relying on the three-dimensional conception of Beetham: the regulatory, morally normative, and social dimensions of legitimacy. Under this approach, legitimacy is concerned with conformity to rules (regulatory indicator), justification in relation to moral norms and values (morally normative indicator), and the consent or representation of those involved or affected (social indicator). The work of the previous chapters referred to above provides the starting point for the exploration below of what new digital tools might mean for legitimacy. The analysis offered will therefore not start from an a priori definition of NGO legitimacy, but will be developed on the basis of several core legitimacy dimensions. While these dimensions will be reflected on from an ICT perspective, the discussion will start from what could be called sources of legitimacy. And as will be shown, in applying the legitimacy dimensions to the use of interactive digital tools, these dimensions will often be constructed from a mix of such sources rather than one strict constellation.

Before considering the legitimacy sources that might be relevant in the light of the use of digital tools, one more observation must be made. When discussing the link between digital tools and NGO legitimacy, two approaches need to be considered. The first is the possible legitimizing effects of the application of digital tools. This approach addresses the role new interactive communication technologies might play in fulfilling the criteria developed for NGO legitimacy. Here the discussion centres around the question in what respect the new tools might play a role in the overall legitimacy of an organization. The second approach concerns the legitimacy of the particular digital tools themselves, including the way they are applied by NGOs. Here the discussion focuses on questions such as: how do NGOs legitimate the strategies and goals that are based on the use of interactive digital tools, and under what circumstances can particular digital activities become illegitimate? The discussion below aims to address both approaches. And in linking the observation that digital tools challenge the legitimacy issue, it will seek to apply both theoretical approaches and empirical findings with regard to NGO legitimacy from other chapters in this book as well as earlier work on the concept of legitimacy.

3.2.   *Legitimizing effects of digital tools*

Publications on the status of NGOs testify that they play an increasingly important role in the international policy arena and 'to some extent this is being reflected in their formal status' (Kamminga 2005). Nevertheless, the capacity of NGOs to influence the international policy agenda is mainly based on other—more informal—ways. In some situations, such informal instruments are expressly provided for in treaties or resolutions (Kamminga 2005, 105-107). In the majority of cases, however, the role of NGOs has no legislative or regulatory backup. Consequently, the legitimacy of their existence and activities is for a large part based on other criteria. These may include factors such as membership (and thus representation), consent of people to initiate a certain strategy, or transparent and predictable decision-making procedures. Clearly, ICT might play an important role here, and many of the initiatives discussed earlier in this chapter as well as in Chapter 3 illustrate that NGOs are beginning to recognize the potential of digital instruments and strategies.

But there is more. According to Vedder (2006), the legitimacy of NGOs cannot be debated along the lines of procedural criteria alone. There is a need for invoking moral values as well, given that the aforementioned rationally satisfying factors for assessing the legitimacy of NGOs 'must include some form of reference—however modest—to certain moral starting points that can be agreed upon by virtually everyone'. The reason for this is that the application of procedural criteria of legitimacy itself seems to presuppose moral values. An interesting question would then be what digital tools might offer in the light of the formulation and acceptability of certain substantive norms. For example, could the new tools influence a larger (worldwide) acceptability of a particular normative starting point and thus make it easier to find common moral ground? In order to find answers to these and other legitimacy-related questions and given the specific characteristics of interactive digital tools, the discussion will centre around types of activities that function as what could be called the primary sources of legitimacy.[5]

A first source might be communication. Commentators have argued that legitimation seems to be created through a process of communication (Steffek 2003). Communication is crucial in explaining to the general public what an NGO ultimately claims to represent and how aims and actions relate to each other. As such, communication is of particular importance to the procedural form of legitimacy (Collingwood and Logister 2005). From this argument it follows that digital tools might not only be beneficial in that they allow for new campaigning opportunities. They also facilitate communication on certain objectives pursued as well as the underlying arguments. For example, NGOs engaged in bringing certain claims against states or companies can inform the public accordingly and explain their reasons for doing so. Interactive communication and debating facilities may provide new opportunities here in that they can help explain to the public that putting human rights

---

5   These sources see to specific types of behaviour or activity (observation, communication, etc.) that influence the interaction between actors (people, organizations). Given this influence, the sources could best be seen as the practical means that operationalize and affect the dimensions of legitimacy. The sources selected for discussion in this section have relevance with regard to the characteristics of interactive digital tools.

on the international agenda requires a carefully prepared process that takes time and effort. Moreover, in the wake of globalization and the increase in cross-border judicial procedures on such issues as human rights and environmental protection, the borderless and international environment of the Internet appears a highly appropriate instrument in communicating with individual supporters, groups, and stakeholders all over the world. Communication as a source of legitimacy may also benefit from digital tools because they allow for improved global networking and information sharing. For example, scholars have emphasized that learning from the field is a foundation for improved accountability, and for this learning need to become institutionalized, ICT might offer important facilities (Madon 1999). Communication by means of interactive digital tools that use multimedia opportunities may also encourage more people to become politically or socially active, for example because a simulation tool shows them the connection between their daily lives and a certain environmental problem.

Communication is also crucial in the light of accountability and, subsequently, control. Accountability is said to relate to several distinct elements. 'First, the account giving in the attenuated sense of narration is followed by a questioning or debating of the issues and finally by an evaluation or a passing of judgment and—possibly—consequences for the actor' (Curtin 2006). Accountability mechanisms may vary: they can be specifically determined (control by courts) or institutionally specific (parliament) but may also be more informal (public approval) (Bovens 2006). Seen from this perspective and depending on the specifics of the context, the legitimacy of NGOs can be said to be closely connected to the acceptance, recognition, and approval by various relevant actors, among them the general public. This implies that when an NGO exposes human rights violations or other abuses, legitimacy requires it to be transparent and verifiable. In using digital tools, an NGO can account for its dealings by communicating and explaining—on a worldwide scale and by means of low-threshold facilities—its ambitions, principles, arguments, procedures, and politics. The new interactive multimedia games and simulation media in particular can be instrumental in trying to argue, promote, or even prove that the adopted strategies are right. In addition to making the decision-making process more transparent and verifiable, digital tools might also enhance transparency on such crucial accountability issues as the NGO's governance structure, its internal or external quality control procedures, and the self-supervision mechanisms. And, last but not least, updated, timely, and detailed information can be provided—and even be debated—with regard to the ways used to acquire funding and to spend budgets. In sum, this new type of communication might be instrumental in opening up NGO dealings to critical assessment by the world at large.

Given that interactive digital tools provide new consultative and debating instruments, the second relevant source of legitimacy is public participation and consensus-building. Active participation has been put forward as one of the building blocks of popular legitimacy: 'Participatory structures are important because people have the best ideas about how they want to manage their environment' (Collingwood and Logister 2005, 22). Also, in the interviews presented in Chapter 2 of this book, NGOs expressed that public support and popular mobilization is essential to achieving change and can be used to put pressure on powerful actors such as governments and corporations. In other words, without public support the case halts. It is precisely the interactive, multimedia dimension of new digital tools that might play a crucial role in mobilizing people and convincing them that action is needed. Simulation tools can help visualize human rights violations or potential environmental disasters. Virtual games can help advance new arguments or deal with complex interactions far more easily than an abstract, analytical approach could. And in using interactive websites that include discussion and comment facilities, NGOs could arrange for online consultation on a wide variety of issues. From these websites, NGOs could subsequently respond to and report on action taken. E-consultation might also facilitate active public participation in strategic and political deliberations and agenda setting of NGOs. As such active public participation by means of e-consultation facilitates the representative structure of NGOs in the sense that the voices of members or supporters can be heard as well as consulted. Moreover, using the Internet in consultation and consensus building would allow not only the people known to the NGO (members), but in fact every (potential) website visitor, to directly participate in a discussion.

When the arguments outlined above are applied to the different aspects of legitimacy as described in Chapters 2 and 3 of this book, interactive tools could fulfil three functions. First, they could create a channel through which NGOs could communicate their views on certain issues and interests, the adopted strategy and any actions taken. This might advance the regulatory aspect of legitimacy. Second, interactive technology could strengthen the social aspect of legitimacy. It could do so by facilitating coordinated discussion through open lists inviting the public to sign. Members or supporters would be heard and debate would ensue between NGOs and the outside world about the merits and demerits of certain strategies, actions, or campaigns of NGOs. Third, the public and all relevant NGO partners could be enabled to directly address an NGO, and relevant input and expertise could be provided. These options could influence the quality of the work of the NGO or its ability to achieve the intended goals. This function could increase both the social aspect of legitimacy and the performance of the NGO. Combined, the three functions offer an important potential for legitimacy that goes beyond more efficient delivery of information on NGO aims, ambitions, and campaigns. In essence, the functions of interactive tools offer an opportunity to fortify the justification of positions and actions, and, as a result, enhance the legitimacy of an NGO.

The third and final relevant source of legitimacy is what could be called e-observation. Recommender systems in particular might be an important factor. As was mentioned earlier, these systems would allow organizations to complement and enhance the collective observation and decision processes of 'human consciousness' (Masum 2002). If the line of reasoning of the creator of TOOL (discussed above) is pursued, recommender systems will become essential for directing human attention and incentivizing society. In some situations, NGOs draw legitimacy from the fact that they represent the views of either their members or the people on whose behalf they are acting. Representation then implies that what an organization claims to represent or puts on its agenda is perceived in society as a societal problem, an unjust or inadequate situation or a cause fighting for. This again means that an NGO must be able to monitor closely the interests and values it claims to represent. This not only implies close links with the grassroots, but also input from certain accepted norms and values that prevail in society. Given that these norms and values might change over time depending on the political situation or other circumstances, an NGO must implement instruments and strategies to make sure that it addresses issues that are worth pursuing. Recommender systems may play a role in that they could identify issues, provide feedback on what an NGO claims and what society feels, or verify whether the NGO works on the basis of or within the boundaries of the accepted values of its members, supporters, or beneficiaries.

At the outset of this chapter, the work of Vedder was referred to, who argues that NGO legitimacy cannot be debated along the lines of procedural criteria alone: the application of procedural criteria of legitimacy ultimately requires the invocation of certain substantive values. This implies that legitimacy need not necessarily rest on the consent and acceptance of NGO members, but might instead refer to certain beliefs and values that may be accepted and shared by all involved. What could then be pointed out here is that recommender systems have the potential to influence the process of legitimization in that they facilitate (or even enhance) the process in which people try to find some shared values or ideals. Of course, this potential should be considered with caution. It may be wondered whether the potential of recommender systems to influence a larger (worldwide) acceptance of a particular normative starting point, would ever lead to a situation where NGOs justify their activities on the basis of the universal validity of a computer-generated moral claim. Recommender systems do, however, offer NGOs the opportunity of finding common ground in selected individual situations, for example by communicating objective information. In sum, when applying the opportunities to the different aspects of legitimacy, recommender systems could play a role with regard to the social aspect (i.e., hearing the voices of members and beneficiaries) and moral legitimacy (in the sense that they signal or verify certain moral values in society).

3.3.   Legitimate use of digital tools

The above shows that interactive digital tools might play a role in forming, explaining and defending strategies and activities of NGOs and could therefore enhance or at least influence several of the legitimacy dimensions. Also, the availability of these tools with their particular modalities of facilitating interactive information distribution might generate new opportunities for finding shared normative perspectives.

However, it should be realized that it is not merely the adoption and use of digital instruments themselves that might help generate legitimacy. It is the way they are used that is crucial. And it is at this point that the second line of thought (discussed above) with regard to digital tools and legitimacy—the legitimacy of how NGOs use these tools—enters the discussion. As was argued in Chapter 3 (and in other publications), the Internet has a number of qualities that are potentially damaging to the legitimacy of NGOs. Research has demonstrated that the vast and ever-growing quantity of information located and available on the Internet, the ease with which this information can be disseminated, and the limitless interpersonal communication capabilities pose specific risks to legitimacy. Also, while the quantity of information people are exposed to can increase, the quality or accuracy of that information may not always be assessed.

It is submitted that when NGOs employ strategies based on interactive digital tools, additional challenges arise. The extent to which interactive digital tools entail specific legitimacy challenges has much to do with the specific characteristics and features of these tools. To date, the use of the new kinds of digital tools described in this chapter is still primarily driven by private, profit, and sometimes public motives. But what if the use of these tools were driven by objectives in the areas of social justice, democratic values, human rights, and the environment? Given the specific characteristics of these tools—they highly depend on input of people rather than treat them as a passive audience, and they nurture the creation of knowledge rather than regard it as standard information—the question arises in what respect the adoption of these new tools engenders new modes of addressing, influencing, or even persuading people. When interactive and visual digital tools are applied, the opinions advocated are likely to have more impact or be more influential and as a result will receive greater consideration. In fact, the visual and interactive features available to users of simulation games could allow for the creation of almost autonomous new worlds (e.g., on the issue of climate change), or suggest a dimension of a conflict, problem, or abuse that does not necessarily reflect the real dimension of the issue at stake. As was shown above, virtual games and simulation tools enable NGOs as well as their members or supporters to explore, test, and operationalize ideas and positions, which may cause them to modify or reverse earlier opinions. In this way, these tools can serve as test beds, learning tools, or debating facilities. But of course, gaming and simulation offer much more. Educating and learning implies instructing people. And, to a large extent, instruction is based on subjective notions and perspectives—in the domain of societal issues and problems, at least. Interactive digital tools may thus become profoundly political tools. And they might even draw attention to pathways to solutions that go beyond accepted codes of ethics. Alternatively, they may become advocates and communicators of thought-provoking comparisons or political opinions. Sometimes, the socioeconomic or socio-political lessons incorporated in games might be obvious and clear, but they could also be hidden. And NGOs can exploit feelings of individuals that arise when they are confronted with an imagined scenario represented in virtual games. Clifford (2002) refers to the 'harsh, Darwinian marketplace' of NGOs where 'legions of desperate groups vie for scarce attention, sympathy, and money.' Under pressure in the fierce competition for global audiences and in their quest to sell their causes to the world, NGOs may be inclined to use digital tools in strategic ways that undermine their original goals and legitimizing base.

It is these ramifications that make games and simulation tools—as well as the organizations using them—vulnerable, when political lessons are embedded especially. The legitimate use of digital tools in an NGO's strategy therefore needs to be based on a carefully prescribed process of demarcation and justification. It requires a clear perspective on the procedures that must guarantee not merely the reliability of the information, but also the perspectives distributed by means of these tools. One could argue that in the end an adequate and balanced use of digital tools relies on reason and good arguments. For example, the adoption and self-enforcement of etiquette on the use of digital tools, might thus determine whether strategies applying these tools will flourish or not. But this is easier said than done. For even if manipulation is not in evidence, it will often be difficult for NGOs to define the conditions for a suitably controlled online scenario or experiment (e.g., with regard to human rights violations). What works for one scenario (e.g., one specific country or culture), does not necessarily translate easily into another. In other words, it might very well be that in the end, the legitimacy of the specific use of digital strategies by NGOs will be tested through instruments and criteria well-known in the offline world as well as through the recognition and acceptance by the general public.

The use by NGOs of flashy new tools as gaming, political simulation, and virtual worlds also entails a legitimacy risk in view of the fact that in developing countries these tools are inevitably far less common or even beyond the reach of certain people and organizations. Due to a lack of financial resources or required knowledge, only a handful of groups may have the ability to capitalize on the opportunities the new digital tools might hold. Often, these groups will be Western-based or supported by wealthy NGOs. There is a clear risk that money and technological expertise may thus make the difference, allowing wealthier organizations to pay for the development and use of these new tools, while they remain beyond the reach of others. Pessimistic observers may also regard the new digital means as yet another step in the worrisome development where money, international media events, diplomacy training sessions, and charismatic leadership—instead of the cause itself—gain importance as key determining factors in an NGO's struggle for international attention and support (Clifford 2002). Seen from this perspective, the new digital tools may also reinforce existing inequalities between NGOs, and leave poor and small organizations even further behind. Legitimate use of new digital tools thus requires that attention is given to the reinforcing effect it may have on the digital divide.

Another issue that relates to the matter of legitimacy is the credibility of the forms of participation: is the participation of supporters genuine? Expressions of opinion through a virtual game on the one hand and real commitment to the cause on the other are two different things. With e-participation the environment in which people participate is considerably more loose than it is in a classic participation setting. And the use of digital tools appears to be manifesting more fragmentation in the participation of people than the traditional ways of participation. Although this does not imply that interactive tools do not allow for social bonding and creating an identity, they will definitely change the relations between an NGO's constituency and the organization itself. Also, supporters of a certain cause might, for instance, be inconsistent in expressing themselves in simulation games. Sooner or later, an NGO wants to know whom it represents or whether it is connected to the people on whose behalf it acts. It would therefore appear that NGOs cannot simply draw legitimacy from the fact that people express their commitment through digital tools. Simply put, any digital tool is useless unless its use is firmly embedded in a functional offline civil society.

A related implication could be that the use of digital tools, which by their very essence largely depend on the input of a large range of participants, could aggravate a problem signalled earlier, namely that NGOs no longer maintain control of their agendas (Townsend 2002). Another consequence could be that the use of digital tools further encourages the present shift from a member model towards a supporter model.[6] Both consequences imply that NGOs using digital tools must realize that a digital tool is not merely an instrument in itself, facilitating certain strategies in isolation. The use of these tools has an effect on society and on how members of the general public participate, which in turn has an impact on dimensions of legitimacy.

Finally, every significant new technology can be used constructively and destructively, and the tools described here are no exception. Ear-

---

6   As became clear from the empirical work of Collingwood and Logister, NGOs are exploring ways to drum up popular support that reach beyond the traditional membership concept to include temporary supporters (supporter model) (Collingwood and Logister 2005, 25-26).

lier, it was suggested that NGOs armed with flashy interactive multi-media tools could, for example, more effectively mobilize support and thus eventually force policy shifts and even changes with greater ease than organizations that do not use these tools. In a more provocative and, perhaps, exaggerated scenario, the use of recommender systems by NGOs might shape the overall movement of information and expression within society and even put social diversity at stake: one political or societal message could dominate the whole discourse. As described earlier, recommender systems signal correlations in people's preferences by connecting two or more perceptions, notions or other views based on user feedback. 'They are tuned to pick up cultural notions and are blind to whether those notions are politically correct or not. So, a political recommendation might simply reflect what enough people in society think on a deeper level.'[7] It is characteristic of recommender systems that the myriad of individual differences is reduced to one or a few categories, which serve as the sole basis for determining political opinions, social perceptions, and so forth. In other words, the use of recommender systems by NGOs could generate a dangerous dimension in that it may force people into restraining, one-dimensional models of society, based on the criteria set by technology and those who apply the technology.

3.4.   Conclusion

This chapter has sought to explore how the emergence of new kinds of interactive and multimedia-oriented digital tools, with their particular modalities of information distribution and circulation, impinges on the position of NGOs using these tools, generates particular opportunities and risks, and shapes the different legitimacy dimensions explored in this book. In short, how should the impact of these tools on NGOs, their legitimacy and that of their dealings be approached and under-stood? From the discussion presented in this chapter, it is apparent that there is no easy answer. The tools discussed in this chapter are not yet commonplace in the strategy of NGOs, meaning that empirical research to grasp the power and implications of these new tools is lacking. The value of interactive digital tools for NGO legitimacy has thus not been proved and it remains unclear how legitimacy will be affected by these

---

7   See http://www.rashmisinha.com/archives/06_01/walmart-recommend-er.html#000175.

tools. Some might say that interactive digital tools have few specific gains to offer other than the known advantages of a more efficient way of obtaining and disseminating information and for carrying out collective campaigns or other activities.

However, it can be argued that the opportunities these new tools might offer need to be followed closely, an important reason for this being that they have a potential for legitimacy that goes beyond more efficient delivery of information on NGO aims, ambitions, and campaigns. Given that they enable the use of new consultative, learning and debating instruments, the new tools might stimulate or enhance both the quantity and the quality of public participation and consensus-building. Also, these tools have the potential to influence the involvement and commitment of people and could even—a possibly somewhat farfetched scenario for the time being—signal or verify certain moral values prevalent in society and use them to decide certain strategies or aims. In essence, digital tools thus offer NGOs a chance to enhance the quality of justification for their positions and actions, and as a result their legitimacy.

A look at the arguments used by both commercial businesses and public sector bodies to opt for the implementation of these tools in their service provision strategies reveals useful illustrations of many abstract arguments presented in this chapter. Moreover, once digital tools become incorporated into the normal practices of daily life, the present clear distinction between traditional campaigning instruments and digital tools will disappear. A crude technological determinism is therefore beside the point. Findings on the effect of Internet use on the general willingness of people to participate in social activity show that the online and offline domains are far from distinct worlds and that online participation positively influences offline involvement: 'The more people are on the Internet, and the more they are involved in online organizational and political activity, the more they are involved in offline organizational and political participation' (Wellman et al. 2001). It may therefore be suspected that the effects of digital tools on legitimacy might in the end be supplementary to those of other instruments.

Another effect might be that through the use of new technologies, the relationship between NGOs and their counterparts might change. In a complex society where NGOs start using the techniques described in this chapter, it may no longer be valid to assume that NGOs have the well-known position in the web of relationships in which they participate. Perhaps in ways similar to the relationship between consumers and producers (Prins 2003), the traditional relationship between NGOs and their partners may shift—not in clearly defined ways and directions, but in subtle and often contradictory ways. The gross outcome of such a shift is still unclear, but it might very well be that NGOs will become less dependent on other parties while realizing their ambitions and aims. For instance, the Internet enables NGOs to communicate their message to a worldwide audience without the help of third parties or hindered by traditional borders.

By way of a tentative, theoretical conclusion on how digital tools might influence NGO legitimacy, it could be argued that the criteria for legitimacy cannot be analyzed irrespective of the particular forms, practices, and strategies that NGOs use in their dealings. In particular, this is the case with the procedural legitimacy criteria: they all presuppose that NGOs implement practical arrangements to make the criteria work. But the substantive criteria—legitimization in terms of shared values and norms—ultimately also require the implementation of actions and strategies, such as making people aware of the prevalence of certain moral values. Given the emergence of new digital tools, then, their deployment automatically relates to procedural as well as substantive moral criteria for legitimacy. It would, however, be too simplistic to subsequently produce an overall perspective on how the new tools actually do transform practices of legitimatization. To grasp the implications of the new tools requires an understanding of the particular specifics and dynamics of the tools' application. This again necessitates further study of the effects of interactive digital tools on NGOs to chart the benefits and impacts in concrete applications. As part of this study, it should also be explored in what respect and to what extent the effects of these tools are impeded or influenced by other technological applications. It may very well be that the elaborate filtering techniques, highly efficient blocking strategies, and monitoring tools that have been put in place by certain governments (e.g., China and Iran) undermine the potential of the new tools.[8]

---

8   Techniques monitor and control how citizens use the Internet, mobile techniques, text messaging and MSN. And following earlier examples set by Yahoo! and Google, other service providers and software companies might also play along with these practices, arguing that they are obliged to respect the local laws and customs of the countries in which they do business. In the interest of their own business interests, they could thus restrict users' ability to post critical comments on their weblogs, edit out

It can therefore be argued that further critical studies of the effects of interactive digital tools on NGO legitimacy should focus on an evaluation of the use of digital strategies and the development of possible tools for such an evaluation. Systematic and critical evaluation efforts may provide feedback on whether digital tools make a difference, the ratio between input (e.g., investments) and output (e.g., improved procedures for decision-making or transparency of policies), the global distribution of the benefits of digital tools (what actors are affected, who benefits, and what does this mean in the light of equity), and what changes or improvements can or must be made in the light of the answers to these questions? Without critical empirical and theoretical reflection on these questions and thus on the difference the new tools really make, their impact on the legitimacy of NGOs cannot be captured and understood.

the objectionable text or prevent the posting of messages entirely if they show that the user engages in civil disobedience. And, in fear of losing the licence required to offer their digital communications services, providers could readily submit information about their customers, including account numbers, phone numbers, and IP addresses. These and other measures have been effective in China since 2000. See http://www.seed-wiki.com/wiki/participatory_media_and_collective_action/government_control?wpid=224722.

Chapter 5. Regulatory legitimacy of the role of NGOs in global governance: Legal status and accreditation

*Peter van den Bossche**

1.   Introduction

Over the last decades, NGOs have become significant actors in global affairs. Their role in international governance has increased considerably. At present, many NGOs seek to shape—or at least influence—the outcome of international policy deliberation and decision-making processes. An increasing number of NGOs strive to do this 'from the inside', i.e., through direct involvement in the policy deliberation and decision-making processes of international governmental organizations.

While not always wholeheartedly, international organizations have responded positively to the call of NGOs for more involvement and currently allow—to different extents and in different ways—NGOs to participate in their activities. The Cardoso Report of June 2004 on *We the People: Civil Society, the United Nations and Global Governance* examined the relationship between NGOs and the United Nations system and made numerous proposals for improving this relationship (UN General Assembly 2004). As stated in the Background Paper for the Cardoso Report, 'well handled' involvement of NGOs in the policy deliberation and decision-making processes of international organizations 'enhances the quality of decision-making, increases ownership of the decisions, improves accountability and transparency of the process and enriches

*   The author is indebted to Dr. Sergey Ripinsky, formerly of the Faculty of Law of Maastricht University, now at the British Institute of International and Comparative Law, London. The author also thanks Bertram Boie, Nina Buttgen, Lorin Van Nuland and Jill Roche for their helpful research assistance.

Anton Vedder et al., *NGO Involvement in International Governance and Policy*, pp. 135-173.
Printed in the Netherlands. ISBN 978 90 04 15846 7.

outcomes through a variety of views and experiences' (United Nations 2003). However, 'handled badly, it can confuse choices, hamper the intergovernmental search for common ground, erode the privacy needed for sensitive discussions, over-crowd agendas and present distractions at important meetings' (United Nations 2003).

As reflected in the discussions leading to and generated by the Cardoso Report as well as other reports (e.g., WTO 2005), the increased role of NGOs in international organizations has given rise to difficult questions regarding the legitimacy of the role of NGOs in international governance in general and in international organizations in particular. As discussed in Chapter 1, the concept of legitimacy, as used in this study, is a three-dimensional one; it has a moral, sociological and regulatory dimension. This chapter focuses on the regulatory dimension of the legitimacy of NGO involvement in international organizations. Chapter 6 also deals with the regulatory dimension of legitimacy but focuses primarily on specific aspects and issues.

As explained in Chapter 1, the regulatory dimension of legitimacy refers to the degree in which the involvement of NGOs in international organizations conforms to legal rules. To the extent that the involvement of NGOs conforms to the relevant rules, this involvement has regulatory legitimacy. Conformity with the relevant rules does, however, not allow for any conclusion on the moral and/or sociological legitimacy. To reach a conclusion on the overall legitimacy of the involvement of NGOs in international governance, the sociological dimension and the moral dimension of legitimacy must, of course, also be examined. However, the latter dimensions of legitimacy are not within the author's legal expertise and are not within the scope and ambition of this chapter.

The central questions addressed in this chapter are what the relevant rules on the involvement of NGOs in international organizations are and whether NGO involvement conforms to these rules. To keep the length of this chapter within reasonable limits, the inquiry into the existing legal rules, and their application, has been limited to eight representative international organizations active on socio-economic, health and environmental issues. They are:

- the United Nations
- the United Nations Conference for Trade and Development (UNCTAD)
- the United Nations Environment Programme (UNEP)
- the World Health Organization (WHO)
- the International Labour Organization (ILO)

–   the International Bank for Reconstruction and Development (IBRD)
–   the International Monetary Fund (IMF)
–   the World Trade Organization (WTO.)

In addition, this chapter focuses on the involvement of NGOs in the policy deliberation and decision-making processes of these international organizations. It does not cover other types of NGO involvement, such as involvement in the planning, implementation and evaluation of development projects or humanitarian aid operations. The involvement of NGOs in the dispute settlement mechanisms of international organizations is equally outside the scope of this chapter.

The relevant legal rules on the involvement of NGOs in the above-mentioned organizations can be divided up in two categories:

1.   The rules defining the legal status of NGOs in those organizations, i.e., the rules providing a legal basis for the involvement of NGOs, and the rules setting out the various forms of this involvement.
2.   The rules on the accreditation of NGOs by these organizations, i.e., the rules that must ensure that only NGOs, which 'add value' to the policy deliberation and decision-making processes, 'enjoy' specific forms of involvement and associated right. This category of rules can be subdivided into:
     –   substantive rules setting out the requirements an NGO must meet to be accredited;
     –   procedural rules for taking decisions regarding accreditation and the subsequent monitoring of accredited NGOs.

2.   Rules on the legal status of NGOs

The first rules examined in this chapter are the rules on the legal status of NGOs. As explained above, these are the rules providing a legal basis for the involvement of NGOs and rules setting out the various forms this involvement may take. For the regulatory legitimacy of the involvement of NGOs in international organizations, it is important that the treaty establishing the international organization allows for this involvement. Ideally, the constituent treaty *explicitly* provides for the involvement of NGOs, and defines the form or forms this involvement may take. The latter can also be done in secondary regulation. Involvement of NGOs in the policy deliberation and decision-making processes raises serious concerns regarding the regulatory legitimacy of this involvement, when this involvement is:

– without a legal basis (involvement *sine legem*); or
– in a form not provided for (involvement *ultra legem*); or
– in a form inconsistent with relevant rules (involvement *contra legem*).

This section successively examines the legal basis for the involvement of NGOs as well as the rules defining the forms of that involvement in the UN, UNCTAD, UNEP, the WHO, the ILO, the IBRD, the IMF and the WTO.

2.1.   *United Nations*

Article 71 of the UN Charter, placed in Chapter X entitled 'Economic and Social Council', states:

> The Economic and Social Council may make suitable arrangements for consultation with non-governmental organizations which are concerned with matters within its competence. Such arrangements may be made with international organizations and, where appropriate, with national organizations after consultation with the Member of the United Nations concerned.

The UN Charter thus explicitly provides for the involvement of NGOs in the policy deliberation and decision-making processes of the United Nations. This is important for the regulatory legitimacy of the involvement of NGOs in the UN. However, the location and language of Article 71 have two important legal consequences for the scope of application of this provision.

First, Article 71 is limited to 'matters within the competence' of the Economic and Social Council (ECOSOC). In other words, Article 71 limits NGO involvement to the activities of the ECOSOC itself. Article 71 *cannot* be interpreted to mean that ECOSOC may make suitable arrangements for NGO participation in the work of the United Nations *as a whole*. This means that the UN Charter does *not* have a legal basis for interactions between NGOs and other principal UN organs. The founding members of the UN were not prepared to allow NGOs to 'participate' in the UN General Assembly—an organ with a general competence to debate all issues falling within the ambit of the UN Charter—and even less in the Security Council. Indeed, there have been calls for formal recognition of NGO involvement beyond economic and social matters; this idea was also supported in the Cardoso Report (UN General Assembly 2004, para. 124).

Secondly, Article 71 does not apply to other UN organizations and specialized agencies. They have their own arrangements for relations with NGOs, some of which are discussed below. However, it is said that Article 71 set a benchmark for other UN agencies (Charnovitz 1997, 253). They may have a formal consultative system similar to that of ECOSOC, but commonly work with a smaller number of more specialized NGOs.

Pursuant to the mandate given to ECOSOC in Article 71 of the UN Charter, it adopted on 25 July 1996 Resolution 1996/31 on the 'Consultative Relationship between the United Nations and Non-Governmental Organizations' (UN ECOSOC 1996). Resolution 1996/31, which is currently still applicable, significantly updated the arrangements previously set out in Resolution 1296 (XLIV) of 23 May 1968. Resolution 1996/31 *defines* an NGO as any 'organization that is not established by a governmental entity or intergovernmental agreement [...], including organizations that accept members designated by governmental authorities, provided that such membership does not interfere with the free expression of views of the organization' (UN ECOSOC 1996, para. 12). This definition is extremely broad and does not take into account many of the factors established in Chapter 1 of this book, including financing sources and structure stability. However, these factors are reflected in the substantive requirements for accreditation by ECOSOC discussed below.

Article 71 of the UN Charter refers to 'consultation' with NGOs, and accordingly, Resolution 1996/31 provides for granting NGOs 'consultative status'. There are three types of such status: general consultative status, special consultative status, and inclusion on the Roster. Each type of status corresponds with a different set of rights. It is important for the regulatory legitimacy of the NGOs' involvement in ECOSOC activities that the forms of involvement are carefully set out in Resolution 1996/31.

A select number of NGOs have 'general consultative status'. The rights and privileges associated with this status are the most far-reaching of the three types of consultative relationship. Every NGO enjoying general consultative status:

– is informed of the provisional agenda of the Council and may propose to the Council Committee on Non-governmental Organizations (NGO Committee) that the Committee request the UN Secretary-General to place items of special interest on the provisional
   agenda of the Council (UN ECOSOC 1996, paras. 27-28);
– may orally present to the Council introductory statements of an
   expository nature on items included on the Council's agenda at the
   proposal of the NGO (UN ECOSOC 1996, para. 32 (b));
– may sit as an observer at public meetings of the Council and its
   subsidiary bodies (UN ECOSOC 1996, paras. 29 and 35);
– may submit written statements with a maximum of 2000 words
   for circulation to the Members of the Council (UN ECOSOC 1996,
   para. 30); and
– may make oral statements to the Council (at the recommendation
   of the NGO Committee and subject to the approval of the Council)
   (UN ECOSOC 1996, para.32 (a)).

NGOs with 'special consultative status' enjoy some of the same privileges granted to NGOs with general consultative status. They are informed
of the provisional agenda of the Council (UN ECOSOC 1996, para. 27);
they may be observers at public meetings of the Council and its subsidiary bodies (UN ECOSOC 1996, paras. 29 and 35); and they may submit
written statements with a maximum of 500 words for circulation to the
Members of the Council (ECOSOC 1996, para. 31 (e)). However, NGOs
with special consultative status cannot propose items for the agenda of
the Council, neither can they make oral statements at meetings of the
Council (UN ECOSOC 1996, para. 38 (a)). However, they may speak at
meetings of the Council's subsidiary bodies that deal with subject matters of specific interest to them (UN ECOSOC 1996, para. 32 (a)).

NGOs on the Roster are informed of the provisional agenda of the
Council and may attend the meetings of the Council and its subsidiary
bodies concerned with matters within their field of competence (UN
ECOSOC 1996, paras. 27 and 29). NGOs on the Roster are consulted at
the request of the Council or its subsidiary bodies (UN ECOSOC 1996,
para. 24).

Although Resolution 1996/31 grants access to public meetings to
NGOs with consultative status, it does not provide for participation in
the informal meetings preceding public meetings of the Council and its
subsidiary bodies. It is at these meetings though that much of the diplomatic negotiations on future decisions or policies take place.

Resolution 1996/31 also governs the participation of NGOs in international conferences convened by the UN and their preparatory process (UN ECOSOC 1996, paras. 41-54). NGOs in any type of consultative status will be accredited to participate upon request; other NGOs may request approval (UN ECOSOC 1996, para. 42). An NGO accredited for a conference may attend the conference *and* its preparatory sessions, although such participation 'does not entail a negotiating role' (UN ECOSOC 1996, para. 50). An accredited NGO may be given an opportunity to briefly address the preparatory committee and the conference and may also make written presentations during the preparatory process (UN ECOSOC 1996, para. 66).

Besides the involvement of NGOs in ECOSOC and its subsidiary organs and participation in international conferences convened by the UN, Resolution 1996/31 also authorises NGOs in any type of consultative status to consult with officers of the UN Secretariat. Such consultations may be conducted upon the request of the NGO or upon the request of the Secretary-General (UN ECOSOC 1996, para. 65). Also, the Secretary-General may request an accredited NGO to carry out specific studies or prepare specific papers (UN ECOSOC 1996, para. 66). At UN meetings, NGOs are allowed to distribute their publications/materials outside the meeting rooms. Usually a number of tables are provided for this purpose. Additionally, the Secretary-General is authorised to offer facilities to accredited NGOs including: access to UN grounds, facilities (including conference space) and UN press documentation services and arrangement of informal discussions on relevant special interest topics (UN ECOSOC 1996, para. 67). Over time, a practice has evolved to allow a certain degree of informal participation by NGOs in the work of the General Assembly's main committees and several of its subsidiary bodies, as well as in special sessions of the Assembly (United Nations 2001, paras. 13-20). However, in the absence of a legal basis in the UN Charter (or Resolution 1996/31), this practice is *sine legem*. Hence, it lacks the degree of regulatory legitimacy of NGO involvement in ECOSOC activities, UN conferences and NGO links with the UN Secretariat.

2.2.   UNCTAD

The United Nations Conference on Trade and Development (UNCTAD), established in 1964, is the key organization within the United Nations for promoting development-friendly integration of developing countries into the world economy. It is a forum for intergovernmental deliberations and the exchange of experiences, supported by discussions with experts (UNCTAD 2005). UNCTAD was established in the UN General Assembly Resolution 1995 (XIX). This Resolution provides that the Trade and Development Board (TDB) may allow NGOs concerned with matters of trade and development to participate (without vote) in its deliberations and those of the subsidiary bodies and working groups established by it (UN General Assembly 1964, para. 11). The *explicit* provision for involvement of NGOs in the policy deliberation and decision-making processes of UNCTAD is an important element in the discussion on the regulatory legitimacy of this involvement.

Pursuant to the mandate given to the TDB by UN General Assembly Resolution 1995 (XIX), the TDB set out the rules governing UNCTAD's relations with NGOs in Rule 77 of its Rules of Procedure. Rule 77 provides that NGOs concerned with matters of trade, especially trade as related to development, and approved by the TDB, may designate representatives to sit as observers at public meetings of the Board, its sessional committees and subsidiary organs. Upon invitation and subject to the approval of the Board or the subsidiary organ concerned, NGOs may make oral statements on matters within the scope of their activities. NGOs may also submit written statements related to items on the agenda of the Board or of its subsidiary organs. These statements are then circulated to the members of the Board or the subsidiary organ concerned. However, NGO rights laid down in Rule 77 apply only to public meetings of the TDB and its subsidiary organs. Accordingly, NGOs cannot participate in any of the many informal meetings. In addition, NGOs do not have the opportunity to influence the agenda of the meetings of the TDB.

At the Quadrennial Conference held every four years, Member States meet at ministerial level to formulate UNCTAD's mandate and work priorities. The legal basis for NGO participation in this ministerial conference is Rule 81 of the Rules of the Procedure of the Conference (UNCTAD 1968), which is modelled after Rule 77 of the Rules of Procedure of the TDB. The rights conferred to NGOs in the context of the Conference are substantially the same as those listed above. However, in contrast to the TDB meetings where NGOs typically speak on their own behalf, at the Conference NGOs usually deliver joint statements.

The arrangements concerning the involvement of NGOs in the deliberations and decision- making processes of UNCTAD are further outlined in Board Decision 43 (VII) of 20 September 1968, which distinguished three categories of NGOs: the General Category, the Special

Category and the Category of NGOs entered in the Register. The NGOs in the first two categories are called NGOs with *observer status* (or NGOs in status). The difference in rights between NGOs in the General Category and NGOs in the Special Category lies in the range of meetings in which NGOs may participate. NGOs in the General Category may participate in all public meetings of *all* UNCTAD intergovernmental organs including all three Commissions and their subsidiary bodies. NGOs in the Special Category may participate in the meetings of the Conference, TDB and in the meetings of the Commission to which they were assigned at the time of accreditation, as well as the subsidiary bodies of that Commission. NGOs in the third Category, i.e., NGOs entered in the Register, only enjoy the right to receive UNCTAD documentation.

The careful and detailed manner in which the forms of NGO involvement in UNCTAD activities is set out in secondary regulation significantly contributes to the regulatory legitimacy of this involvement. However, it must be noted that UNCTAD also interacts with NGOs in ways which are not explicitly provided for.

In practice, NGOs are involved with UNCTAD policy formulation through Civil Society Forums *and* Civil Society Hearings. Civil Society Forums emerged in 1996 as a global NGO forum linked to the UNCTAD Quadrennial Conference. NGO forums adopt joint statements embodying NGO views on Conference agenda items. These civil society statements are subsequently delivered to the Conference, at the plenary meeting and at the meetings on substantive issues, and diffused as official Conference documents. Consensus for joint statements develops during the preparatory processes leading to the forum, which may involve several regional and global preparatory meetings.

Civil Society Hearings are consultations between civil society and UNCTAD, and have regularly occurred since 1988. These consultations have covered a range of topics often of immediate relevance to preparations for upcoming UNCTAD Conferences and have provided important opportunities for the UNCTAD Secretariat and NGO representatives to exchange information and analysis on core trade and development issues (Hill 2002, 55). Today, the Hearings are held annually in connection with TDB sessions to debate issues before the Board. This is not an inter-NGO event like a civil society forum, but a meeting where NGOs engage in discussions with Member States. Outcomes of the Hearings are summarised by the Secretariat for submission as input into the discussions of the TDB. To participate in the Hearings, an NGO either has to have observer status with UNCTAD or receive a special accreditation for the Hearings.

No matter how useful and beneficial, the fact that the Civil Society Forums and the Civil Society Hearings are forms of interaction with NGOs not explicitly provided for in UNCTAD regulations, raises questions regarding their regulatory legitimacy. However, since UNCTAD is explicitly allowed to involve NGOs in its policy deliberation and decision-making processes, it can and should be argued that UNCTAD is definitely allowed to organize its debate with NGOs outside its formal processes.

2.3.   UNEP

The United Nations Environment Programme (UNEP), created by a UN General Assembly Resolution in 1972, serves as the focal point for the activities of the United Nations family in environmental issues (UN General Assembly 1972). Reflecting the fact that NGOs have played and continue to play a central role in shaping the global environmental agenda, the UNEP constitutive instrument, UN General Assembly Resolution 2997 (XXVII), invited

> those non-governmental organizations that have an interest in the field of the environment to lend their full support and collaboration to the United Nations with a view to achieving the largest possible degree of cooperation (United Nations 1972, para. IV.5).

It could be argued that this provision does not give UNEP an *explicit* legal basis to involve NGOs in its activities. However, it definitely constitutes an *implicit* legal basis for such involvement. The two major areas of UNEP-NGO engagement are policy development and implementation of UNEP's work programme. Only the former will be discussed for the purposes of this chapter. The main forms of NGOs involvement in UNEP policy development are, firstly, through participation in sessions of the Governing Council/Global Ministerial Environmental Forum (GC/GMEF) and, secondly, through the Global Civil Society Forum (GSCF) organized immediately prior to the GC/GMEF sessions.

The Rules of Procedure of the Governing Council contain several references to NGOs as participants of the Governing Council process (see, in particular, Rules 7, 9.3, 10 and 69). According to Rule 69, accredited NGOs have a right to:

- sit as an observer at the GC/GMEF meetings;
- make oral statements subject to the approval of the GC/GMEF and chairman; and
- circulate written statements (in an official language) on issues on the agenda of the GC/GMEF or of its subsidiary organs, limited to 2000 words and taking into consideration comments from the Executive Director.

Furthermore, since 2004, accredited NGOs have been given greater rights concerning the process *leading up* to the GC/GMEF. Accredited NGOs can now:
- receive the provisional agenda and the unedited working documents of the UNEP GC/GMEF at the same time as the Committee of the Permanent Representatives (CPR); and
- submit suggestions for changes to the unedited working documents to be circulated to the Committee of Permanent Representatives prior to finalization of the documents.

However, this increase in NGO involvement has not found any reflection (yet) in the Rules of Procedure of the Governing Council.

The Global Civil Society Forum (GCSF) is a two-day event that immediately precedes sessions of the GC/GMEF. Agenda items for the GCSF are the same as those on the ministerial agenda. The UNEP strategy paper, *Enhancing Civil Society Engagement in the Work of the United Nations Environment Programme*, underscores that the GSCF does not have any decision-making role in UNEP (UNEP 2002, 10). Initially, the aim of the GCSF was to produce a report and/or a statement, which would convey the views and recommendations of civil society to the GC/GMEF. However, due to the fact that, since 2004, it has become easier for NGOs to deliver oral statements at the sessions of the GC/GMEF, the GCSF changed its function. It now functions more as a platform where NGOs meet, network, exchange views on policy issues, coordinate and prepare common positions in light of the upcoming session of the GC/GMEF. A joint NGO statement is produced during the 'global drafting meeting'. Prior to the GCSF, each of the six UNEP regional offices facilitates a regional CSO meeting to ensure regional input is considered at the GCSF. These regional CSO meetings elaborate a preparatory statement on the UNEP's work program and international environmental governance, elect regional representatives to attend the GCSF, and select two individuals to participate in the 'global drafting meeting' (UNEP 2004, 4). The twelve selected participants draft a global civil society statement to be provided to the governments in preparation for the upcoming GC/GMEF session (UNEP 2002, 10). More than 100 civil society representatives from 49 countries attended the 6th GCSF in 2005. Approximately 30% of the civil society representatives attending this GCSF were from developing countries.

The GCSF is not explicitly provided for in UN regulations. From a regulatory legitimacy perspective, this is to be regretted. However, UN General Assembly Resolution 2997 (XXVII), inviting NGOs to 'lend their full support and collaboration to the United Nations with a view to achieve the largest possible degree of cooperation', should give UNEP sufficient 'legal cover' for organizing the GCSF.

2.4.   *WHO*

The World Health Organization (WHO), established in 1948, is the United Nations specialized agency for health. The WHO's constituent instrument—the 1946 Constitution of the World Health Organization—contains an *explicit* legal basis for the WHO's collaboration with NGOs. Article 71 of the WHO Constitution provides:

> The Organization may, on matters within its competence, make suitable arrangements for consultation and co-operation with non-governmental international organizations and, with the consent of the government concerned, with national organizations, governmental or non-governmental.

This provision is similar to the one found in Article 71 of the UN Charter. It offers a possibility to the WHO, if it deems appropriate, to establish 'suitable' modalities for engagement with NGOs, primarily international ones.

At its first meeting in 1948, the World Health Assembly adopted a set of working principles governing admission of NGOs into official relations. These principles were later further amended and expanded (see the World Health Assembly's Resolutions WHA1.130, WHA3.113, WHA11.14 and WHA21.28). The current version of the Principles Governing Relations between WHO and Non-governmental Organizations (the 'Principles') was adopted by the World Health Assembly in 1987 (see the World Health Assembly Resolution WHA40.25). This document is the principal WHO legal instrument for relations with NGOs.

In 2001, the WHO Director-General established the Civil Society Initiative to undertake a review of official and informal relations between the WHO and civil society organizations. The review process established that the current Principles are in many respects inadequate to meet the needs of the WHO and the needs and aspirations of civil society (WHO 2002, para. 14). Therefore, a new draft policy on WHO relations with NGOs was negotiated to replace the current Principles, but the World Health Assembly has decided to postpone consideration of the new policy (WHO 2004a; 2004b). Modifications envisaged in the draft policy will be referred to below when appropriate. Lastly, participation of NGOs in meetings of the World Health Assembly and meetings of the Executive Board are governed by (in addition to the Principles) the Rules of Procedure of the World Health Assembly and by the Rules of Procedure of the Executive Board respectively (see Rules 19 and 49 of the Rules of Procedure of the World Health Assembly and Rule 4.2 of the Rules of Procedure of the Executive Board).

The Principles distinguish between two forms of NGO involvement: involvement of NGOs with 'working relations' with the WHO and involvement of NGOs with 'official relations' with the WHO. NGOs with 'working relations' cooperate in WHO operational activities, including acting as advisors, disseminators of WHO information, service providers, data collectors and providers, risk assessors, human resources developers, fund raisers, co-authors or peer reviewers of publications and more (Burci and Vignes 2004, 90-91). The status of 'NGO with working relations' is a *mandatory* pre-requisite for an NGO to obtain the status of 'NGO with official relations'. The 'official relations' status is the only category of formal relationship recognised by the Principles and is essentially similar to the 'consultative status' at ECOSOC, discussed above (WHO 2006, para. 2.1). NGOs with 'official relations' status must continue to engage in WHO operational activities but are also granted participatory privileges in the governing bodies' meetings.

The new draft Policy for Relations with NGOs avoids the division of 'working relations' and 'official relations' and establishes instead, two other forms of WHO relations with NGOs: accreditation and collaboration. Accreditation will give NGOs access to WHO governing bodies while collaboration (for which accreditation is not required) allows links to be established on the operational level. Neither of the two forms serves as a pre-requisite for the other and it is possible for an NGO to obtain both statuses concurrently (WHO 2004a, para. 3).

Rules 19 and 49 of the World Health Assembly's Rules of Procedure allow participation privileges for NGOs with 'official relations' status at the World Health Assembly. Rule 19 prescribes that invited NGOs may attend plenary sessions; Rule 49 entitles NGOs to attend both the plenary meetings and meetings of the Assembly's main committees. Additionally, the Principles provide that NGOs with an 'official relations' status have the right to make a statement and the right to submit a written memorandum (WHO 2006, para. 6.1). However, note with regard to the latter right, that the Chair decides on the nature and the scope of the circulation of written NGO memoranda. This may explain why NGOs make very little use of this right (WHO 2006, para. 6.1, and Lanord 2002, 8). NGOs with 'official relations' status also have these rights in the context of meetings of the Executive Board of the WHO.

Finally, NGOs with 'official relations' status may display their documents and literature on tables in proximity of the Executive Board Room and are entitled 'to non-confidential documentation and such other documentation as the Director-General may see fit to make available through such special distribution facilities as WHO may establish' (WHO 2006, para. 6.1 (ii)).

From a regulatory legitimacy perspective, the fact that the WHO Constitution explicitly provides for the involvement of NGOs in its activities and that secondary regulation clearly defines the forms that this involvement may take, is to be applauded.

2.5.   ILO

The International Labour Organization (ILO), established in 1919 and incorporated into the UN in 1946, is the specialized agency of the United Nations for the promotion of social justice and internationally recognized human and labour rights. Within the UN system, the ILO has a unique tripartite structure with workers' and employers' organizations participating as equal partners with governments in the work of the ILO's organs (ILO 2005a). The meetings of the International Labour Conference, the ILO Governing Body and subsidiary ILO bodies thus include representatives of civil society. In addition, the 1919 ILO Constitution in Article 12(3) provides for *consultative* relationships with 'recognized' NGOs:

> The International Labour Organization may make suitable arrangements for such consultation as it may think desirable with recognized non-gov-

ernmental international organizations, including international organizations of employers, workers, agriculturists and co-operators (ILO 2005a).

The ILO Governing Body has adopted, over time, a number of decisions that laid down rules and procedures detailing and classifying the arrangements for NGO involvement. ILO rules for NGO involvement are not collected in a single document, but scattered throughout many Governing Body decisions dating from late 1940s up to the present (for a useful compilation of a number (but not all) of these decisions, see ILO 2005b, 81-89). Participation of international NGOs in various ILO meetings is further governed by standing orders adopted for each type of meeting. The Standing Orders of the International Labour Conference, the Standing Orders of the Governing Body, the Rules for Regional Meetings and the Standing Orders for Sectoral Meetings are the most important legal instruments in this respect (ILO 2005c).

With respect to the arrangements for consultation, the ILO distinguishes between three categories of international NGOs. The first category, i.e., the category of NGOs with *consultative status*, includes international NGOs with an important interest in a wide range of the ILO's activities. These NGOs are granted either general or regional consultative status. NGOs granted *general* consultative status may participate in all ILO meetings. NGOs granted *regional* consultative status may participate in all regional meetings.

The second category, the Special List of Non-Governmental International Organizations, includes international NGOs other than employers' and workers' organizations which also share the principles and objectives of the 1919 ILO Constitution and 1944 Declaration of Philadelphia. Inclusion of NGOs on this Special List depends on their demonstrated interest in the ILO's programme of meetings and activities. NGOs on the Special List are not considered to have consultative status and do not automatically receive participation rights in ILO meetings. However, it is easy for them to secure an invitation to participate in specific ILO meetings; once they have obtained an invitation they possess the same rights as NGOs with consultative status for that particular meeting. They may also attend meetings of the International Labour Conference as observers.

Finally, certain NGOs fall into a third category. The ILO Governing Body extends invitations to these NGOs to attend specific ILO meetings for which these organizations have demonstrated a particular interest (ILO 2005d).

The fact that the ILO Constitution explicitly provides for the involvement of NGOs in its activities and that secondary regulation clearly defines the forms that this involvement may take, contribute significantly to the regulatory legitimacy of NGO involvement in the ILO.

2.6.   World Bank

The International Bank for Reconstruction and Development (IBRD), commonly referred to as the World Bank, was established in 1945. The World Bank is the specialized agency of the United Nations for the reduction of poverty through promotion of sustainable development by providing loans, guarantees, and analytical and advisory services (World Bank 2005a). The 1944 IBRD Articles of Agreement, the constituent instrument of the World Bank, does not provide for consultation of, or cooperation with, NGOs. Article V, Section 2(v) of the Articles of Agreement provides for cooperation with 'other international organizations', but this is commonly (and correctly) understood as referring to cooperation with international governmental organizations, not to cooperation with NGOs. Consequently, there is no legal basis for the involvement of NGOs in the activities of the World Bank. Nevertheless, the World Bank maintains regular relations with NGOs as part of its relations with civil society organizations (CSOs). CSOs include, in addition to NGOs, community-based organizations, indigenous peoples' organizations, labour unions, faith-based groups, and foundations. The World Bank engages in policy dialogue with CSOs and involves CSOs in the planning, implementation and evaluation of projects which the IBRD finances (World Bank 2000a). The latter type of NGO involvement is beyond the scope of this chapter. With regard to the former type of engagement with NGOs, the World Bank developed non-binding 'best practice' guidelines for consultations with civil society (World Bank 2000b).

To keep CSOs informed about recent developments that involve and/or may be of interest to civil society, the World Bank publishes a monthly electronic newsletter, the *Civil Society Engagement eNewsletter*. More importantly, the World Bank in cooperation with the IMF, organizes twice a year, in the context of their Annual Spring Meetings, Civil Society Dialogues. At these events, World Bank and IMF officials engage into discussions and consultations with participating NGOs on a broad range of topics. During the week of the Annual Meetings, accredited CSOs may also attend events of the Program of Seminars. This

Program includes roundtable discussions, seminars, and regional briefings with the participation of senior World Bank and IMF officials, private sector representatives, government delegates and representatives of civil society. NGOs may also be accredited to observe the concluding plenary session of the Board of Governors during the Annual Meetings. However, CSOs may only *observe* this session; they have no further participatory rights. Reportedly, most CSOs find it more beneficial to attend the parallel Civil Society Dialogues.

In 2000, it was decided to convene annually a World Bank – Civil Society Forum with the objective of 'conven[ing] representatives of NGOs [...] and other organized expressions of civil society with relevant expertise in issues identified as the annual focus of the forum' (World Bank 2000c). A Joint Facilitation Committee (JFC) was established to assist with the organization of the annual Forum. The JFC comprises 14 regional and international civil society networks and World Bank officials (including senior managers). The JFC has become a formal arrangement for permanent engagement with NGOs. The first World Bank – Civil Society Forum was organised in April 2005, a few days after the 2005 Spring Meeting. This 2-day event brought together some 200 civil society leaders, government officials, parliamentarians, donor agency representatives and IMF and World Bank officials. The majority of the CSOs present came from (over 50) developing countries (World Bank 2005b). While the World Bank Civil Society Forum was envisaged as a permanent arrangement, to date there has been insufficient momentum and CSO pressure for it to continue on an annual basis. The Forum did not take place in 2006.

Although there is no legal basis for any kind of NGO involvement in the policy deliberation and decision-making processes of the World Bank, the latter has decided that engagement with NGOs is permissible as long as the general provisions of the Articles of Agreement are observed (World Bank 2005c, 7). From the regulatory legitimacy perspective the existing practice of engaging with NGOs—while perhaps not *contra legem*—is nevertheless problematic.

2.7.   IMF

The International Monetary Fund (IMF) was established in 1945 as a specialized agency of the United Nations, to provide temporary financial assistance to countries to help ease the balance of payments adjustment. The IMF also provides technical assistance to build human and institutional capacity to design and implement effective macroeconomic and structural policies (IMF 2005a). The 1944 Articles of Agreement of the International Monetary Fund, the constituent instrument of the IMF, does not provide for the consultation of or cooperation with NGOs. Despite this, the IMF, like the World Bank, maintains regular relations with NGOs.

The engagement of the IMF with CSOs at the *global level* takes different forms. First, there are regular contacts between IMF management and representatives of CSOs in both small meetings and larger forums. Second, there are meetings, seminars and consultations with IMF staff and Executive Directors on specific policy or country issues. Third, the IMF invites CSOs to contribute to reviews of its policies by attending seminars or by providing comments to papers posted on its external website (IMF 2005b). Fourth, as referred to above, the IMF jointly organizes a series of Civil Society Dialogues with the World Bank. Finally, to keep CSOs informed of recent developments, events, papers and discussions, the IMF publishes the quarterly *IMF Civil Society Newsletter*. Note that unlike the World Bank, the IMF does not have a formal arrangement for permanent engagement with NGOs, comparable with the Joint Facilitation Committee of the World Bank.

The global engagement is supplemented by the IMF-CSO contacts at a *country level*. The importance of the latter is clearly reflected in the 2003 *Guide for Staff Relations with Civil Society Organizations* (IMF 2005c). When the IMF Managing Director or IMF staff visit a country, they meet with representatives of CSOs. Resident IMF representatives regularly meet and exchange information with local CSOs (IMF 2005b).

As for NGO involvement with the World Bank, no explicit legal basis is provided for NGO involvement in the IMF constituent document. While the IMF may—as does the World Bank—take the position that engagement with NGOs is permissible as long as the general provisions of its constituent instrument are observed, the existing practice of engaging with NGOs is from a regulatory legitimacy perspective quite problematic.

2.8.   WTO

The World Trade Organization (WTO), established in 1995, is the key international organization concerned with trade relations among countries. Unlike the international organizations discussed above, the WTO is not part of the United Nations family. The WTO facilitates the implementation of 20 international trade agreements, provides the forum for negotiations among its 150 Members concerning their multilateral trade relations, and settles international trade disputes. The 1994 Marrakesh Agreement Establishing the World Trade Organization (WTO Agreement) in Article V:2 explicitly empowers the WTO to engage with NGOs:

> The General Council may make appropriate arrangements for consultations and cooperation with non-governmental organizations concerned with matters related to those of the WTO.

Pursuant to Article V:2 of the WTO Agreement, in July 1996 the General Council adopted a set of Guidelines regarding the relations between the WTO and non-governmental organizations (WTO 1996). In the 1996 Guidelines, it was agreed that interaction with NGOs should be developed through various means such as the organization of symposia for NGOs on specific WTO-related issues, as well as the establishment of informal arrangements enabling interested delegations to receive information that NGOs may wish to make available. Further initiatives encompass a continuation of the practice of the WTO Secretariat to respond to requests for general information and briefings about the WTO and participation of the Chairpersons of WTO councils and committees in discussions and meetings with NGOs in their personal capacity.

The 1996 Guidelines also make the limits of NGO involvement clear. In the concluding paragraph of the Guidelines, the General Council states that 'it would not be possible for NGOs to be directly involved in the work of the WTO' (WTO 1996, para. 6). NGOs cannot attend any of the meetings of the organs of the WTO with the exception of the plenary sessions of the bi-annual meeting of the Ministerial Conference, the WTO's governing body. However, NGO representatives are not allowed to make any statements and can only attend the formal plenary meetings where heads of governments and trade ministers read out short prepared statements. Access to the working meetings is denied. During the sessions, NGOs are kept informed about the issues under discussion through briefings by the WTO Secretariat.

In the autumn of 1998, the WTO Secretariat created a special section on the WTO website, the 'NGO Room', to post a monthly list of the NGO position papers received by the Secretariat (WTO 2004). Since 2001, the WTO Secretariat has also organised an annual symposium for NGOs and delegations of Members, which was renamed into Public Forum in 2006. Finally, in 2003 under the personal initiative of the then WTO Director-General, Dr. Supachai Panitchpakdi, the Informal NGO Advisory Body was established. To form this Advisory Body, the Director-General selected ten NGOs that he considered to be influential and broadly representative, seeking, where possible, to maintain regional balance and balance between NGOs from developed and developing countries. The main function of the Advisory Body is to advise the WTO Director-General and to channel the positions and concerns of civil society on international trade. Members of the informal NGO Advisory Body include Consumers International, Consumer Unity and Trust Society, the International Federation of Agricultural Producers, World Wide Fund for Nature (WWF) International, Third World Network, Christian Aid, the International Confederation of Free Trade Unions, Public Services International, the International Center for Trade and Sustainable Development, and the International Institute for Sustainable Development. Interestingly enough, Friends of the Earth International and Oxfam International have rejected the invitation to become members, supposedly because of fears of criticism from their peers and potentially bad publicity. Perhaps for the same reason, the NGOs that had agreed to participate reportedly asked the Director-General to abstain from publicizing the existence of the Advisory Body on the WTO website.

The Marrakesh Agreement, the constituent instrument of the WTO, includes an explicit legal basis for the involvement of NGOs in the WTO. As is reflected in the 1996 Guidelines and later practice, the use of this legal basis is fairly modest. While the legal basis in the Marrakesh Agreement is broad enough to allow for this, NGOs do not have formal consultative status in WTO bodies. This may be regretted but from a regulatory legitimacy perspective, the current involvement of NGOs in the WTO is unproblematic.

2.9.   Concluding remarks on the legal status of NGOs

The above analysis of the legal status of NGOs in international organizations shows that the situation differs considerably among international organizations. The constituent instrument of a number of organizations, including the United Nations, UNCTAD, the WHO, the ILO and the WTO explicitly provides a legal basis for NGO involvement in the policy deliberation and decision-making processes of these organizations. The constituent instrument of at least one other organization, the UNEP, contains language which can serve as an implicit legal basis for NGO involvement. The constituent instruments of the World Bank and the IMF do not provide for a legal basis for NGO involvement. Nevertheless, the World Bank and the IMF engage in relations with NGOs. The regulatory legitimacy of this engagement without legal basis (involvement *sine legem*) is problematic, even when this engagement remains 'modest' and does not include active involvement in the policy deliberation processes.

With respect to the involvement form or forms of the NGOs, the above analysis again shows considerable differences among organizations both with regard to the existence of rules setting out the involvement form or forms of an NGO, the binding nature and the degree of detail of these rules; and the extent to which the practice of NGO involvement conforms to these rules or goes beyond them. NGO involvement in the WHO, ILO and the WTO seems to remain within the limits set by the relevant rules. This cannot be said of NGO involvement in the United Nations, UNCTAD, UNEP, the World Bank and the IMF. These organizations engage with NGOs in ways which have not been regulated and/or go further than existing rules allow for. From a regulatory legitimacy perspective, a form of NGO involvement which is *sine legem* or *ultra legem* is a problem. NGO involvement in direct contradiction with existing rules (involvement *contra legem*) would obviously be an even bigger problem but the above analysis has not revealed any such involvement.

3.   Rules on the accreditation of NGOs

In addition to the rules defining the legal status of NGOs, the rules on the involvement of NGOs in international organizations also include rules on the accreditation of NGOs by these organizations. An increasing number of NGOs, with very different objectives, wish to be involved in international organizations' policy deliberation and decision-making processes. For good reasons, international organizations want to keep the number of NGOs involved in their processes 'manageable' and also want to avoid the involvement of NGOs which could potentially harm them in their efforts to achieve their objectives. Therefore, they need to select among the NGOs that want to engage with them. As discussed above, accreditation rules are rules to ensure that only those NGOs which 'add value' to the policy deliberation and decision-making processes 'enjoy' specific forms of involvement and associated rights. The rules on the accreditation include:

– substantive rules setting out the requirements that an NGO must meet to be accredited; and
– procedural rules for taking decisions regarding accreditation and the subsequent monitoring of accredited NGOs.

For the involvement of an NGO in an international organization to have regulatory legitimacy, the international organization must ensure that the NGO concerned meets the accreditation requirements *and* continues to do so.

This section successively examines the existing substantive and procedural rules on accreditation of NGOs by the UN, UNCTAD, UNEP, the WHO, the ILO, the IBRD, the IMF and the WTO.

3.1.   United Nations

ECOSOC Resolution 1996/31 on the 'Consultative Relationship between the United Nations and Non-Governmental Organizations' (UN ECO-SOC 1996), sets out the basic substantive requirements that an NGO must meet to be conferred consultative status in the framework of the Council. In accordance with Resolution 1996/31, the NGO must, first of all, be concerned with matters falling within the (very broad) competence of the Council and its subsidiary bodies (UN ECOSOC 1996, para. 1). Firstly, it must be able to demonstrate that its programme of work is of direct relevance and can contribute to the mission of the United Nations (UN ECOSOC 1996, paras. 3, 8). The aims and purposes of the NGO must be in conformity with the spirit, purposes and principles of the UN Charter (UN ECOSOC 1996, para. 2). This requirement may be used to exclude NGOs that advocate violence, racial discrimination or disrespect for human rights. Secondly, the NGO must also have recognized standing within its field of competence (UN ECOSOC 1996, para. 9). Thirdly, the NGO must have an established headquarters with an executive officer (UN ECOSOC 1996, para. 10); a democratically adopted constitution (UN ECOSOC 1996, para. 10); a representative and accountable inner structure (UN ECOSOC 1996, para. 12); and the authority to speak for its members (UN ECOSOC 1996, para. 11). Fourthly, as regards the funding of the NGO, the basic resources must be derived from either national affiliates or from individual members (UN ECOSOC 1996, para. 13). This requirement may be waived if an

NGO provides a satisfactory explanation in accordance with paragraph 12 of Resolution 1996/31. Finally, the NGO must attest its existence for at least two years as of the date of receipt of its application for consultative status (UN ECOSOC 1996, para. 61 (h)). Consultative status may be granted to international, regional, sub-regional and national organizations (UN ECOSOC 1996, para. 5). Participation of NGOs from developing countries must be encouraged as far as possible, in order to help achieve a just, balanced, effective and genuine involvement of NGOs from all regions and areas of the world (UN ECOSOC 1996, para. 5).

As explicitly stated in paragraph 20 of Resolution 1996/31, decisions regarding arrangements for consultation should be guided by the principle that they are made, *on the one hand*, for the purpose of enabling the Council or one of its subsidiary bodies to secure expert information or advice from NGOs having special competence in the relevant subjects, and, *on the other hand*, to enable international, regional, sub-regional and national NGOs that represent important elements of public opinion to express their views. Therefore, the arrangements for consultation made with each NGO should relate to the subjects in which that NGO has special competence or in which it has a special interest (UN ECOSOC 1996, para. 20). Consequently, the decisive factor in which form of consultative status will be granted (general, special, or roster) is the scope of the NGOs activities and competence. For the general status, it must be as broad as, or at least comparable to, that of ECOSOC; for special status the NGO's scope must cover a few relevant fields; for roster status, a narrower scope is permitted. In 2004, 134 NGOs qualified for general consultative status, 1474 NGOs for special consultative status and 923 NGOs were included on the roster.

With regard to the requirements for NGO accreditation to international conferences convened by the UN, it follows from paragraphs 43-45 of Resolution 1996/31 that these requirements are essentially the same as those for accreditation to ECOSOC. Additionally, it is explicitly provided that NGOs in any of the three types of consultative status shall, as a rule, be accredited for participation (UN ECOSOC 1996, para. 41).

Resolution 1996/31 prescribes the procedure for obtaining consultative status with the ECOSOC and its subsidiary bodies. In order to obtain consultative status, an NGO must submit an application, which is then reviewed by ECOSOC's Committee on NGOs (or NGO Committee). The NGO Committee consists of 19 Member States that are elected every four years by the Council on the basis of equitable geographical representation (UN ECOSOC 1996, para. 60). The Committee, which meets twice each year, in practice discusses all new applications during informal meetings prior to its formal sessions. NGO applications are grouped into two lists. List 1 includes 'unproblematic' NGOs; List 2 features those NGOs that give rise to questions from one or more delegations. These questions are sent to the NGOs concerned so that they may respond before the formal session of the NGO Committee begins. In many instances, these questions have little to do with the compliance of the NGO with the established accreditation criteria, but concern more political sensitivities of particular states. To give just one example, at the January 2006 session of the NGO Committee, Cuba posed the question to an NGO that focused on human rights violations 'in the Global South' as to whether this NGO considered that there were no human rights violations 'in the Global North'. If Member States are not satisfied with answers received from a particular NGO, its application is deferred and additional questions are posed. After deliberating on each NGO, the Committee chairperson usually suggests recommending special consultative status and if there are no objections or proposals to change the type of status (into general or roster) from Member States, this recommendation will be transmitted to ECOSOC for final approval. In difficult cases, the NGO Committee may turn to voting before submitting their recommendation. At its session in January 2006, the NGO Committee considered 99 NGOs and recommended that 60 were put on List 1 and 39 on List 2. The final decision is taken by ECOSOC itself. As discussed above, Resolution 1996/31 provides for three types of consultative status. There is, however, no danger of an NGO applying for the wrong category. The NGO Committee automatically reclassifies the application when appropriate. An NGO may at any time request reclassification.

When national NGOs apply for consultative status, a decision on granting this status will only be made after consultation with the Member State concerned (UN ECOSOC 1996, para. 8). Although only consultation with, and not the consent of, the Member State is required, ECOSOC is unlikely to grant consultative status to national NGOs when the Member State concerned has serious reservations regarding the granting of consultative status.

An NGO granted general or special consultative status with ECOSOC is under an obligation to submit a report on its activities every four years (UN ECOSOC 1996, para. 61 (c)). This report, commonly referred to as the quadrennial report, allows the NGO Committee to review whether the NGO concerned continues to satisfy the substantive criteria of consultative status as set out above. If the Committee is of the opinion that this is not the case, it can recommend reclassification or withdrawal of the NGOs consultative status to ECOSOC. Under 'exceptional circumstances', the Committee can ask for a report between the regular reporting dates. The Committee may ask for such special report when it is informed of an act or a pattern of acts of the NGO concerned which could lead to suspension or withdrawal of the consultative status.

There are three cases in which the consultative status of an NGO may be suspended for up to three years or withdrawn:

1. if an NGO clearly abuses its status by engaging in a pattern of acts contrary to the purposes and principles of the UN Charter, including unsubstantiated or politically motivated acts against Member States of the United Nations incompatible with the Charter's purposes and principles;

2. if there is substantiated evidence of influence from proceeds resulting from internationally recognized criminal activities such as illicit drugs trade, money-laundering or illegal arms trade;

3. if, within the preceding three years, an organization made no positive or effective contributions to the work of the United Nations and, in particular, to the work of ECOSOC or its subsidiary organs (UN ECOSOC 1996, para. 57).

A decision to suspend or withdraw the consultative status of an NGO is made by the Council, upon recommendation of the NGO Committee (UN ECOSOC 1996, para. 58). An NGO whose consultative status is withdrawn may only re-apply for consultative status after three years (UN ECOSOC 1996, para. 59).

To date, few NGOs have seen their consultative status suspended or withdrawn. In 2000, for example, the NGO Committee considered a total of five cases. In only one of these cases the consultative status of the NGO concerned was eventually suspended by the Council (United Nations 2000a; 2000b). Between 2000 and 2005 there have been five suspensions recommended to the Council by the NGO Committee (United Nations 2000a; 2000b and UN ECOSOC 2001; 2002a; 2002b, paras. 82-96; 2003; 2004a, paras. 98-127; 2005, paras. 58-70).

With regard to international conferences convened by the UN, Resolution 1996/31 provides that the accreditation of NGOs is the prerogative of Member States. This prerogative is exercised through the preparatory committee of the conference, which acts upon recommendation of the secretariat of the conference (UN ECOSOC 1996, paras. 41-47). Note that the preparatory committee shall decide on all recommendations for accreditation within 24 hours after the recommendations of the secretariat have been received. In the event of a decision not being made within this period an interim accreditation will be accorded until there is a decision (UN ECOSOC 1996, para. 48).

As the analysis above shows, the United Nations and, particularly the ECOSOC, have detailed substantive accreditation rules to ensure that NGOs 'add value' to the policy deliberation and decision-making processes of the United Nations. They also have elaborate procedural rules for deciding on whether an NGO conforms, and continues to conform to these substantive rules. The United Nations thus *ensures* that an NGO 'adds value' and continues to do so. This gives the involvement in the United Nations of the NGO concerned a high degree of regulatory legitimacy.

3.2.   UNCTAD

Rule 77 of the Rules of Procedure of the UNCTAD Trade and Development Board provides that for an NGO to be granted observer status, the NGO must be concerned with matters of trade and, in particular, with matters of trade as related to development. Board Decision 43 (VII) establishes more detailed criteria, including:

– the aims and purposes of the NGO must be in conformity with the spirit, purposes and principles of the UN Charter;
– the NGO must be of recognized standing and should represent a substantial proportion of the organized persons within the particular field in which it operates;
– the NGO must be international in its structure;
– the NGO must have an established headquarters with an executive officer;
– the NGO must have a conference, convention or other policy-making body;
– members of the NGO must exercise voting rights in relation to its policies or action; and
– the NGO must have authority to speak for its members through its authorized representatives.

NGOs seeking observer status with UNCTAD complete a special questionnaire and provide additional documents for UNCTAD to assess whether they meet the above criteria. Although Decision 43 (VII) does not have any explicit requirements relating to funding sources, this must be disclosed in the questionnaire and submitted together with their annual budget.

An NGO determined to fulfil these criteria will be placed in either the General or Special Category based on the extent to which the scope of the NGOs activities coincide with those of UNCTAD. The General Category refers to international NGOs that are interested in, or engage in, activities related to the majority of UNCTAD's institutional concerns. Nearly all development-related NGOs officially recognized by UNCTAD are in this category. The Special Category of international NGOs covers NGOs with special competence in one or two UNCTAD activities areas. NGOs in the Special Category may attend sessions of the Trade and Development Board and also sessions of selected subsidiary bodies. As discussed above, besides the General Category and Special Category, there is a third category reserved for national NGOs, namely the Category of NGOs entered in the Register. To be entered into the Register, national NGOs are not formally required to meet the common criteria set out above. According to Decision 43 (VII) there are only two conditions for their admission: they must have recognised standing and they must provide a significant contribution to UNCTAD's work. In April 2004, there were 192 NGOs recognized by UNCTAD: 107 in the General Category, 85 in the Special Category and 20 national NGOs in the Register (UNCTAD 2004, para. 4).

The Secretary-General of UNCTAD, in consultation with the Bureau of the Trade and Development Board, must from time to time prepare a list of NGOs for the Board's approval. The list is prepared on the basis of information on objectives, activities, structure, membership and funding that NGOs seeking observer status (which is granted to NGOs falling within the General and Special Category) are required to provide through the special questionnaire. Observer status is conferred by the Trade and Development Board, membership of which is open to all UNCTAD Members. Entry into the Registry (reserved for national NGOs) does not have to be approved by the Trade and Development Board; the decision on entry is taken by the Secretary-General of UNCTAD after consultations with the member state concerned.

There are no separate accreditation rules and procedures for the participation of NGOs in the UNCTAD Civil Society Forums. As these

Forums are convened in conjunction with Quadrennial Conferences, NGOs eligible for participation in the Conference take part in the Forum. To participate in the Civil Society Hearings, an NGO either has to have an observer status with UNCTAD or receive a special accreditation for the Hearings.

While less detailed than the rules of the United Nations/ECOSOC, UNCTAD has fairly elaborate substantive accreditation rules to ensure that NGOs 'add value' to its policy deliberation and decision-making processes. It has procedural rules for deciding on whether an NGO conforms to these substantive rules but has no rules/procedures for monitoring continued conformity with the substantive accreditation rules. The latter negatively affects the degree of regulatory legitimacy of the involvement in UNCTAD of a given NGO.

3.4.   UNEP

It follows from Rule 69 of the Rules of Procedure of the Governing Council of UNEP that there are only three requirements for accreditation. An organization must:

–   be an NGO (understood as any non-profit making entity, i.e., not a business entity);
–   be international, that is, have an international scope of work; and
–   have an interest in the field of environment.

With regard to the latter requirement, note that the list of NGOs accredited by UNEP seems to suggest that an NGO does not have to primarily focus on environmental protection but that this can be just one of the many areas of its activities/interests. In practice, the most difficult accreditation requirement for NGOs to fulfil is demonstrating their international scope. To assess this, UNEP looks at whether the NGO's headquarters and regional offices are located in different countries, whether the NGO has projects and programmes in multiple countries and whether such projects have international implications. Note that an NGO with consultative status with ECOSOC is only required to provide documentation concerning its interest in the environmental field.

To be granted accreditation to the Governing Council/Global Ministerial Environmental Forum (GC/GMEF), an NGO must file an application for accreditation (including all requested documents demonstrating the substantive requirements are met) with the Major Groups and Stakeholders Branch of the UNEP Secretariat. After reviewing the application, it is sent to the Secretariat for Governing Bodies with a recommendation on whether to grant accreditation. The Secretariat for Governing Bodies makes the final decision on the accreditation and alerts the NGO of the result. As of October 2005, 150 international NGOs were accredited as observers to the Governing Council of UNEP.

For the Global Civil Society Forum, UNEP does not select participants but sets approximate limits on the number of different groups of participants in order to finance the event and ensure balanced representation. However, NGOs who are willing to cover their own costs may also participate. Invitations are extended to all NGOs accredited to UNEP's Governing Council, which includes five representatives of each of the six UNEP regions (including one youth representative), 20-40 representatives from the hosting region selected by the Civil Society Host Committee, and about 20 private sector and trade union representative (UNEP 2005).

In comparison with the substantive accreditation rules of the United Nations/ECOSOC and UNCTAD, the substantive accreditation rules of UNEP are quite basic. In addition, the procedural rules for deciding on whether an NGO conforms to these substantive rules are not very elaborate and UNEP does not have rules/procedures for monitoring continued conformity with the accreditation rules. This is an unsatisfactory situation from the perspective of the regulatory legitimacy of the involvement of a given NGO in UNEP activities.

3.5.   WHO

The substantive requirements with which NGOs must comply to be admitted to 'official relations' with the WHO are set out in the Principles Governing Relations between WHO and Non-governmental Organizations (the 'Principles'). In an extensive list, the Principles include the following requirements for accreditation:
-   The main area of competence of the NGO must fall within the purview of WHO objectives. The NGO's activities must centre on development work in health or health-related fields (WHO 2006, para. 3.1).
-   The NGO's aims and activities must be in conformity with the spirit, purposes and principles of the WHO Constitution (WHO 2006, para. 3.1).
-   The NGO must be free from concerns that are primarily of a commercial or profit-making nature (WHO 2006, para. 3.1).

- The NGO shall generally be international in its structure and/or scope (WHO 2006, para. 3.2). As a general rule, an NGO would be considered international if it has activities and/or members in more than one WHO region (WHO 2004c, para. 12).
- The NGO must represent a substantial proportion of the persons globally organised for the purpose of participating in the particular field of interest in which it operates (WHO 2006, para. 3.2).
- Regarding organization, the NGO must have a constitution or similar basic document, have a directing or governing body and an administrative structure at various level of action, and have an established headquarters (WHO 2006, para. 3.2).
- The NGOs have the authority to speak for its members through authorized representatives as evidenced by its constituent documents. NGO members must also be able to exercise voting rights in relation to its policies or actions (WHO 2006, para. 3.3).
- Prior to an application for admission into 'official relations', the NGO must normally have at least two years of successfully completed 'working relations' with the WHO (WHO 2006, para. 3.6).

Note that for granting a 'working relations' status (which precedes an 'official relations' status), the WHO assesses applicant-NGOs on the basis of the same requirements. However, an 'imperfect' NGO may be admitted to a 'working relations' status on the understanding that in order to be granted the 'official relations' status later, it will have to effect the required changes in problematic areas.

The process for entering into 'official relations' with the WHO usually takes between three to four years. The process comprises three stages: 'first contacts', 'working relations' and 'official relations'. 'First contacts' primarily consist of information exchange and reciprocal participation in technical meetings. To establish 'first contacts', NGOs may approach a WHO technical department directly or may seek the help of the Civil Society Initiative or its counterpart in a WHO regional office. The latter put NGOs into contact with interested WHO departments to explore the possibility of informal exchanges. At this point NGOs must submit an explanation of how its work relates to WHO priorities, a copy of its constitution, membership lists, identity of elected officers, composition of governing bodies, annual reports, and academic and media publications (WHO 2005). Collaboration may be increased to 'working relations' after a number of specific joint activities have been identified by an exchange of letters. Such letters set out the agreed basis for the collaboration, indicating details of the activities to be undertaken during the period. A joint assessment of the outcome of the collaboration is completed at the end of the period of 'working relations' by the parties concerned, which also includes consideration of the future relationship (WHO 2006, para. 2.4). Depending on the result of the joint assessment and a 'working relationship' of at least two years, the NGO may apply for 'official relations' status. In addition to a positive assessment, the NGO must present a joint three-year programme of collaboration, agreed on with a technical WHO department. The NGO must also submit a completed questionnaire designed to assess whether the NGO fulfils the substantive requirements listed above.

The Executive Board of the WHO is the organ responsible for deciding on the admission of NGOs into 'official relations' with the WHO (WHO 2006, para. 2.5). The Executive Board has a Standing Committee on Non-governmental Organizations (NGO Committee), composed of five WHO Members, which considers applications from NGOs and makes recommendations to the Board. The NGO Committee recommends to the Board that the application in question be approved, rejected or postponed, depending on whether the NGO meets the criteria for obtaining the 'official relations' status. The latter option may be used especially in cases where the NGO does not meet the criteria but, despite this, the NGO Committee considers that a continuing partnership in a framework of future collaborative activities is desirable (WHO 2006, para. 4.2). The NGO Committee takes its decisions by consensus. After considering the recommendations of the NGO Committee, the Executive Board decides whether a NGO is to be admitted into 'official relations' with WHO. As of May 2005, 184 NGOs were in 'official relations' status with the WHO.

The WHO has a monitoring system in place. The Executive Board, through its NGO Committee, reviews collaboration with each NGO in 'official relations' every three years to determine the desirability of maintaining 'official relations' (WHO 2006, para. 4.6).

Currently there are three grounds for the Executive Board to discontinue or suspend 'official relations':
–   if the Board considers that such relations are no longer appropriate or necessary in the light of changing programmes or other circumstances;
–   if the NGO no longer meets the criteria that applied at the time of the establishment of such relations; or

– if the NGO fails to fulfil its part in the agreed programme of collaboration. This includes failure on the part of NGOs to submit
  their three-year report, although a grace period is usually provided
  (WHO 2006, paras. 4.6-4.7).

In general, these grounds for suspension/discontinuance of official relations give the Executive Board a broad margin of discretion when considering this matter. Note also that the WHO Secretariat also plays a
significant role, as it may unilaterally determine whether or not it would
be beneficial to continue collaboration with a given NGO.

Like the United Nations/ECOSOC, the WHO also has detailed substantive accreditation rules to ensure that NGOs 'add value' to the policy deliberation and decision-making processes of the WHO. Moreover,
it also has elaborate procedural rules for deciding on whether an NGO
conforms—and continues to conform—to these substantive rules. The
WHO thus *ensures* that an NGO 'adds value' and continues to do so.
This gives the involvement in the WHO of the NGO concerned a high
degree of regulatory legitimacy.

3.6.   ILO

As discussed above, the ILO distinguishes three categories of international NGOs:
– NGOs with general consultative status (which may participate in all
  ILO meetings) or NGOs with regional consultative status (which
  may participate in all regional meetings);
– NGOs on the Special List of Non-Governmental International
  Organizations, (which do not automatically receive participation
  rights in ILO meetings but can easily secure an invitation to participate in specific ILO meetings); and
– NGOs to which the ILO Governing Body extends invitations to
  attend specific ILO meetings for which these organizations have
  demonstrated a particular interest (ILO 2005d).

To be granted general or regional consultative status, an NGO must:
– demonstrate the international nature of its composition and activities, and be represented or have affiliates in a considerable number
  of countries;

- have aims and objectives that are in harmony with the spirit, aims and principles of the 1919 ILO Constitution and the 1944 Declaration of Philadelphia;
- have formally expressed an interest—clearly defined and supported by its statutes and by explicit reference to its own activities—in the activities of the ILO (ILO 2005e; 2005f).

The ILO currently grants general consultative status to eight NGOs and regional consultative status to 18 NGOs (ILO 2006a and ILO 2006b).

With respect to the ILO's Special List of Non-Governmental Organizations, it should be noted that admission of an NGO to this List depends primarily on whether the aims of the NGO are in harmony with the spirit, aims and principles of the ILO Constitution and the Declaration of Philadelphia, on the international nature of the NGO (determined through membership of national organizations, geographical coverage of the NGO, and scope of activities) and on evidence that the NGO has an apparent interest in at least one of the activities of the ILO (ILO 2005a). Further factors include the length of existence, membership, and practical achievements of the NGO. The fact that an NGO has consultative status with the ECOSOC, or a UN specialized agency, is relevant but does not necessarily imply admission to the Special List (ILO 2006a and ILO 2006b). There are currently more than 150 NGOs on the Special List, including NGOs concerned with the promotion of human rights, poverty alleviation, social security, professional rehabilitation, gender issues and youth matters (ILO 2006c).

The procedures for conferring general or regional consultative status and for the admittance to the Special List of NGOs have not been spelt out in a legal document. Applicants for general or regional consultative status must submit their constituent documents and latest annual report. Consultative status is granted by the Governing Body on the recommendation of its officers. The majority of NGOs with general and regional status have been affiliated with the ILO for decades. As regards the Special List, an NGO must submit the same documents to the Bureau for External Relations and Partnerships (EXREL). EXREL then makes a preliminary assessment as to whether the NGO satisfies the requirements. The application can be rejected at this stage, if there is a manifest inconsistency with one or more of the requirements. When the NGO is considered to be eligible, EXREL compiles general data in an information note about them and circulates this to relevant technical departments of the ILO for comments. This internal consultation process results in a recommendation to the Director-General who has the power to include or refuse the NGO on the Special List. The whole procedure usually takes less than a year.

While defined, the substantive accreditation rules of the ILO lack in specificity. The procedural rules for deciding on whether an NGO conforms to these substantive rules are not spelled out in a legal document, although fairly elaborate procedures exist. The ILO does not have rules/procedures for monitoring continued conformity with the accreditation rules. From the perspective of the regulatory legitimacy of the involvement of a given NGO in ILO activities, the current situation could certainly be improved.

3.7.   *World Bank*

The World Bank does not grant consultative status to NGOs. With the exception of the concluding plenary session of the Board of Governors during the Annual Meetings, the World Bank does not even allow NGOs to attend the meetings of its bodies. As discussed above, the World Bank does, however, engage with CSOs, including NGOs, in a policy dialogue in the context of the World Bank-Civil Society Forum. For participation in the Forum, no specific accreditation criteria have been formulated. For the 2005 Forum, the World Bank stressed on its website that participation was by invitation only, but provided no guidelines on the criteria for NGOs wishing to secure such an invitation. The Joint Resolution establishing the Forum states that the Forum 'will attempt to be as inclusive as possible and, depending on the issues discussed, it will convene representatives of NGOs [...] with relevant expertise in issues identified as the annual focus of the forum' (World Bank 2000c, para. 1). The civil society members of the Joint Facilitation Committee (JFC), established to facilitate the organization of the Forum, rotate every year according to the topic of the annual Forum (World Bank 2000c, para. 5). No further criteria for the selection of the civil society members of the JFC were defined.

Participation in the annual Civil Society Dialogues, organized jointly with the IMF, is for all practical purposes unrestricted and only subject to a registration requirement.

In order to receive accreditation to attend the concluding plenary session of the Board of Governors during the Annual Meetings of the World Bank/IMF, NGOs must engage with the World Bank and the IMF on a broad range of development operations and in policy dialogue at a local, national, and global level (World Bank 2005d). Note that since the 2005 World Bank/IMF Spring Meetings, CSOs who wish to be accredited for the Annual Meetings can send a request to the External Relations Office of the World Bank (or the IMF), which will clear the requests. The Executive Directors of the country from which the request originates have the opportunity to review the list of approved/rejected CSOs. Accreditation is deemed approved in the absence of objection from the Directors after five working days (World Bank 2005d).

The absence of clearly formulated substantive accreditation rules and rules/procedures to apply these substantive rules seriously affects the regulatory legitimacy of the involvement of NGOs with the World Bank.

3.8.   IMF

Like the World Bank, the IMF does not allow NGOs to participate in the meetings of its bodies (with the exception of the concluding plenary session of the Board of Governors during the Annual Meetings). However, the IMF engages with CSOs (including NGOs) on a global level in different ways. IMF senior staff has regular contacts with CSOs; they hold meetings, seminars and consultations with CSOs on specific issues; they request CSOs to contribute to reviews of IMF policies; and they organize, jointly with the World Bank, the annual Civil Society Dialogues. In spite of this rather significant degree of engagement, the IMF has not formulated any detailed criteria for the selection of the CSOs it engages with. Selection takes place on an *ad hoc* basis. However, the IMF *Guide for Staff Relations with Civil Society Organizations* does provide nonbinding guidelines on consultation policy and selection of CSOs to form relationships. The Guide encourages IMF staff to maintain contact with multiple and diverse sectors of civil society, including both local and transnational representatives, and to foster relationships with CSOs across the political spectrum and beyond familiar actors (IMF 2003, paras. V.F.1 and 2; section 'Legitimacy Concerns' of the Summary). The features suggested by the Guide to determine which CSOs to interact with include national legal status, the morality of their objective, efficacy, membership base, and governance style (IMF 2003, paras. V.F.1 and 2; section 'Legitimacy Concerns' of the Summary). Finally, as stated above, participation in the annual Civil Society Dialogues, organized jointly with the IBRD, is subject only to a registration requirement.

As for the World Bank, the absence of clearly formulated substantive accreditation rules (beyond the non-binding Guidelines) and rules/procedures to apply these substantive rules seriously affects the regulatory legitimacy of the involvement of NGOs with the IMF.

3.9.   WTO

Similarly to the World Bank and the IMF, the WTO engages with NGOs in a number of ways but has not formulated any detailed criteria for the selection of the NGOs it engages with. Article V:2 of the WTO Agreement provides for consultation and cooperation with NGOs *concerned with matters related to those of the WTO*. The 1996 Decision of the General Council (WTO 1996), regarding NGO involvement, does not provide for any further accreditation criteria. When the WTO was first confronted with the problem of accrediting NGOs on the occasion of the first session of the Ministerial Conference in Singapore in December 1996, the WTO Secretariat accredited all non-profit NGOs that could point to activities related to those of the WTO. The applicant-NGOs were not submitted to any further examination of their objectives, membership, institutional structure or financing. It has been suggested that such examination was beyond the resources of the WTO Secretariat.

Besides the criterion of 'WTO-related activities', the only additional accreditation criterion applied at the time was the 'non-profit character' of the NGO. Private companies and law firms were refused accreditation on this basis. This practice continued at subsequent Ministerial conferences. In fact, rather than a system of accreditation, the WTO has only a simple system of *ad hoc* registration for one event, namely the bi-annual session of the Ministerial Conference. The accreditation/registration of NGOs for the bi-annual sessions of the Ministerial Conference is basically left to the discretion of the WTO Secretariat, although the WTO General Council, of course, can address any issue concerning accreditation/registration that may arise in the run-up to a session of the Ministerial Conference.

As for the World Bank and the IMF, the absence of clearly formulated substantive accreditation rules and rules/procedures to apply these substantive rules seriously affects the regulatory legitimacy of the involvement of NGOs with the WTO.

3.10. Concluding remarks on the rules on the accreditation of NGOs

The analysis above shows that the situation with regard to substantive accreditation rules and rules/procedures for the application of these rules differs significantly among the international organizations examined. The United Nations/ECOSOC and the WHO have well-defined and elaborate substantive accreditation rules to ensure that NGOs 'add value' to their policy deliberation and decision-making processes. They also have elaborate procedural rules for deciding on whether an NGO conforms—and continues to conform—to these substantive rules. The United Nations/ECOSOC and the WHO thus *ensure* that an NGO 'adds value' and continues to do so. As a result, the involvement of the NGO concerned in the United Nations/ECOSOC and the WHO has a high degree of regulatory legitimacy. UNCTAD also has detailed substantive accreditation rules and rules/procedures for granting accreditation. However, it lacks rules/procedures for monitoring whether accredited NGOs continue to satisfy the accreditation requirements. This negatively affects the regulatory legitimacy of the involvement in UNCTAD of a given NGO. From the perspective of regulatory legitimacy, the involvement of NGOs in the UNEP and the ILO is even more problematic. Both international organizations have only a rudimentary list of requirements for accreditation, rules/procedures for granting accreditation which are bare-bone and/or are not spelled out in a legal document, and no rules/procedures for monitoring whether accredited NGOs continue to satisfy the accreditation requirements. The situation is even worse as far as the World Bank, the IMF and the WTO are concerned. These organizations have no, or only very basic, substantive accreditation rules (going beyond non-binding guidelines) and no formally established procedures for granting accreditation and subsequent monitoring. The fact that NGO involvement in these organizations is quite restricted because NGOs are not granted consultative status may explain the quasi-absence of accreditation rules and procedures. However, regulatory legitimacy depends on, and does not exist without, rules. The quasi-absence of substantive and procedural accreditation rules, therefore, makes the regulatory legitimacy of the involvement of a given NGO in the activities of the World Bank, the IMF and the WTO problematic.

4.   Conclusion

This chapter has focused on the regulatory legitimacy of NGO involvement in the policy deliberation and decision-making processes of international organizations, and in particular of the UN, UNCTAD, UNEP, the WHO, the ILO, the IBRD, the IMF and the WTO. The concept of 'regulatory legitimacy', as used in this study, refers to the degree to which the involvement of NGOs in international organizations conforms to legal rules. The inquiry above reveals a rather diffuse image. The regulatory legitimacy of NGO involvement varies strongly from one international organization to another.

The relevant legal rules on the involvement of NGOs in the policy deliberation and decision-making processes of international organizations can be divided into two categories:

1.   first, the rules defining the legal status of NGOs in those organizations, i.e., the rules providing a legal basis for the involvement of NGOs and rules setting out the various forms of this involvement; and

2.   secondly, the rules on the accreditation of NGOs by these organizations, i.e., the rules that must ensure that only NGOs that 'add value' to the policy deliberation and decision-making processes 'enjoy' specific forms of involvement and associated rights.

With regard to the first category of rules, the inquiry above shows that the constituent instrument of most of the international organizations examined provides for an explicit legal basis for NGO involvement in policy deliberation and decision-making processes. From a regulatory legitimacy perspective, this is to be applauded. However, the inquiry also reveals the *sine legem* practice of NGO involvement in the IMF and the World Bank. Notwithstanding the modest character of NGO engagement in the policy deliberation and decision-making processes of the IMF and the World Bank, the lack of an explicit legal basis is still to be deplored. The inquiry into the rules setting out the form or forms that NGO involvement may take (the binding nature and the degree of detail of these rules) and the extent to which practice conforms to these rules, shows furthermore considerable differences between the respective international organizations examined. NGO involvement within the WHO, ILO and the WTO appears to conform to the relevant rules. However, international organizations such as the United Nations, UNCTAD, UNEP, the World Bank, and the IMF engage with NGOs in forms *not* provided for, or engage with NGOs more intensively than provided for, in the relevant rules. From a regulatory legitimacy perspective, these *sine legem* and *ultra legem* practices of NGO engagement practices are troublesome. The inquiry has not revealed instances of NGO involvement *contra legem*, i.e., forms of engagement in direct violation with existing rules.

With regard to the substantive rules on accreditation and rules/procedures for the application of the substantive rules, the inquiry shows once again that there are significant differences among the international organizations examined. Only the United Nations/ECOSOC and the WHO have well-defined and elaborate substantive accreditation rules to ensure that NGOs 'add value' to the policy deliberation and decision-making processes of the international organizations concerned. They also have elaborate procedural rules for deciding on whether an NGO conforms—and continues to conform—to these substantive rules. The United Nations/ECOSOC and the WHO thus ensure that an NGO 'adds value' and continues to do so. This gives the involvement of a given NGO in policy deliberation and decision-making processes of the United Nations/ECOSOC and the WHO a high degree of regulatory legitimacy. UNCTAD has detailed substantive rules on accreditation but lacks procedural rules to monitor the continued conformity with these substantive rules. From a regulatory legitimacy perspective, the latter is unfortunate. UNEP and the ILO have only elementary substantive rules on accreditation and accreditation procedures are rudimentary, not spelled out in a legal document or plainly missing. From the perspective of the regulatory legitimacy of the involvement of a given NGO in ILO and UNEP activities, the situation is therefore unsatisfactory. The situation regarding the World Bank, the IMF and the WTO is even less satisfactory. The World Bank, the IMF and the WTO have no, or very basic accreditation rules and no formally established procedures of accreditation, let alone monitoring procedures. The fact that NGO involvement in the policy deliberation and decision-making procedures of these organizations is modest offers perhaps an explanation for this situation. However, it does not remedy the lack of regulatory legitimacy, as regulatory legitimacy depends on, and does not exist without, rules.

The overall conclusion of this chapter has to be that there is still considerable room for improvement of the regulatory legitimacy of NGO involvement in international organizations.

Chapter 6   What makes an NGO 'legitimate' in the eyes of states?

Menno T. Kamminga

1.   Introduction

Under the system of sovereign states in which we live, states serve as the gatekeepers of the status of NGOs.[1] On both the domestic and international level, they decide which NGOs may join them as participants in the public sphere. They also decide on the benefits associated with this status. At the domestic level, the principal status available to NGOs is legal personality. On the international plane its equivalent is consultative or similar status to an intergovernmental organization. While NGOs can exist without these qualifications, in practice this entails serious disadvantages. NGOs not admitted to one or both of these may even be prohibited from operating at all.

To decide whether or not an NGO qualifies for domestic legal personality or consultative or similar a status with an intergovernmental organization, states either explicitly or implicitly employ certain criteria. The term 'legitimacy' tends not to be used as a justification for these criteria. However, when deciding whether an NGO qualifies for domestic or an international legal status, states are in fact carrying out their own legitimacy test (legitimacy in this context means conformity to legal rules (see Chapter 1). The criteria employed in this test therefore, are an important element in any inquiry into the legitimacy of NGOs, particularly because much of the criticism regarding the NGOs perceived lack of legitimacy is from states.[2]

---

1   For a definition of an NGO, see Chapter 1.
2   See for example Slim (2002).

Anton Vedder et al., *NGO Involvement in International Governance and Policy*, pp. 175-195.
Printed in the Netherlands. ISBN 978 90 04 15846 7.

The purpose of this paper is to identify the criteria employed as part of these qualifying procedures. As will become apparent, two sets of criteria can be distinguished. First, there are the domestic standards used by states to decide whether an NGO deserves to be awarded domestic legal status. These standards differ from one state to another but there are certain common features. The Council of Europe has recommended some standards of good practice for states in their dealings with NGOs. Second, there are criteria employed by intergovernmental organizations to decide whether an NGO should be granted consultative or similar status. These criteria differ from one organization to another but again, there are certain common characteristics.

The limited availability of data imposes some restrictions on the scope of this chapter. Among international organizations only the Council of Europe and the Organization for Security and Co-operation in Europe (OSCE) have systematically collected information on the criteria for the domestic recognition of NGOs employed by their member states. The scope of this part of the paper is therefore limited to approximately 60 states in Europe and North America. However, because this sample includes a wide range of states in different stages of development and, with different types of regimes, this restriction should not significantly undermine the general applicability of our findings. In recent years, the Council of Europe has admitted a large number of states as members that do not have a reputation for being tolerant towards NGOs. These members include Armenia, Azerbaijan, Moldova, Russia, Serbia and Ukraine.

As regards the criteria for admission to consultative status, this chapter will be restricted to those developed by the United Nations and the Council of Europe. This is because it is generally considered that these two organizations have the most advanced procedures in respect of NGO participation in their work. They are regarded as a model by other international organizations.

The inquiry will not be limited to laws and rules but will also focus on actual governmental practice implementing these instruments as far as information on such implementation is available. As will be illustrated, actual state practice often provides a more reliable picture of states' real attitudes towards NGOs than mere 'paper' laws do.

An exclusive focus on what makes NGOs legitimate in the eye of states entails obvious limitations. After all, since many governments perceive NGOs as a threat to their own hold on power they have an ambivalent attitude towards NGOs. As an alternative to state-sponsored regulation of NGOs, attention will also be devoted to NGOs initiatives to strengthen their own legitimacy by way of self-regulation.

2.   Domestic legal personality

From the point of view of an NGO, acquisition of legal personality may be crucial because it enables it to act in its own right. An NGO with legal personality can enter into contracts and obligations independently from its members or its officers. Members and officers of such an NGO are not liable for any debts or obligations incurred by the organization (they may, of course, be individually liable for any negligence or misconduct). Moreover, an NGO with legal personality may enjoy certain benefits, such as preferential tax treatment (in some states, this may require a separate registration procedure).

The recognition process so that an NGO can acquire a legal personality under the domestic law of a state is often called 'registration'.[3] In democratic states, NGOs usually have a choice whether or not to apply for legal personality through registration. In some of these states, the acquisition of NGOs legal personality happens automatically when it is established. On the other hand, in less democratic states, NGOs may be obliged to register. In such states, NGOs that have not been registered are prohibited from carrying out any activities. Therefore, registration is a powerful tool which enables states to prevent the operation of NGOs of which they disapprove.

The competent authority for carrying out registration may be a court or a government department (e.g., the Ministry of Justice or the Ministry of the Interior). In more liberal states, such an agency does not possess a discretionary power to accept or reject an application for registration. In these cases registration is then simply an administrative process that occurs by filing a declaration in a register established for this purpose. There is often a central, publicly accessible register where information is kept on NGOs that have acquired legal personality.

Exceptionally, NGOs may also be deprived of their registration if they no longer meet the criteria for registration or if they have provided fraudulent information in their application. If registration is denied or revoked by an administrative body, there should be a possibility of appeal to an independent judicial body.

---

3   See generally: OSCE (1998). The information contained in this and the following paragraph is derived from this paper.

There are no worldwide standards specifically relating to the recognition of the legal personality of NGOs. The only relevant international standards are in three instruments adopted within the context of the Council of Europe: the European Convention on Human Rights (1950), the European Convention on the Recognition of the Legal Personality of International Non-Governmental Organisations (1986) and the Fundamental Principles on the Status of Non-Governmental Organisations in Europe (2003) which builds on the two earlier instruments. Each of these documents will be discussed in turn.

3.   European Convention on Human Rights

Under Article 11 of the European Convention on Human Rights, no restrictions may be placed on the exercise of the right to freedom of association—which includes the right to establish an NGO—'other than such as are prescribed by law and are necessary in a democratic society in the interests of national security or public safety, for the prevention of disorder or crime, for the protection of health or morals or for the protection of the rights and freedoms of others'.

While there has been considerable case law under the European Convention on Human Rights concerning the refusal of national authorities to register political parties and trade unions, there has been much less jurisprudence concerning refusals to register NGOs. In *Sidiropoulos* v. *Greece*[4] and *United Macedonian Organisation Ilinden and Others* v. *Bulgaria*[5] the Court considered complaints concerning the refusal of the authorities to register associations aiming to promote Macedonian culture and minority rights. Both Greece and Bulgaria have sizeable Macedonian minorities that strive towards greater autonomy. In its judgments, the Court pointed out that associations such as these were important to the proper functioning of democracy. Consequently, the restrictions cited above were to be interpreted restrictively and in determining whether there was a 'necessity' within the meaning of Article

---

4   European Court of Human Rights, Judgment of 10 July 1998, *Sidiropoulos and Others* v. *Greece*. http://www.echr.coe.int/echr.

5   European Court of Human Rights, Judgment of 19 April 2006, *United Macedonian Organisation Ilinden and Others* v. *Bulgaria*. http://www. echr.coe.int/echr.

11, states have only a limited margin of appreciation.[6] The Court found that in both of these cases the authorities had violated Article 11 by their refusal to register the association in question.

Article 22 of the International Covenant on Civil and Political Rights similarly provides for the right to freedom of association. But the provision has not yet generated case law clarifying its application in respect of registration of NGOs. The Human Rights Committee, the supervisory body of the Covenant, has not yet adopted a General Comment on its interpretation of Article 22.

4.   European Convention on the Recognition of the Legal Personality of NGOs

Contrary to the expectations created by its title, the European Convention on the Recognition of the Legal Personality of International Non-Governmental Organisations does not provide criteria for the recognition of NGOs either on the domestic or the international plane.[7] The Convention merely provides for the mutual recognition of NGOs that have already been recognized in one of the states parties. According to Article 2, the legal personality acquired by an NGO in the state party in which it has its headquarters must also be recognized in the other states parties. The limited usefulness of this convention is reflected in the fact that only nine: Austria, Belgium, France, Greece, Macedonia, Portugal, Slovenia, Switzerland and the United Kingdom of the 46 member states of the Council of Europe have become parties so far.

5.   Fundamental Principles on the Status of NGOs in Europe

On 16 April 2003, the Council of Europe's Committee of Ministers 'took note with appreciation' of a document entitled Fundamental Principles on the Status of Non-Governmental Organisations in Europe (herein-

---

6   European Court of Human Rights, Judgment of 10 July 1998, *Sidiropoulos and others v. Greece*, para. 40; Judgment of 19 April 2006, *United Macedonian Organisation Ilinden v Bulgaria*, para. 61.

7   European Convention on the Recognition of the International Legal Personality of International Non-Governmental Organisations, 24 April 1986, ETS No. 124, entered into force 1 January 1991.

after the Fundamental Principles).[8] The Fundamental Principles were elaborated at three 'multilateral meetings' held in Strasbourg in 2001 and 2002. Although the Fundamental Principles do not employ the term 'legitimacy', in practice they represent the most sophisticated rendition available of what the Council of Europe expects from NGOs. But in spite of their impressive title, the Fundamental Principles are not legally binding on member states. They merely 'recommend the implementation of a number of principles which should shape relevant legislation and practice'.

Even though they were not 'adopted' but merely 'taken note of' by the Committee of Ministers, the Fundamental Principles deserve to be taken seriously because they result from thorough consideration over a long period of time[9] and because they carry the support not only of member states, but also of NGOs associated with the Council of Europe. In assessing the relevance of the Fundamental Principles it should furthermore be kept in mind that membership of the Council of Europe these days includes not only West European States but also states such as Russia, Tajikistan, Azerbaijan that do not have a long tradition of being sympathetic towards NGOs. The Fundamental Principles therefore reflect the official views of a wider range of states than may be assumed at first sight.

The Fundamental Principles are ambitious because they cover all types of NGOs and are not limited to certain categories of associations. However, they seem quite realistic in terms of their general expectations. Their outset is that 'the operation of NGOs entails responsibilities as well as rights' (COE 2003a, preamble). As regards their internal structure, the Explanatory Memorandum accompanying the Fundamental Principles provides that this is 'entirely a matter for the NGO itself' (COE 2003a, para. 33. See also para. 55). There is therefore no requirement of internal democracy and NGOs do not need to be membership-based (COE 2003a, para. 3). As regards transparency and accountability, the Explanatory Memorandum states that it is 'good practice' for an NGO

---

8   Fundamental Principles on the Status of Non-Governmental Organisations in Europe, taken note of with appreciation by the Council of Europe's Committee of Ministers on 16 April 2003. https://wcd.coe.int/ViewDoc.jsp?Ref=RAP-ONG(2003)4&Sector=secCM&-Language=lanEnglish.

9   Six consultative meetings were held over a seven year period to discuss the legal status of NGOs (Explanatory Memorandum to the Fundamental Principles, para. 6).

to submit an annual report to its members on its activities and its accounts. NGOs that have received public support 'can be expected to account to the community concerning the use made of public funds' (COE 2003a, para. 66). Thoughtfully, however, the Explanatory Memorandum adds that 'reporting requirements must be tempered by other obligations relating to respect for privacy and confidentiality' (COE 2003a, para. 67). As regards supervision, the Explanatory Memorandum points out that self-regulation is the best way of ensuring responsible conduct by NGOs (COE 2003a, para. 70). No indications are given on how such self-regulation should be carried out.

Although they do not specifically say so, the Fundamental Principles seem to take the view that legitimacy of NGOs is a matter of degree. They do not take an absolutist approach. For example, Principle 3 provides that NGOs are 'usually' organisations which have a membership but this does not necessarily need to be the case. Principle 64 provides that NGOs should 'generally' have their accounts audited by an independent institution but this is not an absolute requirement.

The Fundamental Principles explicitly attempt to fill the gap left by the Convention on the Recognition of the Legal Personality of NGOs by providing criteria for the registration of NGOs. The Fundamental Principles require that registration should, in principle, be approved. This should only be refused in the case of clearly defined circumstances, for example, 'if a name has been used that is patently misleading or is not adequately distinguishable from that of an existing natural or legal person in the country concerned, or if there is an objective in the statutes which is clearly incompatible with the law' (COE 2003a, para. 31).

However, in spite of the use of the word 'only' this list of conditions is not intended to be exhaustive. According to the Explanatory Memorandum attached to the Fundamental Principles, states may lay down additional grounds for refusal in their legislation, as long as they are 'based on clear and objective considerations' (COE 2003a, para. 45). This obviously is a reference to the case law of the European Court of Human Rights. An additional ground for refusal, for example, may be that the NGO lacks the required minimum number of founding members. This number varies between states. In some states one to five founders are sufficient, in others up to 30 may be required.[10]

---

10   Bosnia and Herzegovina requires 30 founders, Romania 20 and Poland 15 (OSCE 1998, para. 6.1.1).

6.   Implementation of the Fundamental Principles

During the course of 2004, the Council of Europe submitted to its member states a detailed questionnaire on the implementation of the Fundamental Principles within their respective domestic legal orders. An analysis of the responses to this questionnaire prepared by Jeremy McBride (University of Birmingham) revealed a number of instances in which the Fundamental Principles clearly were not complied with (McBride 2005). Because only 16 out of 46 member states responded to the questionnaire it may be assumed that the real situation is even less favourable.[11]

When applying for registration, the requirement that an NGO's objectives as defined in its statutes must be compatible with the law may be one of the most difficult hurdles for an NGO to pass.[12] Mercifully, the Fundamental Principles do not require NGOs applying for registration to accept existing laws and governmental policies as they are. Of course, such a requirement would exclude most NGOs that engage in advocacy from registration. It would, for example, prevent branches of Amnesty International from registration that campaign for the abolition of the death penalty and the release of prisoners of conscience. The Fundamental Principles provide explicitly that NGOs are free to take positions contrary to stated government policies and that they may be established to pursue changes in the law (COE 2003a, para.10 and 11). However, many governments find it difficult to comply with this principle if they perceive it as a threat to their own interests.

For example, on 10 January 2006, Russian President Putin signed amendments to the Russian law on association that significantly tightened requirements for the registration of NGOs. The amendments provided the authorities with wide-ranging powers to close the offices of any foreign NGO implementing a project that does not have the aim of 'defending the constitutional system, morals, public health, rights and lawful interest of other people, guaranteeing the defence capacity and security of the state' (Human Rights Watch 2006). Following pressure

---

11   Responses to the questionnaire were received from Belgium, Bulgaria, Croatia, Germany, Hungary, Lithuania, Luxembourg, Norway, Portugal, Romania, Serbia and Montenegro, Slovenia, Sweden, Switzerland, The Former Yugoslav Republic of Montenegro and Ukraine.

12   Principle 10 provides that an NGO is free to pursue its objectives 'provided that both the objectives and the means employed are lawful'.

exerted by Western states, the amendments were later withdrawn and subjected to further consideration by the Russian Government.

Although sixteen respondents to the Council of Europe question-naire indicated that it was possible for NGOs to pursue changes in legislation in their countries, one respondent (Germany) replied that this was not possible if the NGO intended to be recognized as a chari-table organization (McBride 2005, 30). This means for example, that an environmental NGO wishing to maintain its charitable status may not campaign for changes in emission laws. Apparently, the thinking behind this policy of otherwise liberal states is that while they will not oppose granting a legal personality to NGOs that oppose their policies, they are not prepared to offer them financial advantages. Such a nar-row-minded approach which the United Kingdom also adheres to, is not compatible with Fundamental Principle 12. That Principle provides that involvement in political activities may be a relevant consideration in any decision to grant financial benefits to an NGO.

In response to the questionnaire, several member states, including Bulgaria, Croatia, Kosovo and 'The Former Yugoslav Republic of Mace-donia' reported that they impose a blanket prohibition on NGOs which support political parties in (McBride 2005, 42). This prohibition, which is clearly incompatible with Principle 12, typically reflects the concern of governments that NGOs may become too closely associated with politics and thereby pose a threat to their own hold on power. Principle 12 provides that an NGO may support a political party as long as it is 'transparent in declaring its motivation'.

In sum, the Fundamental Principles reflect governmental concern that NGOs should not become involved in politics. Involvement in poli-tics is seen as an attempt to promote changes in laws and governmental policies and support for political parties and candidates. While an NGO may not be refused registration on these grounds it may be penalised by refusing the financial benefits associated with its charitable status. Even then, several member states of the Council of Europe impose restric-tions on political activities by NGOs that go beyond what is permitted by the Fundamental Principles.

7.   Consultative or similar status

Unlike on the domestic level, there is no procedure for NGOs to gain legal personality on the international level. Moreover, unlike other non-state actors, such as intergovernmental organizations and multinational enterprises, NGOs have been unable to obtain a degree of international legal personality implicitly, for example by concluding treaties on an equal footing with states. Intergovernmental organizations including the United Nations and its agencies have concluded so-called headquarter agreements with their host states which regulate matters such as taxation, visa requirements and policing powers. Some multinational enterprises have concluded agreements with states regarding oil concessions. When such agreements are governed by international law rather than the domestic law of the state in question they resemble treaties concluded on a foot of equality between the parties. However, the only NGO which has concluded such agreements with states is the International Committee of the Red Cross (Kamminga 2002).

The closest thing to the conferral of legal personality to NGOs on the international level has been the awarding of consultative status by intergovernmental organizations. However, consultative status should not be confused with international legal personality because the benefits are quite limited and its scope is restricted to the intergovernmental organization that has awarded it. Conditions of consultative status vary from one organization to another. Nevertheless, the conditions of consultative status provide some further clues as to what makes an NGO legitimate in the eyes of states. As explained in the introduction, the scope of inquiry will be limited to the two organizations that have developed the most sophisticated systems for regulating NGO participation in their work: the United Nations and the Council of Europe.

8.   United Nations

At the United Nations, an NGO may be permitted to participate in the UN's work through four separate mechanisms: by receiving *accreditation* for a certain UN conference, by establishing *working relations* with certain UN bodies, by *associating* itself with the UN Department of Information and by acquiring *consultative status* with the UN Economic and Social Council. Of these four mechanisms, consultative status entails the most extensive privileges (Aston 2001, 943-944). Consultative status entitles an NGO to attend meetings of ECOSOC and its sub-organs such as the Commission on Human Rights, to circulate written statements at these meetings and to make oral statements with the permission of the chair (UN ECOSOC 1996, paras. 36-38). Accreditation merely allows access to a particular conference, while the acquisition of working relations or associative status amounts to little more than just being put on a mailing list of the UN department or body in question.

Article 71 of the UN Charter provides:

> The Economic and Social Council may make suitable arrangements for consultation with non-governmental organizations, which are concerned with matters within its competence. Such arrangements shall may be made with international organizations and, where appropriate, with national organizations after consultation with the members of the United Nations concerned.

It follows from this provision that consultative arrangements can only be made with the Economic and Social Council, a relatively unimportant UN organ, and not with UN organs that matter, such as the Security Council or the General Assembly. It also follows that consultative status can be obtained not only by international NGOs but also by domestic ones. Apparently, according to the founding fathers of the United Nations, an NGO does not need to derive its legitimacy from its worldwide representativity.

The 'suitable arrangements for consultation' referred to in Article 71 have been elaborated in ECOSOC Resolution 1996/31. This resolution contains, inter alia, the eligibility requirements for admission to consultative status, the rights and duties of NGOs in consultative status and the procedure for suspension or withdrawal of consultative status. Some of the criteria for the admission of an NGO to consultative status are as follows (UN ECOSOC 1996, paras. 9-13):

> [...]
>
> 9. The organization shall be of recognized standing within the particular field of its competence or of a representative character. Where there exist a number of organizations with similar objectives, interests and basic views in a given field, they may, for the purposes of consultation with the Council, form a joint committee or other body authorized to carry on such consultation for the group as a whole.
>
> 10. The organization shall have an established headquarters, with an executive officer. It shall have a democratically adopted constitution, a copy of which shall be deposited with the Secretary-General of the United Nations, and which shall provide for the determination of policy by a confer-

ence, congress or other representative body, and for an executive organ responsible to the policy-making body.

11. The organization shall have authority to speak for its members through its authorized representatives. Evidence of this authority shall be presented, if requested.

12. The organization shall have a representative structure and possess appropriate mechanisms of accountability to its members, who shall exercise effective control over its policies and actions through the exercise of voting rights or other appropriate democratic and transparent decision-making processes. Any such organization that is not established by a governmental entity or intergovernmental agreement shall be considered a nongovernmental organization for the purpose of these arrangements, including organizations that accept members designated by governmental authorities, provided that such membership does not interfere with the free expression of views of the organization.

13. The basic resources of the organization shall be derived in the main part from contributions of the national affiliates or other components or from individual members. Where voluntary contributions have been received, their amounts and donors shall be faithfully revealed to the Council Committee on Non-Governmental Organizations. Where, however, the above criterion is not fulfilled and an organization is financed from other sources, it must explain to the satisfaction of the Committee its reasons for not meeting the requirements laid down in this paragraph. Any financial contribution or other support, direct or indirect, from a Government to the organization shall be openly declared to the Committee through the Secretary-General and fully recorded in the financial and other records of the organization and shall be devoted to purposes in accordance with the aims of the United Nations.
[...]

The requirement of a democratic internal structure is remarkable among these criteria. Only a handful of the more than 2700 NGOs currently in consultative status with ECOSOC could be said to meet this requirement. Most NGOs are not like Amnesty International with its extensive decision-making structure involving more than one million members. Members and donors of such NGOs have no voting rights, and the only way in which they can hold the organization's leadership accountable is by discontinuing their membership or their donations. However, apparently states do not consider the absence of internal democracy and accountability important enough grounds for refusing consultative status. This makes sense because many NGOs in consultative status with ECOSOC play a useful role because of their technical expertise and not because they represent a large segment of public opinion. This shows that the decision-making process on consultative status is politicized, and that it is not a matter of simply applying the criteria.

9.   Withdrawal and suspension of UN consultative status

When trying to find out what states consider 'legitimate' NGO activity the practice of ECOSOC with regard to withdrawal and suspension of consultative status is of considerable interest. ECOSOC Resolution 1996/31 provides that consultative status can be suspended for up to three years or even withdrawn if an NGO engages in 'a pattern of acts contrary to the purposes and principles of the Charter of the United Nations including unsubstantiated or politically motivated attacks against Member States of the United Nations incompatible with those principles and purposes' (UN ECOSOC 1996, para. 57). Pursuant to this provision, several NGOs have had their consultative status suspended for periods of up to three years. ECOSOC's practice in this field and its Committee on Non-Governmental Organizations give a good indication of the sensitivities involved.

In 1994 ECOSOC for the first time suspended the status of an NGO. The International Lesbian and Gay Association was suspended after the United States had complained that one of the association's affiliates had advocated paedophilia (ECOSOC Res. 1994/50). This appears to have opened Pandora's Box. In 1999, Christian Solidarity International had its consultative status revoked at the insistence of Sudan because it had been represented by an alleged Sudanese rebel leader (UN ECOSOC 1999). In 2000, ECOSOC suspended the consultative status of the International Council for the Associations for Peace in the Continents for having made critical statements about Cuba (Council Decision of 18 October 2000). In 2003, ECOSOC suspended the consultative status of Reporters Without Borders because members of the organization had staged a protest against the decision of the Commission on Human Rights to let a Libyan representative chair the Commission. In 2004, the Indian movement Tupaj Amaru had its consultative status suspended for having staged an anti-American demonstration at a session of the Commission on Human Rights (UN ECOSOC 2004b).

It follows that NGOs in consultative or similar status with ECOSOC are currently being suspended at an increasing pace. The decision-making process has become highly politicized. The United States has joined some notoriously repressive states in calling for sanctions against NGOs that are supposed to have misbehaved. In the process, little attention is being paid to the question whether an attack was indeed unsubstantiated or politically motivated as required by ECOSOC Resolution 1996/31. It appears to be merely a question of gathering the necessary votes. While at ECOSOC decisions are generally taken by consensus, decisions on suspension of NGOs are invariably taken by a majority vote (and invariably approved by a small majority).

It is widely recognized that current practice concerning civil society participation in UN affairs is unsatisfactory. In response to criticisms, in 2003 the UN Secretary-General appointed a Panel of Eminent Persons to review existing practices concerning access to, and participation of, civil society in UN deliberations. The subsequent Cardoso Report—named after the Panel's chair, Fernando Henrique Cardoso, former President of Brazil—agreed that existing mechanisms for accreditation were politicized, time-consuming and expensive. It proposed streamlining and de-politicizing the system by the establishment of a single United Nations accreditation process under the aegis of the U.N. General Assembly. It also suggested various mechanisms to speed up the process and reduce political interference but, significantly, it did not propose new criteria for the accreditation of NGOs (UN General Assembly 2004, paras. 120-138). Apparently, this was considered too hot a potato to touch. No changes have been introduced into the system since the publication of the report.

10.   Council of Europe

The Council of Europe has recently revised its system of consultative status for International Non-Governmental Organizations (INGOs) (unlike the UN, the Council of Europe excludes purely domestic organizations). The system is henceforth called participatory status (COE 2003b).[13] All INGOs that previously enjoyed consultative status have

---

13   This system governing participatory status has replaced the old system of consultative status pursuant to Resolution (98) 38. There is also a system

been given participatory status. Participatory status may be granted to
INGOs:

1. which are particularly representative in the field(s) of their compe-
    tence, fields of action shared by the Council of Europe;[14]
2. which are represented at European level, that is to say which have
    members in a significant number of countries throughout greater
    Europe;
3. which are able, through their work, to support the achievement of
    that closer unity mentioned in Article 1 of the Council of Europe's
    Statute;[15]
4. are capable of contributing to and participating actively in Council
    of Europe deliberations and activities;
5. which are able to make known the work of the Council of Europe
    among European citizens.

These rules are considerably less bureaucratic and much easier to follow
than those of the United Nations. The legitimacy test carried out on the
basis of these rules is not very demanding. It is restricted to representativity both in terms of competence and in terms of membership. There is
no penalty provision threatening INGOs that engage in unsubstantiated
attacks with withdrawal of their status. Unlike the United Nations, the
decision-making process is entirely depoliticized because it is carried
out by the civil servants acting under the responsibility of the Council of
Europe's Secretary-General and not by the member states themselves.

Nevertheless, the Council of Europe clearly means business. Less
than a year after the new system was introduced the Secretary-General
announced that 30 INGOs had been deprived of their participatory status because they had failed to comply with their reporting requirements
(COE 2004).

---

of partnership for national NGOs with less demanding criteria for admission. See COE (2003c).

14   This apparently means that participatory status may be granted to the
      most important NGOs that are working on topics that are within the com-
      petence of the Council of Europe.

15   Art. 1(a) of the Statute of the Council of Europe provides: 'The aim of the
      Council of Europe is to achieve a greater unity between its members for
      the purpose of safeguarding and realising the ideals and principles which
      are their common heritage and facilitating their economic and social
      progress.'

11.   A complementary approach: Self-regulation by NGOs

The assumption that states are the best judges of the legitimacy of NGOs has obvious flaws. States are driven by self-interest and their main concern is that NGOs shall not threaten them politically. A complementary approach to standard-setting by states and by intergovernmental organizations is self-regulation by NGOs. Such an approach deserves serious consideration. While self-regulation by multinational enterprises raises immediate and often well-founded suspicions, self-regulation by NGOs should not trigger the same warning signs because NGOs are in the business of promoting the public interest rather than pursuing their private interests. They also tend to be acutely aware that their moral authority depends on their credibility, and thus on their adherence to certain minimum standards of proper conduct.

The underlying assumption of the Fundamental Principles on the Status of NGOs in Europe is that more detailed standard-setting and supervision of compliance with those standards can best be undertaken through self-regulation by NGOs (Explanatory Memorandum to Fundamental Principles, para. 70). Although attempts have been made to draft such codes of conduct for NGOs on a generalized basis, the NGOs themselves appear to feel that it is impossible to devise meaningful standards that apply to each and every NGO. A more realistic approach would be to draft codes of conduct for NGOs working on a particular issue.

12.   Codes of conduct

An example of a 'sectoral' code of conduct is the code adopted in 1995 by a group of NGOs working in the field of disaster relief. The group included: Caritas Internationalis, Catholic Relief Services, The International Federation of Red Cross and Red Crescent Societies, International Save the Children Alliance, Lutheran World Federation, Oxfam, The World Council of Churches, and the International Committee of the Red Cross (ICRC 1994). They set out a code of conduct consisting of the following 10 principles:

1. The Humanitarian imperative comes first.[16]
2. Aid is given regardless of the race, creed or nationality of the recipients and without adverse distinction of any kind. Aid priorities are calculated on the basis of need alone.
3. Aid will not be used to further a particular or religious standpoint.
4. We shall endeavour not to act as instruments of government foreign policy.
5. We shall respect culture and custom.
6. We will attempt to build disaster response on local capacities.
7. Ways shall be found to involve programme beneficiaries in the management of relief aid.
8. Relief aid must strive to reduce future vulnerabilities to disaster as well as meeting basic needs.
9. We hold ourselves accountable to both those we seek to assist and those from whom we accept resources.
10. In our information, publicity and advertising activities, we shall recognize disaster victims as dignified humans, not hopeless objects.

Note that the nature of these standards differs substantially from the ones developed by states. They focus on NGO activities only. They do not address questions of internal structure or funding, but this makes sense because of the large variety of relief organizations. There is no mechanism to supervise the implementation of these principles but that does not appear to be a serious omission in view of the character of the principles.

Apparently, NGOs involved in other, more controversial areas than relief, such as advocacy, have not adopted similar collective codes of conduct.

12.   Coalition building

An entirely different method to increase NGO legitimacy is coalition building around certain issues. Examples of successful NGO coalitions (termed 'caucus' in the United States) are the International Campaign

---

16   The principles explain that this means that the organizations primary motivation is to alleviate human suffering amongst those least able to withstand the stress caused by disaster.

to Ban Landmines (now covering more than 1400 NGOs) (Williams and Goose 1998, 20) and the Coalition for the International Criminal Court (now covering more than 2000 NGOs) (Pace 1999, 189-211). These coalitions exercised a decisive influence on both the wording and the adoption of the Convention against Landmines[17] and the Statute of the International Criminal Court respectively.[18]

Such NGO coalitions lack an internal code of conduct and have no admission requirements. Any NGO wishing to join is welcome to do so. As a result, individual NGOs do not improve their legitimacy by joining such a coalition. On the other hand, coalitions such as those referred to above enjoy a high degree of (social) legitimacy. This is based on the extension of their membership (both geographically and in terms of expertise) and the quality of the positions they adopt. Positions adopted by NGO coalitions tend to be carefully negotiated and non-partisan. Arguably, such coalitions also contribute significantly to the legitimacy of decision-making by intergovernmental gatherings. It is unlikely that the Convention against Landmines and the Statute of the International Criminal Court would have enjoyed the impact and the large number of ratifications without the continuing support of their respective NGO coalitions.

13.   Conclusions

The governmental stamp of approval awarded to NGOs has different labels. Domestically, it may be called 'registration', at the international level it may be called 'accreditation', 'participatory status', or 'consultative status'. 'Registration' is the procedure by which an NGO may acquire domestic legal personality in a particular country thus enabling it to act in its own right. There is no comparable procedure for an NGO to obtain international legal personality. 'Accreditation' is the procedure for an NGO to gain permission to attend an intergovernmental conference. A 'Participatory' or 'consultative' status entitles an NGO to circulate written documents and make oral statements at meetings of certain organs of intergovernmental organizations. For the purposes of

---

17   Convention on the Prohibition of the Use, Stockpiling, Production, and Transfer of Anti-Personnel Mines and on their Destruction, Oslo, 18 September 1997, 36 ILM 1507.

18   Statute of the International Criminal Court, Rome, 17 July 1998, 37 ILM 999.

identifying the legitimacy criteria employed by states the distinctions between these labels have little relevance.

The criteria by which states decide which NGOs may have access to domestic legal personality or status with an intergovernmental organization do not necessarily coincide with the concept of 'legitimacy' as perceived by the general public. Nevertheless, as a starting point for an inquiry into the legitimacy of NGOs, the conditions that states impose on NGOs as part of these admission procedures provide an interesting point of departure.

The official criteria by which states profess to judge the legitimacy of NGOs—as for example in the Fundamental Principles on the Status of Non-Governmental Organisations in Europe—are not excessively demanding. They can be summarized as follows; NGOs are free to determine their own internal structure, they are not required to be internally democratic or membership-based. It is true that the criteria for UN consultative status require that NGOs must have a system of internal democracy and accountability but in UN practice, these criteria are not insisted upon. There is appreciation for transparency of finances and membership but it is understood that this may be subject to necessary restrictions. Self-regulation and self-supervision by NGOs is encouraged.

On paper states accept, be it rather reluctantly and sometimes at the expense of their charitable status, that NGOs may campaign for changes in legislation and in governmental policies. However, in so doing NGOs may not engage in what governments perceive as unsubstantiated or politically motivated attacks. In other words, NGOs may not discard their nongovernmental identities and turn into political parties or liberation movements that pose a direct challenge to governmental power. Such NGO involvement in politics is what states are most concerned about. When they perceive that their own power is threatened, governments may in fact be considerably less forthcoming than is suggested by the relevant international standards.

Of course, this must not be read as a proposal to NGOs wishing to improve their own legitimacy to attempt to comply lock, stock, and barrel with international standards laid down by states, such as those contained in the Fundamental Principles on the Status of Non-Governmental Organisations in Europe. It goes without saying that states are not at all the best judges of the legitimacy of NGOs, since they are motivated primarily by self-interest and are reluctant to cede power and influence to NGOs that could pose a threat to their own power and influence.

At the United Nations, the double standards applicable to states and to NGOs are striking. Contorted requirements are imposed on NGOs before they can acquire the very limited privileges associated with consultative status. One misstep may be sufficient for deprivation of their consultative status. But states only need to comply with the simple requirement that they are peace-loving and able and willing to carry out the obligations of the UN Charter in order to acquire the full rights associated with UN membership (UN Charter, Art. 4). Even if they subsequently turn out to be aggressors, they are unlikely to loose their membership.

It could be argued *a contrario* that NGOs that are supposed to function as a counterbalance to state power cannot, by definition, enjoy public trust if they attempt to meet the legitimacy standards devised by states. In fact, NGOs that have been refused registration by repressive governments may actually enjoy more legitimacy in the eyes of the public than officially registered NGOs.[19] However, this argument does not apply to intergovernmental organizations. NGOs granted consultative status with the United Nations or the Council of Europe tend to proudly display this achievement in their letterheads. NGOs themselves apparently regard such status as contributing to their legitimacy. In the case of the United Nations this may be connected to the fact that the organization conferring the status is the main global intergovernmental organization. In the case of the Council of Europe this may be attributed to the fact that the Council's approval procedure is comparatively objective and transparent.

This paper therefore should not be seen as a plea for states to become the ultimate judges of the legitimacy of NGOs. Should regulation be necessary to help ensure NGOs conduct themselves more responsibly, then the NGOs are in a far better position to undertake that task. Remarkably, NGOs, in particular NGOs engaged in advocacy, have so far, not raised to the challenge. Codes of conduct developed by NGOs to provide standards to judge their own conduct are rare. The method of establishing NGO coalitions is used more frequently. Although not explicitly created to strengthen the collective legitimacy of the participating NGOs they do have this impact. Nevertheless, this mechanism can only be used under appropriate circumstances.

---

19   The draft-report ICHRP (2003) cites the example of human rights NGOs in Mauritania in the 1990s.

The question therefore is: How long can NGOs afford to turn a blind eye to the nagging demand that they improve their legitimacy while at the same time run the increasing risk that states will take the initiative to impose their own criteria on them?

Chapter 7   Towards a defensible conceptualization of the legitimacy of NGOs

*Anton Vedder**

1.   Introduction

The legitimacy of the involvement of NGOs in international govern-ance and policy should be a subject of discussion for the various rea-sons mentioned in Chapter 1. This book aims at drawing the chalk lines within which the debate on the legitimacy of NGOs should ideally take place. It does so by trying to develop a concept of legitimacy that simul-taneously does justice to three types of demands: (1) the practical char-acteristics and—when compared with national states—restrictions of NGOs; (2) the requirements that come with the social, legal, and moral significance of NGOs as powerful players in the international arena; and (3) the basic criteria that are usually applied when theories and accounts of concepts are assessed, such as coherence, consistency, simplicity, and elegance.

In Chapter 1, stipulations of legitimacy and familiar notions were given. In the quest for a defensible account of legitimacy of NGOs, an elementary and broad conception of legitimacy encompassing social, regulatory and moral dimensions was taken as a starting point. The no-tion was borrowed from political theories of the legitimacy of (national) state authorities. In Chapter 1, attention was also paid to the somewhat troublesome and murky route towards the best ways of adapting an existing technical term to new phenomena and developments. In this chapter, this journey will, for the time being, be completed by confront-

*   The author is indebted to Iain Atack (University of Dublin, Trinity College) and Veit Bader (University of Amsterdam) for their valuable comments and suggestions.

Anton Vedder et al., *NGO Involvement in International Governance and Policy*, pp. 197-211. Printed in the Netherlands. ISBN 978 90 04 15846 7.

ing the broad three-dimensional conception of legitimacy with a series of questions that are prompted by the data and conclusions described in Chapters 2 to 6, on the one hand, and by current discussions on the legitimacy of state authorities and the global governance order as a whole, on the other. The issues to be discussed concern the difference between (primarily) normative and descriptive approaches to the legitimacy notion—including a reflection on the mutual relationships between the moral and the other dimensions of legitimacy—the specification of the criteria within the three dimensions, the specific character of legitimacy as a criterion, and the normative content layer of legitimacy in respect of the presumed global moral pluralism. The chapter will be concluded with the presentation of what may be considered a defensible and feasible concept of NGO legitimacy.

2.   Normative versus empirical or legal conceptions of legitimacy

With regard to the debate on the legitimacy of states and global governance structures as a whole, a distinction is sometimes made between empirical and normative approaches to legitimacy (Steffek 2003; see also Bader 1989). Normative approaches refer to ideals (Held 1999; Buchanan 2004), empirical approaches focus on the motives for and causes of the perception of organizations as legitimate (Hurd 1999; Franck 1988; 1995; Bodansky 1999; Hurrell 2002; Clark 2003). Empirical approaches are often inspired by the German sociologist Max Weber (1864-1920). Weber emphasized the importance of the belief in legitimacy—in addition to custom, societal and personal advantage, and ideal motives—as a necessary element for the legitimacy of an authority (Weber 1978, 213). Modern proponents of the empirical conception tend to restrict legitimacy to the criterion of being believed to be legitimate by a relevant reference group.

The terminology used in the distinction is a little awkward. In both the normative and the empirical approach, legitimacy is pictured as a criterion or a set of criteria preferably to be met by organizations or governance structures. In a way, therefore, both are ultimately normative. Nonetheless, there is an important difference between the approaches behind each of the two conceptions.

The difference is that proponents of an empirical view are not intrinsically interested in moral or other normative criteria for the acceptance of an organization or regime. Their focus is on how the perception of legitimacy is actually brought about: psychological, sociological, and political mechanisms. The moral quality of those mechanisms is not their first concern; it may be viewed as a means for bringing about acceptance, but it need not be. Ultimately, the advocates of the empirical view are concerned with legitimacy as a practical phenomenon for reasons of political efficiency and effectiveness. Of course, political efficiency and effectiveness may also be termed ideals, but they need not be morally desirable ones. In this, the advocates of the empirical view are far apart from the proponents of the normative conception. The latter are interested in acceptance, agreement, and, legality to the extent that these conditions meet moral standards. Whereas proponents of the empirical conception can be said to restrict their notion of legitimacy to the dimension of public support and representation or, sometimes, legality, the proponents of the normative conception can be said to embrace the three-dimensional concept while ranking the normative dimension as prioritary.

Serious attempts to bridge the gap between the two approaches have been made by Beetham, on the one hand, and Habermas and Steffek on the other. It may be fruitful for the discussion of NGO legitimacy to have a closer look at their perspectives. Beetham (1991) enriched the Weberian view by adding legality and morality. In Beetham's view, authority is legitimate if it is believed to be legitimate on the basis of its acting in accordance with rules and procedures (legality) that in turn are based on shared moral values and norms (morality). Beetham's conception inspired the broad three-dimensional conception of legitimacy that was chosen as a tentative definition framework for legitimacy in the studies presented in this book, but the differences should not be overlooked. Beetham's conception is a somewhat ambiguous attempt to turn Weber's view into a coherent conception by making the belief in legitimacy ultimately dependent on commonly held moral norms and values via formalized norms and procedures. It is clearly Beetham's intention to shield the Weberian view from accusations of arbitrariness. He even emphasizes that the connection between the belief in legitimacy and shared moral values and norms must be a conceptual connection, not (merely) a psychological one. Thus, he excludes manipulation and coercion as possible motivators of the belief in legitimacy.

Beetham's view has two interesting features. The first is his attempt to map out the mutual relationships between the three elements of legitimacy. The second is his contention about the hierarchical order between the moral and the other elements. Nevertheless, his conception has serious drawbacks, certainly for the purposes of this book.

First—and this is the case with applications of the conception to governmental authorities as well as to NGOs—there is a moral drawback. The conception remains substantially empirical by referring to commonly held moral values and norms. The problem of this reference lies in its traces of a communitarian perspective. A communitarian perspective is a meta-ethical view in which morality is dependent on a specific culture or community so that the validity of the norms is restricted to the domain of that culture or community. Since such a view lacks external justifications and assessment options, the contents of the agreed moral norms and values are arbitrary—at least from an outsider's perspective that is characteristic of a non-relativistic view. The shared moral norms and values are valid within the community or culture involved, but not necessarily valid or even morally acceptable for others or from the perspective of an impartial observer. The stance of the impartial observer is the vantage point that is typical of the traditional universalistic Kantian and utilitarian outlooks. To put it bluntly, in Beetham's view—and this would apply to most empirical conceptions of legitimacy—a government of crooks could still be legitimate, when it is believed to be so by a population of citizens who share their government's vicious moral framework.

Of course, it is not completely silly to use the term legitimacy in this way, for it shows the importance of the congruence between the norms and values by which authorities act and the norms and values by which their supporters live. It cannot be denied, however, that using the term in this way is at least a trifle confusing. For that reason it would not be very helpful to use the term to assess candidates rising to become new actors in global governance, such as NGOs.

Second, Beetham's persistence in clinging to the element of public support and representation that is so characteristic of the empirical conception is extremely problematic for NGOs. As became clear from the interviews with NGOs and their stakeholders (Chapter 2), it is very difficult for NGOs to determine with which persons, groups, and organizations they have some sort of representational or supportive relationship. Who exactly are the relevant stakeholders: workers, members, supporters, beneficiaries, affiliated organizations, or all? How can the very different relationships of each of these groups with the NGO and its activities be understood? Should the potentially highly divergent purposes and objectives of these groups be taken into account? These questions demonstrate that it is very difficult to weigh and estimate the importance of the degree of acceptance by the groups involved.

Third, the communitarianism or moral relativism inherent in Beetham's emphasis on shared norms and values is extremely problematic with regard to NGOs. Not only is it very difficult to establish the exact reference group that should be involved, it is also difficult to detect common ground between all the groups involved. For example, the aims and purposes of an NGO may frequently clash with those of local governments and even large parts of the population affected. Should a human rights NGO that monitors women's rights in a community where women are oppressed not be considered legitimate? Again, especially with regard to internationally operating NGOs, it does not seem to be very realistic to assume that moral values and norms shared by workers, members, supporters, beneficiaries, and other stakeholders, such as companies and governments, can be accurately identified.

The problems issuing from Beetham's insistence on actually shared moral values and norms may to a certain extent be avoided by what could be called the Habermas-Steffek approach. In an attempt to challenge much of the existing literature on the legitimacy of international governance structures that regards a democracy deficit a priori as a core problem, Jens Steffek (2003) tries to deliver a new theoretical approach to the legitimation problems of contemporary international institutions. He tries to make clear that legitimacy of governance beyond the state to a great extent rests on rational assent and conviction. Leaning heavily on Weber and Habermas (Habermas 1979; 1987; 1988; 1996), he tries to explain how legitimacy and support can be received through the use of good justification. According to Habermas (1996, 496), the consensus which brings about legitimacy is a proposition to which all parties could assent in principle. Steffek presents a discourse approach to the study of legitimacy of governance beyond the democratic state, starting from the empirical question of how international organizations legitimate their own activities and how they create perceptions of legitimacy in the absence of democratic participation and control. In essence, he claims that 'the legitimacy of international governance hinges upon popular assent to the justifications of its goals, principles and procedures' (Steffek 2003).

What is won with the Habermas-Steffek approach in comparison with Beetham's perspective, is of course the absence of a requirement of actual agreement, a requirement that many internationally operating NGOs would find very difficult to meet. Nonetheless, Habermas and

Steffek regard assent from the parties concerned still as one of the conditions for legitimacy, and it is not very clear what exactly this means. For one thing, Steffek seems to give more empirical content to this criterion than Habermas does. While Habermas refers expressly to a virtual rational assent (in the sense of an assent that could be given in principle), Steffek, on some occasions, even suggests that he is thinking of actual assent.[1] For this reason, the application of Habermas' approach to NGOs is less probelematic than Steffek's. Unfortunately, however, Habermas, is not very clear about what exactly he means with the parties involved that should be able to assent, or about what it means that they should in principle be willing to assent. The formulation allows of a strict and a broad interpretation. The strict interpretation would be that the parties involved should be able to assent on the basis of their particular views and aims. This interpretation is still problematic for many NGOs because of the broad variety of stakeholders and the broad range of disparate views, aims, and characteristics. The broad interpretation would be at some remove from the empirical conception. It would hold that every party possibly affected or involved ought to be able to assent, not on the basis of its particular aims but by temporarily discarding its particular views and aims. In the broad version, the question is no longer whether the parties actually give their assent. Rather, the real question is whether (the justifications of) the goals, principles, and procedures of an NGO can be assented to by any impartial, rational person, if he would fully understand both the proposition and its justification. In fact, this version comes very close to the idea that a rational, impartial spectator should be able to assent. Also, the people in what Rawls terms the original position are not far off (Rawls 1971). It would appear then that in the first, strict interpretation, the requirement of actual agreement cannot function as a necessary condition for NGOs to be legitimate. In the broad interpretation, however, it can.

The argument so far makes clear that representation and public support as such cannot be necessary conditions for the legitimacy of NGOs. It also suggests that the definition of NGO legitimacy must hinge on a normative condition, not an empirical one. The consensus or compliance on which the legitimacy rests is not empirical or practical,

---

1   Remarkably, Anna-Karin Lindblom (2005, 28), who discusses the contribution of NGOs to the legitimacy of international law, seems to believe that Habermas actually requires real and practical individual assent from all individuals involved.

but hypothetical. This condition, furthermore, is not about values and norms on which only persons from a particular community or culture agree. It is about norms and values that could in principle be shared by any impartial, rational person, and therefore by all. This does not mean that actual agreement or empirically measurable assent is of no importance to the legitimacy of NGOs. Actual agreement can be an empirical indicator of legitimacy, but it does not necessarily need to be. This is why actual agreement and claims for representation and public support should always be tested against norms and values.

A very similar argument can be developed in response to the question whether legitimacy should be considered a primarily legal notion. Although lawful deployment of activities and legal status of an organization can be empirical signs of its legitimacy, ultimately the question is whether the laws involved conform to values and norms to which a rational, impartial person could assent. An NGO that does not act in complete accordance with the laws of a particular country, need not merely for that reason be illegitimate. The observation that it does not can be a sign of defective legitimacy, for instance, when the laws of the country can be assumed to be just. In countries where the law can be assumed to be unjust, the organization's legitimacy need not be compromised. The same holds true for the criteria of legal status and accreditation extensively treated in Chapters 5 and 6. Whether these add to the legitimacy of the NGO ultimately depends on the moral quality of the conditions attaching to the status. From this perspective, it is also perfectly understandable that some NGOs stay aloof from affiliations and accreditations with other international entities in order to avoid the appearance of bias and prejudice.

3.   Reconsidering the three legitimacy dimensions

As was made clear in Chapters 2 and 3, NGOs and their stakeholders, when asked what makes NGOs legitimate, refer to a broad range of sources of legitimacy, from an organization's aims, mission and values, its efficiency and effectivity, to the number of its members and donors. In Chapter 3, it was argued that none of these sources can be categorized as unequivocally and uniquely belonging to one of the dimensions of legitimacy. Some of the sources belong directly or indirectly to more than one dimension. Nonetheless, it is evident that, by and large, all of the sources are covered by the three dimensions. Here is a first categorization:

- Regulatory dimension: references to international law, accreditations, annual reports, financial statistics, audit reports, clear eligibility requirements for support (supervision by steering committees);
- Social dimension: references to grassroots, number of members, references to powerful or knowledgeable organizations, donations by governments, donations by companies;
- Moral dimension: aims, mission and values, efficiency and earlier successes (effectiveness), reliability.

In Chapter 3, it was also pointed out that some sources or legitimacy referred to in the interviews and in the analysis of websites cannot be grouped neatly under a single dimension of the tentative legitimacy concept. Reference to international law (mostly basic international law and human rights) is often made not merely to stress the legality of an organization's activities, but also to show the compliance of the organization's mission with broadly shared basic moral values and norms. These values and norms are then assumed to be embodied in, for instance, human rights. For that reason, references to international law may also be interpreted as constituting a source that belongs to the moral dimension. In addition, the instrumental value of some of the sources covered by the regulatory and the social dimensions for other sources of legitimacy belonging either to the same or to another dimension is sometimes believed to be of more importance than their own intrinsic significance. For instance, accreditations, connections with grassroots organizations, and even donations by governments and companies, are often not mentioned as directly contributing to an organization's legitimacy. They are referred to as (indirect) signs of the authority, expertise, trustworthiness, and credibility. These are qualities which the organization can be assumed to possess, for example because of its correct behaviour, its efficiency and effectiveness, or its role in the realization of certain ideals.

One group of sources of legitimacy deserves special attention because it plays an important role in the (sparse) literature on NGO legitimacy: effectiveness and credibility. These criteria will be referred to as performance criteria. With regard to NGOs focused on bringing about changes in the world directly (e.g., aid organizations, organizations aiming at the protection of the environment by buying and maintaining territories, etc.), effectiveness is often mentioned as an important source of legitimacy. With regard to NGOs focusing on advocacy, reference is often made to credibility as an additional factor or as an even more important factor than effectiveness.

In the categorization given above, performance criteria belong to the moral dimension, because they can be easily seen to coincide with efficiency, past performance, and reliability. Of course, here too, overlaps may be detected with, for example, the regulatory dimension, as grass-root connections can contribute to expertise and reliability, whereas legal status and accreditation can contribute to efficiency and effectiveness and function as signs of credibility.

Here it seems fit to draw attention once more to a distinction made in Chapter 1 between procedural and substantive criteria. Substantive criteria refer to the degree to which an individual or an organization conforms to certain values and ideals, such as respect for human rights, animal well-being, protection of the environment, assistance of the needy and the poor, etc. Procedural criteria refer to the formal aspects of the decision-making procedures of the individuals or the organizations involved.[2] The items in the social and regulatory dimensions are of a primarily procedural character. Issues they address may include the following. Does a decision that will initialize an activity rest on the consent of all people involved? Are the procedures for decisions and policies transparent and can they be checked? Does an NGO have a legal status under national law? Has an NGO successfully passed the accreditation procedures of an international organization? Only the morally normative dimension includes substantive criteria such as the requirement that the actions of the organization involved be justified in terms of values and norms with specific content. As was already noted in Chapter 1, however, the morally normative dimension is not restricted to substantive criteria. It can also contain criteria of responsibility and accountability that are not completely reducible to substantive criteria. In addition, it can occasion the application of procedural criteria that may belong to the social and regulatory dimensions. So, for instance, in order to show that it adheres to (in principle) universally acceptable substantive norms and values, an NGO may strive for transparency and accountability by producing annual reports, gathering public support, and acquiring legal status or accreditation. This, however, does not mean that transparency, formal accountability, public support, democratic decision stuctures, or a status with an international organization are necessary conditions for NGOs to be legitimate, as suggested by Scholte (2004, 230-232). Condi-

---

2   Note that Atack (1999) uses these terms in a different way.

tions such as these may be relevant to the legitimacy of NGOs that are somehow involved in new governance arrangements and participate in public political decision-making, implementation of public policy, and control. They may also be relevant to NGOs that are active in civil society as aid organizations and organizations raising awareness among the public, but they cannot be necessary conditions for the legitimacy of these organizations, since these conditions can conflict with or even nullify their effectiveness and credibility (see also Section 4).[3]

The distinction between procedural and substantive criteria sheds new light on the sources of legitimacy often grouped under performance: efficiency, effectivity, and reliability. Many authors stress the importance of performance for the legitimacy of NGOs.[4] Most of them seem to assume readily that all organizations that refer to themselves as NGOs embrace ideals that could be asserted by almost everyone. Somehow, they seem to overlook the possibility that an NGO's mission may be inconsistent or incoherent, or that an NGO might advocate ideals that individually and as such would be perfectly acceptable, but may become questionable when combined with a despicable overarching ideal. That possibility, however, suggests that performance must not be regarded as a sufficient or even a necessary condition for legitimacy. Regarding NGOs driven by detestable ideals, the world would be much better off with ineffectivity and inefficiency. Performance can only be considered to contribute to the legitimacy of an NGO when the NGO involved is driven by acceptable ideals.

Should performance be considered a necessary condition for legitimacy? Performance of NGOs is very difficult to measure (Landman 2004). Clearly, however, performance is important. It shows that the mission of an NGO is more than a set of hollow phrases. This must not only be taken to mean that NGOs must show to be effective with regard to their main objectives. Equally important is the coherent implementation of the norms which the NGO claims to adhere to within its organizational structure and the manner in which it deploys its activities.[5] At this point, it may be useful to recall Steffek's conception of legitimacy.

---

3   The author is grateful to Veit Bader (University of Amsterdam) for his emphasis on the need for clarification of this point.

4   So, for instance, Edwards (1999), Edwards and Zadek (2003), and Hudson (2000).

5   In this context, Hudson (2000) makes an interesting point in his discussion of chains of legitimacy: an organization must embody its mission not

Steffek defines the core of legitimacy as popular assent to the justifications of an organization's goals, principles, and procedures. In doing so, he misses an important point: legitimacy is not merely about the justifiability of an organization's goals, principles, and procedures; it is also about the extent to which organizations embody and actually realize their goals and aspirations. A rational, impartial observer should not only be convinced of the acceptability of an NGO's values and norms; he should also be able to see that these norms and values are fully integrated into the organization's structures and activities.

4.   The specific character of legitimacy as a criterion

Legitimacy of NGOs is a multi-dimensional, multi-layered notion. Many of the criteria overlap; some relate to others in an instrumental way, some are implementations of others, yet others are indicators that other criteria have—at least to a certain extent—been fulfilled. Thus far, it has been argued that the criteria of the moral dimension can be considered logically primordial. The criteria of the regulatory and social dimensions depend on these fundamental criteria in the sense that the latter must be met before the criteria of the other two dimensions can come into play. The criteria of the moral dimension boil down to the requirements that an NGO's values and norms should be acceptable in principle for all and that those acceptable values and norms are integrated as fully as possible into the NGO's organizational structures and activities.

Attributing primordial status to the moral criteria does not exclude the possibility of conflicts and inherent tensions between the different criteria of the moral dimension or between the criteria of the different dimensions. As will be shown in this section, deficiencies with regard to one criterion can and should sometimes be compensated through compliance with other criteria. Similarly, concrete circumstances do not always allow an NGO to live up to the sometimes opposing requirements of the different criteria. In such circumstances, familiarity with the particularities of the situation, careful practical judgement, and readiness to negotiate substantial trade-offs are called for (compare the approach of Bader and Engelen 2003).

---

only by pointing to the concrete output of its actions but also by explicating in what other ways it implements its mission.

Now the following questions should be addressed. What kind of standard or criterion exactly is applied to an NGO when its legitimacy is examined? Is legitimacy an all-or-nothing concept, or does it allow of degrees? Should legitimacy be viewed as a threshold concept in the sense that it allows a clear line to be drawn between NGOs that meet the criteria of legitimacy to a satisfactory extent and those that clearly do not?

These questions bear the traces of a rather absolutist attitude to the issue of legitimacy, suggesting that the legitimacy of NGOs can be determined regardless of the concrete circumstances. It is doubtful whether such a detached perspective will ever be feasible. The criteria for legitimacy are so subtle and complicated, their mutual relationships so intricate and so dependent on circumstances, that decisions on the legitimacy of NGOs will probably always have to be made in the light of the contexts in which NGOs operate. And even then, it does not seem to make much sense to talk about NGOs qualifying as legitimate, or about some NGOs being more legitimate than others. It seems more appropriate to establish whether, and if so, in what ways the legitimacy of a specific NGO may be doubted. This falsification approach—not trying to prove an NGO's legitimacy, but rather trying to detect clear deficiencies in its legitimacy—may be much more to the point (for a similar view in terms of minimal morality, see Bader 2007). Practically, the identification of NGOs with doubtful and perhaps failing legitimacy is much more urgent than establishing strict conditions for positive legitimacy. The prevention of harm is more urgent than the proliferation of beneficence. Thus, the criteria of legitimacy should provide the grounds for assessing whether the legitimacy of an NGO can be questioned. If there are no doubts about the legitimacy of an NGO, there is no reason to deny an NGO the moral right to expand its activities. If the legitimacy can be questioned, there is reason to reconsider that right.

5.   The legitimacy of NGOs and the legitimacy of the global order

Anna-Karin Lindblom (2005, 34) expresses serious doubts about the significance of the debate on the legitimacy of NGOs:

> Because of the democratic deficit in international law, resulting from both the rules on the representation of populations and from globalisation, diverse and conflicting information, opinions and concerns of different

groups are needed in the fora where international law is made and applied. The criticism often heard about NGOs [with regard to legitimacy deficiencies, AV] thus loses some of its relevance.

This view is understandable in the light of Lindblom's predominant interest in the role and status of NGOs in international law. Contrary to the authors of this book, she focuses on NGOs as a sector rather than on individual organizations. She also sympathizes with a Habermasian view of the international system as a whole. Habermas (2001, 111) seems to suggest that when the system as a whole is oriented towards communicative action—the free exchange of information and views—rather than towards the specific input in the system by individual actors, weaknesses in the legitimacy of those specific actors need not be considered very important.

It seems likely that both Habermas and Lindblom were primarily concerned with NGOs whose legitimacy is flawed because of specific contingencies, such as the presence of an oppressive regime that precludes an NGO from being transparent about its activities, policies, and plans, but that would try to live up to legitimacy criteria as soon as conditions would improve. As was shown in the previous section, however, deficiencies such as these can be accommodated in the conceptualization of legitimacy of individual NGOs. There is no need to consider these NGOs as defective in terms of legitimacy or to silence their voices in the international arena. There may be good reasons for their not being able to live up to all of the conceivable criteria of legitimacy that should ideally be met.

However, the definition of NGO legitimacy cannot accommodate flaws with regard to the moral orientation of NGOs. The criteria of the moral dimension are the touchstones of (non-) conformity with the criteria of the other dimensions. Lindblom's, and, for that matter, Habermas' position seems to allow for the possibility of morally objectionable NGOs disseminating information and voicing opinions in the international arena as part of the international legal order without compromising the legitimacy of that order in any way. This is hard to understand, since it seems natural that the information and opinions provided by objectionable NGOs will be affected or manipulated by the values and objectives of the NGOs. For this reason, even with regard to the legitimacy of the world order as a whole a clear view of the legitimacy of individual NGOs is required. This also applies if the global perspective on legitimacy is based on discursive reason in the vein of Habermas and Lindblom.

6.   Summing up

NGO Legitimacy is a complex notion that remains semantically vague in certain respects. Many of the criteria overlap; some relate to others in an instrumental way, some are implementations of others, yet others are indicators that other criteria have—at least to a certain extent—been fulfilled. The criteria of the moral dimension must be considered logically primordial. They include both compliance with substantive values and norms and conformity to procedural norms—such as transparency, accountability, and verifiability of past performance—that may also take the form of criteria of the regulatory and social dimensions. The criteria of the latter two dimensions depend logically on the moral criteria in the sense that conformity to the criteria of the social and legal dimensions is relevant to the legitimacy of an NGO to the extent that this conformity is an expression of implementation or fulfilment of the criteria of the moral dimension. Deficiencies and flaws with regard to the criteria of the social and legal dimensions can be justified or compensated by fulfilling criteria of the moral dimension. Deficiencies and flaws regarding the social and legal dimensions that cannot be justified by calling on criteria of the moral dimension may compromise the legitimacy of the organization. The criteria of the moral dimension boil down to the requirements that an NGO's values and norms should be acceptable in principle for all, and that those values and norms are integrated into the NGO's organizational structures and activities as fully as possible and in verifiably so.

In order to verify whether an NGO conforms to relevant substantive values and norms that can, in principle, be asserted by all, the mission, aims and performance of the NGO must be optimally transparent and verifiable. Real and actual compliance with relevant substantive values and norms is all-important. Transparency and verifiability are instrumental in enabling verification of this compliance. It is important to note that the degree of transparency and verifiability required may vary with the circumstances. First, the NGO should not be required to take up burdens in order to comply with transparency requirements to such a degree that its capacity to realize its mission is seriously hampered. It seems reasonable to hold that these burdens should be proportionate to the magnitude, character, and financial position of the NGO. Second, in certain contexts, regimes or large groups of the population oppose the in se morally unobjectionable mission and performance of the NGO. In such circumstances, lack of transparency and verifiability may protect the NGO and need not necessarily indicate deficient legitimacy. In other words, the required degree of transparency and verifiability are dependent on the size, character, and financial position of the NGO as well as on what the specific circumstances allow.

It is very difficult to draw a full and clear picture of an NGO that is the legitimate NGO par excellence. This is partly so because of the complexities of the criteria involved and their mutual relationships and priority patterns. Another reason is that the legitimacy of an NGO and its activities seems to depend to a large extent on the specific context of the NGO and its activities. With the conception of legitimacy presented here defective NGO legitimacy may be diagnosed and the significance of referring to a deficiency as a lack of legitimacy may be explained. Above all, it allows NGOs themselves to work on their legitimacy in a positive manner.

About the authors

Vivien Collingwood undertook her doctoral research at the University of Oxford on good governance conditionality, and did post-doctoral research at Tilburg University in the Netherlands. Her interests include the role of non-governmental organizations in international politics, global economic governance, and conditionality, and the Bretton Woods institutions. She is currently working for the Dutch office of *Médecins Sans Frontières*.

Anke van Gorp has an MSc in Material Science and Engineering and a PhD in Ethics and Technology from Delft University of Technology. She was a research fellow at the Tilburg Institute for Law, Technology, and Society of Tilburg University. She is currently working as a researcher for the Innovation Policy group of TNO Quality of Life in Delft.

Menno Kamminga is a Professor of International Law at Maastricht University. He is the Director of the Maastricht Centre for Human Rights and a former Legal Adviser and member of the International Executive Committee of Amnesty International.

Louis Logister holds a doctorate in Philosophy from Radboud University of Nijmegen. He was a research fellow at Tilburg University. He currently teaches Philosophy at Tilburg University and the University of Twente.

Corien Prins holds a degree in Law as well as Slavic Languages and Literature from Leiden University. She has been a Professor of Law and Informatization at Tilburg University since 1994. She serves on the Board of the Social Sciences Division (MAGW) of the Netherlands Organisation for Scientific Research (NWO), and is a member of the Advisory Council of the Netherlands ICT Research and Innovation Authority

(ICTRegie). Furthermore, she was a member of the programme committee of the NWO National Programme on Information Technology and Law (ITeR).

Peter Van den Bossche is a Professor of International Economic Law and Head of the Department of International and European Law of Maastricht University. He holds a PhD from the European University Institute, Florence (1990). From 1990 to 1992, he worked at the European Court of Justice, Luxembourg. From 1997 to 2001, he was a Counsellor to the Appellate Body of the World Trade Organization, Geneva, and in 2001 he served as the Acting Director of its Secretariat. He is a visiting professor at the World Trade Institute, Berne, the *Université libre de Bruxelles*, and the Institute of European Studies of Macau, China. He also serves on the Board of Editors of the *Journal of International Economic Law*.

Anton Vedder is a Senior Lecturer of Ethics and Law at the Faculty of Law of Tilburg University. He holds a doctorate in Philosophy from Utrecht University. In his research and teaching, he mainly focuses on ethics of technology and ethics of international relations.

Bibliography

Aston, Jurij D. (2001) The United Nations Committee on non-governmental organizations: Guarding the entrance to a politically divided house. *European Journal of International Law* 12: 943-962.

Atack, Iain (1999) Four criteria of development NGO legitimacy. *World Development* 27, no. 5: 855-64.

Ayers, Micheal D. (2003) Comparing collective identity in online and offline feminist activists. In *Cyberactivism: Online activism in theory and practice*. Edited by Martha McCaughey and Micheal D. Ayers. London & New York: Routledge.

Bader, Veit (1989) Max Webers Begriff der Legitimität. Versuch einer systematisch-kritischen Rekonstruktion. In *Max Weber heute. Erträge und Probleme der Forschung*. Edited by Johannes Weiss. Frankfurt am Main: Suhrkamp.

Bader, Veit (2007) Moral minimalism and global justice. *Critical Review of International Social and Political Philosophy* 10 (Miller Volume), forthcoming.

Bader, Veit, and Ewald Engelen (2003) Taking pluralism seriously. Arguing for an institutional turn in political philosophy. *Philosophy and Social Criticism* 29, no. 4: 375-406.

Ballantyne, Peter G. (2000) Investing in knowledge: Sharing information resources on the web (ECDPM InfoBrief 3). Maastricht: ECDPM. http://www.ecdpm.org/Web_ECDPM/Web/Content/Navigation.nsf/index2?readform&http://www.ecdpm.org/Web_ECDPM/Web/Content/Content.nsf/0/ECBF9172809CEEB6C1256C52003D21E7 (accessed 26 November 2006).

Beetham, David (1991) *The legitimation of power*. London: Macmillan.

Bodansky, Daniel (1999) The legitimacy of international governance: A coming challenge for international environmental law? *American Journal of International Law* 93 (3): 596-624.

Bovens, Marc (2006) Analysing and assessing public accountability. A conceptual framework. *European Governance Papers*, no. C-06-01 (16 January). http://www.connex-network.org/eurogov (accessed 26 November 2006).

Boyer, Anna-Nicole (2005) Serious play: Cyber tyrant toppling games. *Worldchanging* (15 March). http://www.worldchanging.com/archives/002343.html (accessed 26 November 2006).

Bratton, Michael (1989) The politics of government-NGO relations in Africa. *World Development* 17, no. 4: 53-65.

Bryman, Allan (2004) *Social research methods*. Oxford: Oxford University Press.

Buchanan, Allen (2003) *Justice, legitimacy, and self-determination: Moral foundations for international law*. Oxford: Oxford university Press.

Burci, Gian Luca, and Claude-Henri Vignes (2004) *The World Health Organization*. Deventer: Kluwer Law and Taxation Publishers.

Carens, Joseph H. (2000) *Culture, citizenship, and community: A contextual exploration of justice as evenhandedness*. Oxford: Oxford University Press.

Carens, Joseph H. (2004) A contextual approach to political theory. *Ethical Theory and Moral Practice* 7, no. 2: 117-132.

Cascio, Jamais (2005) Pax warrior. *Worldchanging* (12 February). http://www. worldchanging.com/archives/002093.html (accessed 26 November 2006).

Charnovitz, Steve (1997) Two centuries of participation: NGOs and international governance. *Michigan Journal of International Law* 18, no. 2: 183-286.

Clark, Ian (2003) Legitimacy in a global order. *Review of International Studies* 29: 75-95.

Clark, John D., and Nuno S. Themudo (2006) Linking the web and the street: Internet-based "dotcauses'" and the "anti-globalization" movement. *World Development* 34, no. 1: 50-74.

Clifford, Bob (2002) Merchants of morality. *Foreign Policy* 129 (March/April): 36-45. http://ssrn.com/abstract_= 922037 (accessed 26 November 2006).

COE (2003a) *Fundamental principles on the status of non-governmental organisations in Europe and explanatory memorandum*. http://www.coe.int /t/e/ngo/public/PrincFondam%20en%20engl.pdf (accessed 3 February 2007).

COE (2003b) *Resolution – Participatory status for international non-govern-mental organisations with the Council of Europe.* Adopted by the Committee of Ministers at the 861st meeting of the Ministers' Deputies (Res (2003)8), 19 November.
http://www.coe.int/t/e/ngo/public/EResolution2003_8.asp (accessed 7 February 2007).

COE (2003c) *Resolution – Status of partnership between the Council of Europe and national non-governmental organisations.* Adopted by the Committee of Ministers at the 861st meeting of the Ministers' Deputies (Res (2003)9), 19 November.
http://www.coe.int/t/e/ngo/public/EResolution2003_9.asp (accessed 7 February 2007).

Collingwood, Vivien, and Louis Logister (2005) State of the art: Addressing the INGO 'legitimacy deficit'. *Political Studies Review* 3, no. 2: 175-192.

Curtin, Deidre M. (2006) European legal integration: Paradise lost? In *European Integration and Law.* Edited by Deirdre Curtin, André Klip, Jan Smits, and Joseph McCahery. Antwerp: Intersentia.

Diani, Mario (2001) Social movement networks, virtual and real. In *Culture and politics in the information age.* Edited by Frank Webster. London & New York: Routledge.

Edwards, Michael (1999) Legitimacy and values in NGOs and international organisations: some sceptical thoughts. In *International perspectives on voluntary action: reshaping the third sector.* Edited by David Lewis. London: Earthscan.

Edwards, Michael and Simon Zadek (2003) Governing the provision of global public goods: The role and legitimacy of nonstate actors. In *Providing global public goods.* Edited by Inge Kaul. Oxford, Oxford University Press.

Etzioni, Amitai, and Oren Etzioni (1999) Face-to-face and computer-mediated communities, a comparative analysis. *The Information Society* 15, no. 4: 241-248.

Finucane, Melissa L., Ali Alhakami, Paul Slovic, and Stephen M. Johnson (2000) The affect heuristic in judgments of risks and benefits. *Journal of Behavioral Decision Making* 13, no. 1: 1-17.

Franck, Thomas M. (1988) Legitimacy in the international system. *American Journal of International Law* 82 (4): 705-759.

Franck, Thomas M. (1995) *Fairness in international law and institutions.* Oxford: Clarendon Press.

Garrido, Maria, and Alexander Havalais (2003) Mapping networks of support for the Zapatista Movement: Applying social-networks analysis to study contemporary social movements. In *Cyberactivism: Online activism in theory and practice.* Edited by Martha McCaughey and Micheal D. Ayers. London & New York: Routledge.

Gastil, John, Donald Braman, Dan M. Kahan, and Paul Slovic (2005) The 'Wildavsky heuristic': The cultural orientation of mass political opinion. *Yale Law School Public Law & Legal Theory Research Paper Series,* no. 107. http://ssrn.com/abstract=834264 (accessed 26 November 2006).

Habermas, Jürgen (1979) *Communication and the evolution of society.* London: Heinemann Educational Books.

Habermas, Jürgen (1987) Wie ist Legitimität durch Legalität möglich? *Kritische Justiz* 20 (1): 1-16.

Habermas, Jürgen (1988) *Legitimation crisis.* Oxford: Polity Press.

Habermas, Jürgen (1996) *Between facts and norms: Contribution to a discourse theory of law and democracy.* Cambridge, MA: MIT Press.

Habermas, Jürgen (2001) *The postnational constellation. Political essays.* Cambridge: Polity Press.

Held, David (1999) The transformation of political community: Rethinking democracy in the context of globalization. In *Democracy's Edges.* Edited by Ian Shapiro and Casiano Hacker-Cordón. Cambridge: Cambridge University Press.

Hill, Tony (2002) UNCTAD and NGOs: An evolving cooperation. In *UNCTAD-Civil society dialogue on selected development issues being addressed by the United Nations system.* Edited by Frederick Glover. New York, Geneva: United Nations Press.

Hudson, Alan (2000) Making the connection: Legitimacy claims, legitimacy chains and Northern NGO's international advocacy. In *New roles and relevance: Development NGOs and the challenge of change.* Edited by David Lewis and Tina Wallace. Bloomfield CT: Kumarian Press.

Human Rights Watch (2006) Russia/France summit must spotlight NGO protection. Condemn Kremlin's assault on civil society. http://hrw.org/ english/docs/2006/02/11/russia12656.htm (accessed 31 January 2007).

Hurd, Ian (1999) Legitimacy and authority in international politics. *International Organisation* 53 (2): 379-408.

Hurrell, Andrew (2002) "There are no rules" (George W. Bush): International order after September 11. *International Relations* 16: 185-204.

ICHRP (2003) Deserving trust: Issues of accountability for human rights NGOs. Draft report for consultation prepared under the auspices of the International Council on Human Rights Policy. http://www.ichrp.org/paper_files/119_w_01.doc (accessed 31 January 2007).

ICRC (1994) *Code of conduct for the international Red Cross and Red Crescent Movement and non-governmental organizations (NGOs) in disaster relief.* http://www.icrc.org/Web/Eng/siteengo.nsf/html/p1067 (accessed 31 January 2007).

ILO (2005a) About the ILO. http://www.ilo.org/public/English/about/ index.htm (accessed 7 February 2007).

ILO (2005b) *Report of the Committee on legal issues and international labour standards.* ILO doc. GB.294/9(Rev.). 294th Session, November. http://www.ilo.org/public/english/standards/relm/gb/docs/gb294/pdf/gb-9.pdf, (accessed 7 February 2007).

ILO (2005c) Rules for meetings. http://www.ilo.org/public/english/bureau/leg/reglem.htm (accessed 7 February 2007).

ILO (2005d) Relations with the non-governmental sector. http://www.ilo.org/public/english/comp/civil/ngo/relngios.htm (accessed 7 February 2007).

ILO (2005e) *Information note: Representation of international non-governmental organizations at the International Labour Conference and other ILO meetings.* http://www.ilo.org/public/english/standards/relm/ilc/pdf/note.pdf (accessed 7 February 2007).

ILO (2005f) Appenix III: Representation of international non-governmental organizations at the International Labour Conference. In conference guide presented at the 94th (maritime) session of the International Labour Conference, 23 February 2006, in Geneva, Switzerland. http://www.ilo.org /public/english/standards/relm/ilc/ilc94/guide.pdf (accessed 7 February 2007).

ILO (2006a) Non-governmental international organizations having general consultative status with the ILO. http://www.ilo.org/public/english/comp/ civil/ngo/ngogen.htm (accessed 1 September 2007).

ILO (2006b) Non-governmental international organizations having regional consultative status with the ILO. http://www.ilo.org/public/english/comp/ civil/ngo/ngoreg.htm (accessed 1 September 2007).

ILO (2006c) ILO special list of non-governmental international organizations. http://www.ilo.org/public/english/bureau/exrel/civil/ngo/index.htm (accessed 1 September 2006).

IMF (2003) Guide for staff relations with civil society organizations. http://www.imf.org/external/np/cso/eng/2003/101003.htm (accessed 7 February 2007).

IMF (2005a) About the IMF. http://www.imf.org/external/about.htm (accessed 7 February 2007).

IMF (2005b) The IMF and civil society organizations: A fact sheet. http://www.imf.org/external/np/exr/facts/civ.htm (accessed 7 February 2007).

IMF (2005c) Guide for staff relations with civil society organizations. http://www.imf.org/external/np/cso/eng/2003/101003.htm (accessed 7 February 2007).

Jägers, Nicola (2002) *Corporate human rights obligations: In search of accountability.* Antwerp: Intersentia.

Kamminga, Menno T. (2002) The evolving status of NGOs under international Law: A threat to the inter-state system? In *State, sovereignty, and international governance.* Edited by Gerard Kreijen, Marcel Brus, Jorris Duursma, Elizabeth de Vos, and John Dugard. Oxford: Oxford University Press.

Krahmer, Emiel, Judith van Dorst, and Nicole Ummelen (2004) Mood, persuasion and information presentation. The influence of mood on the effectiveness of persuasive digital documents. *Information Design Journal* 12, no. 3: 219-232.

Kurtz, Jürgen (2002) NGOs, the Internet and international economic policy making: The failure of the OECD Multilateral Agreement on Investment. *Melbourne Journal of International Law* 3: 213-246. http://ssrn.com/abstract_id=364900 (accessed 26 November 2006).

Landman, Todd, and Meghna Abraham (2004) *Evaluation of nine non-governmental human rights organisations.* The Hague: Ministry of Foreign Affairs of The Netherlands.

Lanord, Christophe (2002) A study of WHO's official relations system with nongovernmental organizations. *Civil Society Initiative Documents*, no. CSI/2002/WP4 (15 November). http://www.who.int/civilsociety/documents /en/study.pdf (accessed 7 February 2007).

Lebkowsky, Jon (1999) A few points about online activism. *Cybersociology Magazine*, no. 5. http://www.socio.demon.co.uk/magazine/5/5jon.html (accessed 26 November 2006).

Lindblom, Anna-Karin (2005) *Non-governmental organisations in international law.* Cambridge: Cambridge University Press.

Linden, Greg, Brent Smith, and Jeremy York (2003) Amazon.com recommendations: item-to-item collaborative filtering. *IEEE Internet Computing* (January/February). http://dsonline.computer.org/0301/d/w1lind.htm (accessed 26 November 2006).

Lips, Miriam, Simone van der Hof, Corien Prins, and Ton Schudelaro (2005) *Issues of online personalisation in commercial and public service delivery.* Tilburg: Wolf Legal Publishers.

Madon, Shirin (1999) International NGOs: Networking, information flows and learning. *Journal of Strategic Information Systems* 8, no. 3: 251-261. http://www.sciencedirect.com/science?_ob=PublicationURL&_tock ey=%23TOC%236027%231999%23999919996%2317281O%23FLA%23& _cdi=6027&_pubType=J&view=c&_auth=y&_acct=C000026138&_ver- sion=1&_urlVersion=0&_userid=522558&md5=1f6742eb6ed8415dedcf379 804bbef62 (accessed 26 November 2006).

Masum, Hassan (2002) TOOL: The open opinion layer. *First Monday* 7, no. 7. http://www.firstmonday.org/issues/issue7_7/masum/ (accessed 26 November 2006).

McBride, Jeremy (2005) *Legal framework for the setting-up and functioning of non-governmental organisations in Europe: Analysis of the answers to the questionnaire.* COE doc. ONG (2005) 1 (Strasbourg, 3 February). http://www.coe.int/t/e/legal_affairs/legal_co-operation/steering_commit- tees /cdcj/documents/2005/ONG%20_2005_%201%20E%20Analysis%20q uestionnaire%20McBride.pdf (accessed 7 February 2007).

McCaughey, Martha, and Michael D. Ayers, eds. (2003) *Cyberactivism: Online activism in theory and practice.* London & New York: Routledge.

McGirk, Tim (1999) General analysis: Role of NGOs wired for warfare. *Time Magazine* 154, no. 15 (11 October). http://www.globalpolicy.org/globaliz/cvlsocty/zapatis.htm (accessed 26 November 2006).

Merriam-Webster Online Dictionary (2006) Legitimate. http://www.m-w.com/dictionary/legitimate (accessed 8 September 2006).

Naude, Annelie M.E., Johannes D. Froneman, and Roy A. Atwood (2004) The use of the Internet by ten South African non-governmental organizations—a public relations perspective. *Public Relations Review* 30, no. 1: 87-94.

Nip, Joyce Y.M. (2004) The Queer Sisters and its electronic bulletin board: A study of the Internet for social movement mobilization. In *Cyberprotest: New media, citizens and social movements*. Edited by Wim van de Donk, Brian D. Loader, Paul G. Nixon, and Dieter Rucht. London & New York: Routledge.

Norris, Pippa (2001) Digital Parties: Civic engament and online democracy. Paper presented at joint workshops of the European Consortium of Political Research conference, 6-11 April 2001, in Grenoble, France.

Olesen, Thomas (2004) The transnational Zapatista solidarity network: An infrastructure analysis. *Global Networks* 4, no. 1: 89-107.

Oliviero, Melanie Beth, and Adele Simmons (2002) Who's minding the store? Global civil society and corporate responsibility. In *Global Civil Society Yearbook* 2002. Edited by Marlies Glasius, Mary Kaldor, and Helmut Anheier. Oxford: Oxford University Press.

OSCE (1998) Freedom of association: The question of NGO registration. Background paper presented at the OSCE Human Dimension Implementation Meeting, 5 October 1998, in Warsaw, Poland. http://www.osce. org/documents/odihr/1998/10/1493_en.pdf (accessed 8 February 2007).

Pace, William R. (1999) The relationship between the International Criminal Court and non-governmental organizations. In *Reflections on the International Criminal Court*. Edited by Herman A.M. von Hebel, Johan G. Lammers, and Jolien Schukking. The Hague: T.M.C. Asser Press.

Patton, Michael Q. (2002) *Qualitative evaluation and research methods*. 3rd ed. London: Sage.

Pissalidis, Basile (2002) Playing games with MEASLS: Disaster simulations can be excellent teachers. *Interaction* (8 April). http://www.interaction.org/ library/detail.php?id=371 (accessed 26 November 2006).

Prins, Corien (2003) Consumers, liability, and the online world. *Information and Communications Technology Law* 12, no. 2: 143-164.

Prins, Corien (2006) Property and privacy: European perspectives and the commodification of our identity. In *The future of the public domain. Identifying the commons in information law*. Edited by Lucie Guibault and Bernt Hugenholtz. The Hague: Kluwer Law International.

Rawls, John (1971) *A theory of justice*. Oxford: Oxford University Press.

Rosenkrands, Jacob (2004) Politicizing *homo economicus*: Analysis of anti-corporate websites. In *Cyberprotest: New media, citizens and social movements*. Edited by Wim Van de Donk, Brian D. Loader, Paul G. Nixon, and Dieter Rucht. London & New York: Routledge.

Salter, Lee (2003) Democracy, new social movements, and the Internet: A Habermasian analysis. In *Cyberactivism: Online activism in theory and practice*. Edited by Martha McCaughey and Micheal D. Ayers. London & New York: Routledge.

Scholte, Jan Aart (2004) Civil society and democratically accountable global governance. *Government and Opposition* 39, no. 2: 211-33.

Siurala, Lasse (2000) Changing forms of participation. Paper presented at the New Forms of Youth Participation conference, 4-6 May 2000, in Biel, Switzerland.
http://www.coe.int/t/e/cultural_co-operation/youth/Changing_Form_Participation.doc (accessed 26 November 2006).

Slim, Hugo (2002) By what authority? The legitimacy and accountability of non-governmental organisations. Paper presented at a meeting of the International Council on Human Rights Policy on Global Trends and Human Rights, 10-12 January, in Geneva, Switzerland.

Steffek, Jens (2003) The legitimation of international governance: A discourse approach. *European Journal of International Relations* 9, no. 2: 249-275.

Surman, Mark, and Katherine Reilly (2003) Appropriating the Internet for social change: Towards the strategic use of networked technologies by transnational civil society organizations. (This report was published by the Social Science Research Council as part of the Information Technology and International Cooperation programme.)
http://www.ssrc.org/programs/ itic/civ_soc_report (accessed 26 November 2006).

Swanton, Christine (1992) *Freedom: A coherence theory*. Indianapolis & Cambridge: Hacket Publishing Co. Inc.

The Marine Stewardship Council (2002)
http://www.msc.org (accessed 8 September 2006).

Townsend, Eric J.S. (2002) E-activism connects protest groups. *Hartford Courant* (4 December).
http://www.globalpolicy.org/ngos/advocacy/protest/iraq/2002/1204activism.htm (accessed 26 November 2006).

UN ECOSOC (1996) *Resolution 1996/31—Consultative relationship between the United Nations and non-governmental organizations.* UN doc. A/RES/1996/31. 49th Plenary meeting, 25 July 1996. http://www.un.org/ documents/ecosoc/res/1996/eres1996-31.htm (accessed 2 April 2005).

UN ECOSOC (1999) *NGO loses consultative status with Economic and Social Council.* ECOSOC press release, no. 5876 (26 October). http://www.un.org/News/Press/docs/1999/19991026.ecosoc5876.doc.html (accessed 8 February 2007).

UN ECOSOC (2001) *Report of the Committee on non-governmental organizations on its 2001 regular session (New York, 7-25 May 2001).* UN doc. E/2001/86. Substantive session, 15 June 2001.

UN ECOSOC (2002a) *Report of the Committee on non-governmental organizations on its resumed 2002 session (New York, 8-24 January 2003).* UN doc. E/2003/11. Resumed organizational session for 2003, 18 March 2002.

UN ECOSOC (2002b) *Report of the Committee on non-governmental organizations on its resumed 2001 session (New York, 14-25 January 2002).* UN doc. E/2002/10. Resumed organizational session, 29 April 2002.

UN ECOSOC (2003) *Report of the Committee on non-governmental organizations on its 2003 regular session (New York, 5-23 May 2003).* UN doc. E/2003/32. Substantive session, 26 August 2003.

UN ECOSOC (2004a) *Report of the Committee on non-governmental organizations on the 2004 regular session (New York, 10-28 May and 23 June 2004).* UN doc. E/2004/32, Substantive session, 13 August 2004.

UN ECOSOC (2004b) *Economic and Social Council adopts texts on NGO participation, Israeli occupation, Palestanian women, as it suspends 2004 session.* ECOSOC press release, no. 6136 (23 July). http://www.un.org/ News/Press/docs/2004/ecosoc6136.doc.htm (accessed 8 February 2007).

UN ECOSOC (2005) *Report of the Committee on non-governmental organizations on its resumed 2005 session (New York, 5-20 May).* UN doc. E/2005/32. Substantive session, 15 June 2005.

UN General Assembly (1964) *Resolution 1995 XIX—Establishment of the United Nations Conference on Trade and Development as an organ of the General Assembly.* UN doc. A/RES/19/1995. 19th Session, 30 December 1964. http://daccessdds.un.org/doc/RESOLUTION/GEN/NR0/210/89/IMG/NR021089.pdf?OpenElement (accessed 7 February 2007).

UN General Assembly (1972) *Resolution 2997 (XXVII)—Institutional and financial arrangements for international environmental cooperation.* UN doc. A/RES/27/2997. 27th Session, 15 December 1972. http://www.un-documents.net/a27r2997.htm (accessed 7 February 2007).

UN General Assembly (2004) We, the peoples: Civil society, the United Nations and global governance. Report of the Panel of Eminent persons on United Nations-Civil Society Relations. UN doc. A/58/817. 58th Session, 11 June 2004. http://www.ohchr.org/english/about/ngohandbook/CardosoReport.pdf (accessed 7 February 2007).

UNCTAD (1968) *Rules of Procedure.* UN doc. TD/63/Rev.2. New York, 1 February 1968.

UNCTAD (2004) *List of non-governmental organizations participating in the activities of UNCTAD.* UN doc. TD/B/NGO/LIST/7 and Corr.1. 3 May 2004. http://www.unctad.org/en/docs//tbngolistd7&c1_en.pdf (accessed 7 February 2007).

UNCTAD (2005) About UNCTAD. http://www.unctad.org/Templates/Page.asp?intItemID=1530&lang=1 (accessed 7 February 2007).

UNEP (2002) *Enhancing civil society engagement in the work of the United Nations Environment Programme: Strategy paper.* UN doc. UNEP/GC.22/INF/13. 22th Session of the Governing Council/Global Ministerial Environment Forum, 21 November 2002. http://www.unep.org/dpdl/civil_society/PDF_docs/ Enhancing_Civil_Society_Engagement_In_UNEP.pdf. (accessed 7 February 2007).

UNEP (2004) Engaging civil society in the governing council/global ministerial environment forum. Background document for the regional meetings in preparation of the sixth Global Civil Society Forum, 14 October 2004. http://www.unep.org/DPDL/civil_society (accessed 15 August 2006).

UNEP (2005) Guidelines for the sixth Global Civil Society Forum. http://www.unep.org/DPDL/civil_society/GCSF/index.asp (accessed 15 August 2005).

United Nations (2000a) *Report of the Committee on non-governmental organizations on the first and second part of its 2000 session (New York, 15-19 May and 12-23 June 2000).* UN doc. E/2000/88, Part I. Substantive session, 5 July 2000.

United Nations (2000b) *Report of the Committee on non-governmental organizations on the first and second part of its 2000 session (New York, 15-19 May and 12-23 June 2000).* UN doc. E/2000/88, Part II. Substantive session, 13 July 2000.

United Nations (2001) *Reference document on the participation of civil society in United Nations conferences and special sessions of the General Assembly during the 1990s* (version August 1). Prepared by the Office of the President of the Millennium Assembly. 55th Session of the United Nations General Assembly, 1 August 2001. http://www.un.org/ga/president/55/speech/ civilsociety1.htm (accessed 7 February 2007).

United Nations (2003) UN system and civil society: An inventory and analysis of practices. Background paper for the Secretary-General's Panel of Eminent Persons on United Nations Relations with Civil Society. http://www.un.org/reform/civilsociety/practices.shtml (accessed 7 February 2007).

Van Aelst, Peter, and Stefaan Walgrave (2004) New media, new movements? The role of the Internet in shaping the 'anti-globalization' movement. In *Cyberprotest: New media, citizens and social movements.* Edited by Wim van de Donk, Brian D. Loader, Paul G. Nixon, and Dieter Rucht. London & New York: Routledge.

Van de Donk, Wim, Brian D. Loader, Paul G. Nixon, and Dieter Rucht, eds. (2004) *Cyberprotest: New media, citizens and social movements.* London & New York: Routledge.

Van Genugten, Willem, Rob van Gestel, Corien Prins, and Anton Vedder (2004) *NGO's als 'nieuwe toezichthouders' op de naleving van mensenrechten door multinationale ondernemingen. Een beschouwing vanuit internationaalrechtelijk, bestuursrechtelijk en ethisch perspectief.* The Hague: Boom Juridische Uitgevers.

Van Gorp, Bouke (2003) Bezienswaardig? Historisch-geografisch erfgoed in toeristische beeldvorming. PhD dissertation, Utrecht University. Delft: Eburon.

Vedder, Anton (1998) Considered judgements: Meaning, community and tradition. In *Reflective equilibrium. Essays in honour of Robert Heeger.* Edited by W. van der Burg and T. van Willigenburg. Dordrecht, Boston, London: Kluwer Academic Publishers.

Vedder, Anton (2006) Morality and the legitimacy of non governmental organizations' involvement in international politics and policy making. In *International studies in sociology and social anthropology. Neo-liberal glo-*

balism and social sustainable globalisation. Edited by Eva Nieuwenhuys. Leiden: Brill.

Vedder, Anton, and Robert Wachbroit (2003) Reliability of information on the Internet: Some distinctions. *Ethics and Information Technology* 5, no. 4: 211-215.

Vedder, Anton, ed. (2003) *The WTO and concerns regarding animals and nature.* Nijmegen: Wolff Legal Publishers.

Vegh, Sandor (2003) Classifying forms of online activism. The case of cyber-protests against the World Bank. In *Cyberactivism: Online activism in theory and practice.* Edited by Martha McCaughey and Michael D. Ayers. London & New York: Routledge.

Weber, Max (1978) *Economy and society.* Berkeley: University of California Press.

Wellman, Barry, Anabel Quan Haase, James Witte, and Keith Hampton (2001) Does the Internet increase, decrease, or supplement social capital? Social networks, participation, and community commitment. *American Behavioral Scientist* 45, no 3: 437-455.

WHO (2002) Policy for relations with nongovernmental organizations. Report by the Director-General. WHO doc. EB111/22. 111th Session, 25 November 2002. http://www.who.int/gb/ebwha/pdf_files/EB111/eeb11122.pdf (accessed 7 February 2007).

WHO (2004a) *Draft policy for relations with nongovernmental organizations.* WHO doc. A57/32. 57th World Health Assembly, 1 April 2004. http://www.who. int/gb/ebwha/pdf_files/WHA57/A57_32-en.pdf (accessed 7 February 2007).

WHO (2004b) *Decision WHA57(12) —Decisions and list of resolutions.* WHO doc. A57/DIV/5. Eighth plenary meeting, 22 May 2004. http://www.who.int/gb/ ebwha/pdf_files/WHA57/A57_DIV5-en.pdf (accessed 7 February 2007).

WHO (2004c) *Report of the standing committee on nongovernmental organizations.* WHO doc. EB113/23. 113th Session, 23 January 2004. http://www.who.int/ gb/ebwha/pdf_files/EB113/eeb11323.pdf (accessed 7 February 2007).

WHO (2005) WHO's relations with nongovernmental organisations. http://www.who.int/civilsociety/relations/en (accessed 7 February 2007).

WHO (2006) *Principles governing relations between WHO and nongovernmental organization.* http://www.who.int/civilsociety/relations/principles/en/index. html (accessed 7 February 2007).

Williams, Jody and Stephen Goose (1998) The international campaign to ban landmines. In *To walk without fear: The global movement to ban landmines.* Edited by Maxwell A. Cameron, Brain W. Tomlin, and Robert J. Lawson. Toronto: Oxford University Press.

World Bank (1989) *Operational directive 14.70: Involving NGOs in bank-supported activities.* Washington, DC: The World Bank Group.

World Bank (2000a) Involving nongovernmental organizations in bank-supported activities. *World Bank operational manual, good practices,* no. GP 14.70 (January). http://wbln0018.worldbank.org/Institutional/Manuals/ OpManual. nsf/o/1DFB2471DE05BF9A8525672C007D0950?OpenDocument (accessed 7 February 2007).

World Bank (2000b) *Consultations with civil society organizations: General guidelines for World Bank staff.* Washington, DC: The World Bank. http://lnweb18.worldbank.org/ESSD/sdvext.nsf/60ByDocName/ConsultationswithCivilSocietyOrganizationsGeneralGuidelinesforWorldBankStaffNGOandCivilSocietyUnitWorldBankJune2000PDF754KB/$FILE/ConsultationsWithCSOsGuidelines.pdf (accessed 7 February 2007).

World Bank (2000c) Joint resolution between the World Bank and the NGO Working Group. *Endorsement of the proposal for a World Bank – Civil Society Forum* (6 December). http://www.staff.city.ac.uk/p.willetts/NGOWG/JNT-RES.HTM (accessed 7 February 2007).

World Bank (2005a) Five agencies, one group. http://web.worldbank.org/ WBSITE/EXTERNAL/EXTABOUTUS/0,,content MDK:20122644~menuPK:278902~pagePK:34542~piPK:36600~theSitePK :29708,00.html (accessed 7 February 2007).

World Bank (2005b) World Bank – Civil society global policy forum. http://web. worldbank.org/WBSITE/EXTERNAL/TOPICS/CSO/0,,content MDK:20327929~pagePK:220503~piPK:220476~theSitePK:228717,00.html (accessed 7 February 2007).

World Bank (2005c) *Issues and options for improving engagement between the World Bank and Civil Society organizations.* http://siteresources. worldbank.org/CSO/Resources/Issues_and_Options_PUBLISHED_VERSION.pdf (accessed 25 September 2005).

World Bank (2005d) Annual and spring meetings.
http://web.worldbank.org/ WBSITE/EXTERNAL/TOPICS/CSO/0,,content
MDK:20094168~pagePK:220503~piPK:220476~theSitePK:228717,00.html
(accessed 7 September 2005).

WTO (1996) *Guidelines for arrangements on relations with Non-Governmental
Organizations.* WTO doc. WT/L/162. Decision adopted by the General
Council, 18 July.
http://www.wto.org/English/forums_e/ngo_e/guide_ e.htm (accessed 7
February 2007).

WTO (2004) For NGOs.
http://www.wto.org/english/forums_e/ngo_e/ngo _e.htm (accessed 7
February 2007).

WTO (2005) The Future of the WTO: Addressing institutional challenges in
the new millennium. Report by the Consultative Board to the Director-
General Supachai Panitchpakdi.
http://www.wto.org/english/thewto_e/10anniv_e/ future_wto_e.pdf (accessed 7 February 2007).

Index

Nijhoff Law Specials

For more titles in this series, consult our web site: **http://www.brill.nl**

MARTINUS NIJHOFF PUBLISHERS — LEIDEN • BOSTON

March and/08